The Historian's Handbook

A DESCRIPTIVE GUIDE TO REFERENCE WORKS

The HISTORIAN'S HANDBOOK

A DESCRIPTIVE GUIDE TO REFERENCE WORKS

By HELEN J. POULTON

WITH THE ASSISTANCE OF MARGUERITE S. HOWLAND

FOREWORD BY WILBUR S. SHEPPERSON

UNIVERSITY OF OKLAHOMA PRESS : NORMAN AND LONDON

ISBN: 0-8061-1009-0

Library of Congress Catalog Card Number: 71-165774

Copyright © 1972 by the University of Oklahoma Press, Publishing Division of the University. All rights reserved. Manufactured in the U.S.A. First edition, 1972; second printing, 1973; third printing, 1974; fourth printing, 1977; fifth printing, 1980; sixth printing, 1986.

7 8 9 10 11 12 13 14 15 16 17 18 19 20 21 22 23 24

Foreword

Many students of history rely on zeal and tenacity to overcome a lack of technical expertise in their daily explorations into the catacombs of the library. Perhaps most people who use the library could save much time and frustration and improve their work if they knew how and where to look for historical material. Indeed, some of us have half-seriously suggested to students in our seminars that they first become librarians and then study to be historians.

Fortunately, Helen J. Poulton followed similar advice and acquired advanced degrees in both history and library science. This background enabled her to prepare this volume with precision and authority.

The Historian's Handbook: A Descriptive Guide to Reference Works is designed to aid both students and scholars of the social sciences. It surveys a wide variety of the major reference works in all fields of history, as well as important titles in several allied disciplines. An opening chapter on the organization of the library helps make this study a valuable key in the unlocking of a library's secrets.

WILBUR S. SHEPPERSON

Preface

The history student is required to find and use widely scattered and often complex materials, such as government documents, archives, and legal works, as well as books, newspapers, and periodicals. This volume attempts to select and list the major reference titles which can help the student and researcher select most efficiently from the thousands of titles the specific ones he needs. It is not a catalog of all the materials that might be useful or relevant to a subject.

Many people have helped me, but I wish to express my gratitude in particular to: Quirinus Breen, Professor Emeritus of History, University of Oregon; Angie Debo, formerly of the Oklahoma State University Library; Mrs. Ruth Donovan, Assistant Director, University of Nevada Libraries; Jerome Edwards, Assistant Professor of History, University of Nevada; Mrs. Marguerite S. Howland, Head Documents Librarian and Coordinator, Social Sciences and Humanities Areas, Oklahoma State University Library; James W. Hulse, Associate Professor of History, University of Nevada; Wilbur S. Shepperson, Professor of History, University of Nevada; and James Tigner, Professor of History, University of Nevada.

Helen J. Poulton

Contents

The Historian's Handbook

A DESCRIPTIVE GUIDE TO REFERENCE WORKS

1

The Library
and Its Catalog

Libraries have always played an important role in the transfer of information. They have existed to acquire, to preserve, and to make available recorded information. With today's explosion of information, the role of the library is increasingly important. As Verner W. Clapp has defined it, the function of a research library "is to enable inquirers to identify library materials relevant to their inquiries and to supply them with copies of these materials for their use."[1]

From earliest times the principle of local self-sufficiency and the principle of sharing resources have shaped the growth of the world's libraries. Today the continuing increase in the number of publications, the complexity of languages, and rising costs have caused even the largest and most specialized libraries to recognize the fact that they can not have completeness of resources. Foster E. Mohrhardt, Director of the National Agricultural Library, has said:

As we move rapidly into an era of computer-aided sharing of

[1] Verner W. Clapp, *The Future of the Research Library* (Urbana, University of Illinois Press, 1964), 11; see also, Katharine G. Harris, "Currently Available Tools—Their Adequacy for Today's Needs," in *The Present Status and Future Prospects of Reference Information Service: Proceedings of the Conference Held at the School of Library Service, Columbia University, March 30–April 1, 1966*, ed. by Winifred B. Linderman (Chicago, American Library Association, 1967), 103.

library resources, I feel certain that, within the next decade, the multiple-access computer will be in general use by research libraries. I would assume that possibly in ten years, instead of mailing tapes to libraries throughout the country, we will probably have the computers electronically connected so that each can tap the other's information. We will not have a common computer storing all the information but, among research libraries at least, a commonly joined computer system.[2]

Research libraries have large bibliographic collections to identify the material the user wants, and they use the telephone, teletype, photoduplication, telefacsimile, and delivery and mail services to implement the principle of sharing resources. The student should investigate the interlibrary loan services at his library. Because most libraries follow the American Library Association's National Interlibrary Loan Code of 1968, they do not usually ask to borrow United States books in print of moderate cost, serials if the item can be copied at moderate cost, rare materials, reference materials, genealogical materials, bulky or fragile newspapers, or doctoral dissertations when they are available on microfilm. The borrowing library has the responsibility of identifying the request according to accepted bibliographic practice and citing the source of the reference.

Many libraries have local, state, regional, and national arrangements to facilitate the acquisition of materials not available locally. The University of Nevada Library, for example, follows the Interlibrary Loan Code in obtaining material for its faculty and graduate students working on their theses and dissertations. It also provides material for all the libraries of Nevada, which funnel their requests through the Nevada State Library at Carson City. In addition, the University of Nevada Library has joined the Consortium of Western Universities and Colleges, which, accord-

[2] Foster E. Mohrhardt, "The Library Kaleidoscope: National Plans and Planning," in *The Present Status and Future Prospects of Reference Information Service*, 85, 89.

ing to its bylaws, hopes "to provide, through the close cooperation of the acquisitions and services program [extended interlibrary loans and photoduplication service] of the libraries of member institutions, better research material and study opportunities in the field of international relations and area studies for students and faculty members of the associated institutions." With the University's new two-year medical school, the University of Nevada's Life and Health Sciences Library will be able to participate in the National Library of Medicine system which provides faster interlibrary loan and reference service through MEDLARS (Medical Literature Analysis and Retrieval System) tapes deposited at selected regional centers.

A library should organize its books, serials, documents, tapes, manuscripts, records, and microforms so that its users will be able to find what they want. If the researcher will learn a few basic, common library practices, he will save time and avoid much frustration.

The card catalog is the key to the library. It is an index to the cataloged material in the library. Some library catalogs are dictionary catalogs, that is, author, title, and subject cards are filed alphabetically in one catalog. Other library catalogs may be divided catalogs, with author and title cards filed alphabetically in one section and subject cards filed alphabetically in another section. Filing rules differ in libraries, but the student should note a few of the important variations, especially whether the cards are filed letter by letter or word by word.

Word by Word	*Letter by Letter*
New England	Newell
New era	Newe Metamorphosis
New Mexico	New England
New York	New era
Newe Metamorphosis	Newfoundland
Newell	New Mexico
Newfoundland	Newport

6

Newport	News
News	New York

For author and title cards, if the first word is an article (a, an, the, *le, les, un, une, der, das, die*), it is disregarded in filing. When an article is within the title, it is counted in the alphabetizing. *Le Grand Frederic avant l'avènement* by Ernest Lavisse, for example, is filed under *Grand* and not under *Le*; however, *l'avènement* is filed alphabetically under *l'avènement*.

Abbreviations are arranged as though they were spelled out— *St.* as *saint*, *Dr.* as *doctor*, and *G.B.* as *Great Britain*.

Words beginning with *M'*, *Mc*, and *Mac* are filed as though they were all spelled *Mac* and interfiled with other words beginning *mac*; thus the following arrangement:

> McAdoo, William Gibbs
> Macalih, Basile
> Mac Annan, George Buss
> Macao
> McArthur, Arthur
> MacArthur, Douglas

Numerals are filed as though spelled out: *1066 and All That*, for example, is filed as though it began *Ten Sixty Six*.

Organizations are considered authors if they have issued publications. These organizations include institutions such as the University of California,[3] government agencies such as the United States Department of State,[4] societies such as the American Academy of Political and Social Science,[5] and corporations such as Rand, McNally and Company.[6]

[3] University of California, University at Los Angeles, Committee on Latin American Studies, *Statistical Abstract of Latin America* (Los Angeles, 1955–).

[4] U.S. Department of State, Historical Office, *American Foreign Policy: Current Documents* (Washington, D.C., 1956–).

[5] *The Annals* of the American Academy of Political and Social Science, Vol. 1– (Philadelphia, American Academy of Political and Social Science, 1890–).

The student should also learn how the library files foreign names. What does it do with names with prefixes (*de* and *von*), with names with an umlaut (ä, ö, ü), and with hyphenated names? The library usually disregards prefixes; thus Joachim von Kurenberg is filed under *K* and Maximilien de Bétherne, duc de Sully is filed under *S*. Libraries do file sometimes under *du*; thus Madame du Barry is filed under *Du Barry, Marie Jeanne Bécu, comtesse.* If the student is hunting Müller, for example, he should check both *Mueller* and *Muller* to be safe. In the case of hyphenated names, libraries usually file under the first part of the surname; thus Desmond Chapman-Huston is filed under *Chapman.*

Finding subject headings requires a little knowledge and finesse. The student can learn how. There are four basic types of subject headings. The simplest type is without divisions: History. The next type has subdivisions:

> History—Bibliography
> History—Collections
> History—Curiosa and Miscellany
> History—Dictionaries
> History—Methodology
> History—Periodicals
> History—Philosophy
> History—Sources
> History—Yearbooks

A third type has inverted subject headings: History, Ancient or History, Modern. The fourth type consists of a phrase: History in Art.

Filing may differ in libraries, but the following illustrates a typical arrangement of the four types of subject headings:

> History
> History—Bibliography

⁶ *The World Book Atlas*, 1966 ed. (Chicago, Field Enterprises Corp., 1965).

8

> History—Sources
> History—Sources—Bibliography
> History, Ancient
> History, Modern
> History, Modern—Sources
> History, Modern—18th Century
> History, Modern—19th Century
> History, Modern—20th Century
> History in Art

Note that chronological subdivisions are filed in chronological order after all the form and topical subdivisions.

In the card catalog the student will also find cross references. A reference referring from a form not used to forms used in a *see* reference: History, Medieval *see* Middle Ages—History. A reference from a form used to related headings where additional titles are listed is a *see also* reference: History, Modern *see also* Civilization, Modern; Reformation; Renascence.

Most large, scholarly research libraries follow the list of *Subject Headings Used in the Dictionary Catalogs of the Library of Congress*.[7] By checking this list, the student can learn what subject headings and cross references to look for. While there are revisions to keep the list up to date, some terms may never get in it. For example, the term *cold war* is now so much accepted it is in *Webster's Third New International Dictionary of the English Language*, but the subject heading for Louis Joseph Halle's book, *The Cold War as History*, is History, Modern—1945.

Libraries classify their materials to bring together those on a particular subject. The two most commonly used classification schemes in United States libraries are the Dewey Decimal Classification and the Library of Congress Classification. The Dewey decimal scheme, developed by Melvil Dewey in the 1870's, is based on figures used decimally. Dewey divided all knowledge into ten classes.

[7] Ed. by Marguerita V. Quattlebaum, 7th ed. (Washington, D.C., for sale by the Card Division, Library of Congress, 1966).

Main Classes

000–099	General Works	500–599	Pure Science
100–199	Philosophy	600–699	Technology
200–299	Religion	700–799	The Arts
300–399	Social Sciences	800–899	Literature
400–499	Language	900–999	History

Each main class is divided into ten divisions. For example, the main class History is divided as follows:

History

900–910 History—General Works
910–919 Geography, Travels, Description
920–929 Biography
930–939 Ancient History
940–949 Europe
950–959 Asia
960–969 Africa
970–979 North America
980–989 South America
990–999 Other Parts of the World

Each division is divided into ten sections:

North America

970 North America—General Works
971 Canada
972 Mexico and the Caribbean
973 United States
974 Northeastern States
975 Southeastern States
976 South Central States
977 North Central States
978 Western States
979 Far Western States and Alaska

The Library of Congress Classification System was developed to organize the vast collections of the United States national library. Classifications were tailored to fit its collections, which were especially good in history and political and social science. The Library of Congress system classifies by the use of letters and numbers. The letters up to a maximum of two indicate the classes and divisions. Numerals up to four are used serially to indicate subdivisions. The following is the outline of the twenty main groups into which the fields of knowledge are divided:

Library of Congress

A	General Works. Polygraphy
B	Philosophy. Psychology. Religion
C	Auxiliary Sciences of History
D	History: General and Old World
E–F	History: America
G	Geography. Anthropology. Recreation
H	Social Sciences
J	Political Science
K	Law
L	Education
M	Music and Books on Music
N	Fine Arts
P	Language and Literature
Q	Science
R	Medicine
S	Agriculture
T	Technology
U	Military Science
V	Naval Science
Z	Bibliography and Library Science

The catalog card, usually a Library of Congress card, gives very valuable and highly accurate information: the author's full name, his birth and death dates, the call number of the book, the full title of the book, the imprint, the collation, the Library of Congress card number, the date of the card code number, the Dewey classification number, and the tracing.

In the sample cards for the same book the reader can learn the author's full name (Billington, Ray Allen) and the date of his birth (1903). Because there is no death date and the book appeared in 1967, the author is presumably alive. The full title is *Western Expansion: A History of the American Frontier.*

The call number of a book is made up of the symbols assigned to a book to indicate its location on the shelves of a library. It consists of the class number (E179.5) and the author number or "Cutter number" (B63), which is a letter-number combination of the author's name.

The imprint includes the place (New York), date of publication (1967), and the name of the publisher (Macmillan) or the printer (sometimes both). The name of the publisher of a book can give the informed reader valuable information. The scholar soon learns about the character and scope of publishers. If the firm is a vanity press, it publishes books at the author's expense. If it is a university press, it publishes scholarly and specialized works which commercial presses, fearing a small audience and therefore limited sales, hesitate to publish. If it is a reprint firm, Peter Smith, for example, it publishes books dropped by the original publishers but for which there is a limited demand. The edition of the book appears between the title and place of publication. The fact that this is a third edition tells the student that it is a very important and apparently an up-to-date work.

The collation is the part of the catalog entry which describes the work as a material object, telling its volumes, pages, size, and the type and character of illustrations. This is a one-volume work, twenty-five centimeters high, consisting of 933 pages, with seventeen (xvii) preliminary pages, and maps.

The notes on a card tell the reader whether the book is part of a

Sample cards for the same book

```
E
179.5      Billington, Ray Allen, 1903-
B63            Westward expansion; a history of the Ameri-
1967       can frontier.  3d ed.   New York, Macmillan
           [c1967]
               xvii, 933 p.  maps.  25 cm.

           "Bibliographical notes": p. 761-893.




               1. U. S. - Territorial expansion.  2. U. S. -
           Hist.  3. Mississippi Valley - Hist. - 1803-
           1865.  4. The West - Hist.  I. Title.
```

Author card

```
           Westward expansion.
E
179.5      Billington, Ray Allen, 1903-
B63            Westward expansion; a history of the Ameri-
1967       can frontier.  3d ed.   New York, Macmillan
           [c1967]
               xvii, 933 p.  maps.  25 cm.

           "Bibliographical notes": p. 761-893.




               1. U. S. - Territorial expansion.  2. U. S. -
           Hist.  3. Mississippi Valley - Hist. - 1803-
           1865.  4. The West - Hist.  I. Title.
```

Title card

Subject cards

```
                    U. S. - TERRITORIAL EXPANSION
 E
 179.5           Billington, Ray Allen, 1903-
 B63                 Westward expansion; a history of the Ameri-
 1967             can frontier.  3d ed.   New York, Macmillan
                  [c1967]
                     xvii, 933 p.  maps.  25 cm.

                  "Bibliographical notes": p. 761-893.



                    1. U. S. - Territorial expansion.  2. U. S. -
                  Hist.  3. Mississippi Valley - Hist. - 1803-
                  1865.  4. The West - Hist.  I. Title.
                                    O
```

```
                    U. S. - HISTORY
 E
 179.5           Billington, Ray Allen, 1903-
 B63                 Westward expansion; a history of the Ameri-
 1967             can frontier.  3d ed.   New York, Macmillan
                  [c1967]
                     xvii, 933 p.  maps.  25 cm.

                  "Bibliographical notes": p. 761-893.



                    1. U. S. - Territorial expansion.  2. U. S. -
                  Hist.  3. Mississippi Valley - Hist. - 1803-
                  1865.  4. The West - Hist.  I. Title.
                                    O
```

14

Subject cards

MISSISSIPPI VALLEY - HISTORY - 1803-1865

E
179.5
B63
1967

Billington, Ray Allen, 1903-
   Westward expansion; a history of the American frontier. 3d ed. New York, Macmillan
[c1967]
   xvii, 933 p. maps. 25 cm.

"Bibliographical notes": p. 761-893.

   1. U. S. - Territorial expansion. 2. U. S. -
Hist. 3. Mississippi Valley - Hist. - 1803-
1865. 4. The West - Hist. I. Title.

○

THE WEST - HISTORY

E
179.5
B63
1967

Billington, Ray Allen, 1903-
   Westward expansion; a history of the American frontier. 3d ed. New York, Macmillan
[c1967]
   xvii, 933 p. maps. 25 cm.

"Bibliographical notes": p. 761-893.

   1. U. S. - Territorial expansion. 2. U. S. -
Hist. 3. Mississippi Valley - Hist. - 1803-
1865. 4. The West - Hist. I. Title.

○

series, if there are editors, the changes of title, and if there is a bibliography, an appendix, or a supplement. This book has a bibliography on pages 761–893.

The tracing on a catalog card is the record on the main entry card (at the bottom in small print) of all the additional headings under which the work is represented in the card catalog. Four subject headings were assigned this title: the one given on the subject card, U.S.—History, Mississippi Valley—History—1803–1865, and The West—History. The student can add these to his list of subject headings to check for his report, thesis, or dissertation.

Once the student has learned to use the catalog in his own library, he can use the same techniques in using the great national and research library catalogs.

2

National Library Catalogs and National and Trade Bibliographies

The printed catalogs of great libraries are invaluable bibliographical aids to the scholar. Their catalogs are the nearest approach to universal bibliography in the world today. They are indispensable in verifying and locating items.

NATIONAL LIBRARY CATALOGS

The most useful catalog is that of the Library of Congress, founded in 1800. Since 1870 the Library of Congress has received for deposit a copy of all works copyrighted in the United States and acquired significant books from throughout the world. Its *Catalog of Books*, an author and main-entry catalog, is a facsimile of the printed cards issued by it for some 4.25 million volumes up to July 31, 1942.[1] A supplement was issued covering August 1, 1942–December 31, 1947.[2] This has been continued by the *Library of Congress Author Catalog, 1948–1952*.[3] In 1953 the title was changed to *Library of Congress Catalog, Books: Authors* and in July, 1956, to the *National Union Catalog, A Cumulative Author List*, which included titles reported by other libraries.[4]

[1] 167 vols. (Ann Arbor, Mich., Edwards Bros., 1942–46).
[2] 42 vols. (Ann Arbor, Mich., Edwards Bros., 1948).
[3] 24 vols. (Ann Arbor, Mich., Edwards Bros., 1953).
[4] *1953–1957*, 28 vols. (Ann Arbor, Mich., J. W. Edwards, 1958); *1958–1962*, 54 vols. (New York, Rowman and Littlefield, 1963); *1963–1967*, 72 vols. (Ann Arbor, Mich., J. W. Edwards, 1969). Supplemented by

Libraries use the locations given for a title as a list of institutions from which they may borrow a title on interlibrary loan. It is the most important, single printed source of interlibrary loan information.

In 1950 the Library of Congress began issuing *The Subject Catalog*, the fullest and most up-to-date subject catalog for modern books.[5] It gives many more specific entries than does its British counterpart the British Museum's *Subject Index*, and it is most helpful when the student does not know the author of a book or wants to check to see what books have been written on his topic.

The Library of the British Museum is the British national library. It has a *General Catalogue*[6] and a *Subject Index*.[7] The coverage of the British Museum does not duplicate the listings of the *National Union Catalog*. The British Museum covers books

monthly, quarterly, annual, and quinquennial cumulations. To fill in the gap from 1952 to 1956, when the *National Union Catalog* became a real union catalog, the Library of Congress compiled *The National Union Catalog, 1952–1955: Imprints: An Author List Representing Library of Congress Printed Cards and Titles Reported by Other American Libraries*, 30 vols. (Ann Arbor, Mich., J. W. Edwards, 1961). It includes entries and locations for monographs. To fill in the gap from 1956 back to the beginning of printing, *The National Union Catalog: Pre-1956 Imprints*, 600 vols. (London, Mansell, 1968–) is in progress. The Library of Congress and the National Union Catalog Subcommittee of the Resources Committee of the Resources and Technical Services Division, American Library Association, are co-operating in the compiling and editing of this major work.

[5] *1950–1954*, 20 vols. (Ann Arbor, Mich., J. W. Edwards, 1955); *1955–1959*, 22 vols. (Paterson, N.J., Pageant, 1960); *1960–1964*, 25 vols. (Ann Arbor, Mich., J. W. Edwards, 1965). Quarterly issues with annual cumulations.

[6] British Museum, Department of Printed Books, *General Catalogue of Printed Books: Photolithographic Edition to 1955*, 263 vols. (London, Trustees of the British Museum, 1959–66).

[7] British Museum, Department of Printed Books, *Subject Index of the Works Added to the Library of the British Museum in the Years 1881–1900*, ed. by G. H. Fortescue, 3 vols. (London, Trustees of the British Museum, 1902–1903). There have been ten five-year supplements from 1901 to 1950, which were published in London by the Trustees of the British Museum, 1906–61, in ten volumes.

18

from the fifteenth century to the end of 1955 in all languages, except the Oriental. And, because of its copyright privileges, it has the most complete collection of British publications in the world. The author catalog has catchword title entries, cross references for anonymous works, editors and translators, and analytics for series. Biographical material is entered under personal names, and official publications of a country and works about it are listed under the name of the country. It includes analytics for series and makes cross references from editors and translators. The catalog is kept up to date by annual volumes beginning with the year 1963,[8] and these cumulate in ten-year supplements.

The Bibliothèque Nationale, the French national library, has the largest collection of French books in the world because, according to copyright law, it is supposed to receive a copy of every book published in France. Entries in its catalog, the *Catalogue général*, are arranged alphabetically by personal author; there are no entries for anonymous classics, periodicals, or corporate authors.[9] Each volume includes the titles acquired up to the date of publication of that volume; thus there is a difference in coverage between the first volumes, which include the entries for the early part of the alphabet and which were published around 1900, and later volumes, which cover the middle and latter part of the alphabet and which were published fifty years later. Beginning with volume 189 (Tissonière), no entries after 1959 are included. Quinquennial supplements, beginning with 1960–64, are published to keep the catalog up-to-date. These supplements include corporate entries and anonymous authors.[10]

A great book such as *The Federalist* would probably be found in

[8] British Museum, Department of Printed Books, *General Catalogue of Printed Books, Ten-Year Supplement, 1956–1965*, 50 vols. (London, Trustees of the British Museum, 1968).

[9] Paris, Bibliothèque Nationale, *Catalogue général des livres imprimés: Auteurs*, vol. 1– (Paris, Imprimerie Nationale, 1900–).

[10] Paris, Bibliothèque Nationale, *Catalogue général des livres imprimés: Auteurs-collectivités-Auteurs-anonymes, 1960–1964* (Paris, Bibliothèque Nationale, 1965–).

The Federalist.

The Federalist: a collection of essays, written in favour of the new Constitution, as agreed upon by the Federal convention, September 17, 1787 ... New-York: Printed and sold by J. and A. M'Lean, no. 41, Hanover-square, M,DCC,LXXXVIII.

2 v. 17ᵐ.

First complete edition. *cf.* The Fœderalist ... ₍ed.₎ by Henry B. Dawson. New York, 1863. Introduction: p. xxiii, lv–lxiii.

1. U. S. Constitution.   I. Hamilton, Alexander, 1757–1804.   II. Madison, James, pres. U. S., 1751–1836.   III. Jay, John, 1745–1829.

9—21562

Library of Congress   JK154 1788

———— Copy 2.   2 v. in 1.

₍a37c1₎

The Federalist.

The Federalist: a collection of essays, written in favour of the new Constitution, as agreed upon by the Federal convention, September 17, 1787 ... New-York, Printed and sold by J. Tiebout, 1799.

2 v. 16ᵐ.

1. U. S. Constitution.   I. Hamilton, Alexander, 1757–1804.   II. Madison, James, pres. U. S., 1751–1836, joint author.   III. Jay, John, 1745–1829, joint author.

9–21561

Library of Congress   JK154 1799

———— Copy 2.

The Federalist.

The Federalist, on the new Constitution. By Publius. Written in 1788. To which is added, Pacificus, on the proclamation of neutrality. Written in 1739. Likewise, the federal Constitution, with all the amendments. Rev. and cor. ... New-York: Printed and sold by George F. Hopkins, at Washington's Head. 1802.

2 v. 21⅓ᵐ.

1. U. S. Constitution.   I. Hamilton, Alexander, 1757–1804.   II. Madison, James, pres. U. S., 1751–1836.   III. Jay, John, 1745–1829.

9—21564

Library of Congress   JK154 1802

———— Copy 2.   ₍41j1₎

HAMILTON (Général Alexander). — The Works of Alexander Hamilton, edited by Henry Cabot Lodge. [Federal edition. 2ᵈ edition.] → *New York, G. P. Putnam,* 1904. 12 vol. in-8°, portr.
[8° Z. 16399

———— The Federalist, a commentary on the constitution of the United States, being a collection of essays written in support of the constitution agreed upon September 17, 1787, by the Federal Convention, reprinted from the original text of Alexander Hamilton, John Jay, and James Madison. Edited by Henry Cabot Lodge. — *London, T. F. Unwin,* 1888. In-8°, xlvi-586 p. [8° Pb. 3105

———— Le Fédéraliste, ou Collection de quelques écrits en faveur de la constitution proposée aux États-Unis de l'Amérique par la Convention convoquée en 1787, publiés dans les États-Unis de l'Amérique par MM. Hamilton, Madisson [sic] et Gay [sic]. ... — *Paris, Buisson,* 1792. 2 vol. in-8°. [8° Pb. 238

———— Le Fédéraliste (commentaire de la constitution des États-Unis), recueil d'articles écrits en faveur de la nouvelle constitution, telle qu'elle a été adoptée par la Convention fédérale le 17 septembre 1787, par A. Hamilton, J. Jay et J. Madison. Nouvelle édition française, avec une introduction bibliographique et historique, par Gaston Jèze,... avec une préface de A. Esmein, ... — *Paris, V. Giard et E. Brière,* 1902. In-8°, lv-788 p. [8° Pb. 4427
(Bibliothèque internationale de droit public.)

———— The Federalist : a collection of Essays [signed : Publius, i.e. Alexander Hamilton, assisted by J. Madison and J. Jay] written in favour of the New Constitution, etc. 2 vol. 1788. 12°. *See* PUBLIUS.   **1389. b. 3.**

Above left, The Library of Congress, above right, The Bibliothèque Nationale, bottom, The British Museum.

all the large research libraries of the world. This series of essays supporting the Constitution first appeared in the form of letters to the New York City *Independent Journal*, October 27, 1787–April 2, 1788. The letters, signed "Publius," were written by Alexander Hamilton, James Madison, and John Jay. Hamilton collected and revised the letters for publication in book form in 1788. Because *The Federalist* is a significant contribution to political theory, it has been published and still is being published in various editions. The student can compare some of the entries for it from the printed catalogs of the three great national libraries mentioned above.

In addition to the catalogs of the great national libraries, there are national and so-called trade bibliographies or records of books published in the various countries. These two forms of bibliography are helpful in verifying entries. When a researcher wants to know about the existence of a book, he can check the catalogs of the national libraries, publishers, and dealers.

TRADE BIBLIOGRAPHIES

United States

The following reference aids will help the student find a book published in the United States. Charles Evans' *American Bibliography*, the most important general list of early American publications, is a year-by-year record from 1639 to 1800.[11] It has an index

---

[11] *American Bibliography: A Chronological Dictionary of all Books, Pamphlets, and Periodical Publications Printed in the United States of America from the Genesis of Printing in 1639 down to and Including the Year 1800: With Bibliographical and Biographical Notes*, 12 vols. (Chicago, privately printed for the author by the Columbia Press, 1903–34); vol. 13, comp. by Clifford K. Shipton (Worcester, Mass., American Antiquarian Society, 1955); vol. 14, *Index*, ed. by Roger P. Bristol (Worcester, Mass., American Antiquarian Society, 1959). The Henry E. Huntington Library and Art Gallery in San Marino, California, has published *American Imprints, 1648–1797 in the Huntington Library, Supplementing Evans' "American Bibliography,"* comp. by Willard O. Waters, a reprint from the *Huntington Library Bulletin*, no. 3 (February, 1933). The Rare Book

of authors, an index for classified subjects, and an index for printers and publishers in each volume. Evans stopped with the letter *M* in the entries for 1799, and Clifford K. Shipton started with the letter *N* for 1799 and continued through the alphabet for 1800 with an author and subject index. Roger P. Bristol has edited volume 14, a cumulative author-title index to the whole work, including pseudonyms, attributed authors, government bodies, and group entries for newspapers and almanacs. He has also compiled a *Supplement*, which is arranged chronologically and is being issued in parts, and an *Index of Printers, Publishers, and Booksellers Indicated by Charles Evans in His "American Bibliography."*[12]

Clifford K. Shipton, with James E. Mooney, has compiled the *National Index of American Imprints through 1800: The Short-Title Evans.*[13] The 39,000 Evans items and 10,000 items not in Evans but numbered by Shipton are arranged in one alphabetical list. The entry gives the author when known, his dates, the short title, the place of publication, the printer and publisher, the date of publication, pagination, the Evans number, and the location of the copy reproduced in the microprint edition of *Early American Imprints.* It also lists the libraries that have the microprint cards.

American Bibliography: A Preliminary Checklist[14] is intended to fill the gap between Evans' *American Bibliography* and Orville A. Roorbach's *Bibliotheca Americana, 1820–1861.* One volume, arranged alphabetically by author, has been published for each year between 1801 and 1819. Ralph E. Shaw and Richard H.

Division of the New York Public Library published in 1960 a *Checklist of Additions to Evans' "American Bibliography" in the Rare Book Division of the New York Public Library*, comp. by Lewis M. Stark and Maud D. Cole (New York, New York Public Library).

[12] (Charlottesville, Bibliographical Society of the University of Virginia, 1962–); (Charlottesville, Bibliographical Society of the University of Virginia, 1961).

[13] 2 vols. (Worcester, Mass., American Antiquarian Society and Barre Publishers, 1970).

[14] 22 vols. (New York, Scarecrow Press, 1958–65). Includes one volume of corrections and an author index, one volume of addenda, a list of sources and library symbols, and one volume that is a title index.

Shoemaker checked secondary sources, such as the records of the American Antiquarian Society and the catalogs of selected large libraries, for their entries for books, periodicals, newspapers, sermons, speeches, and government documents of historical importance. The information given for each title varies but generally includes the author, title, imprint, and at least two locations. The index volumes include one for authors, one for titles, and one for a list of sources and library symbols.

Richard Shoemaker is compiling *A Checklist of American Imprints*, one volume for each year, to cover materials, except periodicals and newspapers, for the years 1820–25.[15] He has used the same method of compiling from secondary sources that he and Shaw used in their *American Bibliography*, and he gives the same information about author, title, imprint, and location. This work overlaps Roorbach, updates it, and includes many more entries.

Orville A. Roorbach's *Bibliotheca Americana, 1820–1861*[16] and James Kelly's *American Catalog of Books (Original and Reprints) Published in the United States from Jan. 1861 to Jan. 1871*[17] cover sketchily the periods 1820–61 and 1861–71. Both Roorbach and Kelly list less than half as many titles per year as Evans (who lived in a period when there was much less publishing), and they fail to give locations for their less accurate and more incomplete entries.

Roorbach compiled his work for publishers and booksellers rather than for scholars. The first volume, covering 1820–52, includes periodicals and sections on law books, state reports, and digests. The second, covering October, 1852–May, 1855; the third, May, 1855–March, 1858; and the fourth, March, 1858–January, 1861, are less comprehensive. All four are arranged alphabetically by author and title, and the entry includes the publisher and occasionally the date of publication.

Kelly continued Roorbach's work. His first volume covers the

---

[15] Vol. 1– (New York, Scarecrow Press, 1964–).
[16] 4 vols. (New York, O. A. Roorbach, 1852–61).
[17] 2 vols. (New York, Wiley, 1866–71).

Civil War period, 1861–65, and all the titles, except a separate list of forty-two, were published in the North. The second volume, 1866–70, includes some items omitted from the first volume and from Roorbach. Both volumes include reprints and originals with author, title, and series entries interfiled alphabetically. Although inaccurate and incomplete, Roorbach and Kelly were the only reference aids of their kind available for their period until Shoemaker began his *Checklist of American Imprints.*

Joseph Sabin's *Dictionary of Books Relating to America from Its Discovery to the Present Time* (sometimes referred to as *Bibliotheca Americana*) includes books, pamphlets, and periodicals printed in America and works about this country printed elsewhere down to 1892, with the location of libraries that have copies.[18] Sabin, an Oxford man who became an authority on rare books about America, completed only thirteen volumes, published between 1868 and 1881, before his death. Wilberforce Eames finished the next seven volumes by 1892, and R. W. G. Vail finally completed the series for the Bibliographical Society of America in 1936. The entries, arranged alphabetically by author, usually give author, full title, place, publisher, and date of publication. If there are printings of a title in more than one country, complete bibliographical information is given for each. References to reviews are often given, as are locations for rare books. Since there are no title or subject indexes, the user must use an author approach to this monumental and fairly comprehensive work.

The *American Catalog of Books* is the standard list for the period 1876–1910.[19] It was begun by Frederick Leypoldt as a trade bibliography of books in print and for sale to the public. The *United States Catalog: Books in Print*[20] and the *Cumulative Book*

[18] 29 vols. (New York, Joseph Sabin, 1868–92; Bibliographical Society of America, 1928–36).

[19] *American Catalog of Books, 1876–1910,* 9 vols. in 13 vols. (New York, Publishers' Weekly, 1876–1910).

[20] 1st ed., 2 vols. (New York, H. W. Wilson Co., 1899); 2d ed. (New York, H. W. Wilson Co., 1902); 3d ed. (New York, H. W. Wilson Co., 1912); 4th ed. (New York, H. W. Wilson Co., 1928).

Index, commonly known as the *CBI*,[21] constitute an indispensable record of American publications from 1898 to date. The fourth edition of the *United States Catalog* lists all the books published in English in the United States and Canada in print in 1928, and the *CBI* lists books published anywhere in the English language. The *CBI* excludes government documents and ephemeral material. Both are dictionary catalogs listing entries for authors, titles, and subjects in one alphabet, and both give full bibliographic information for an item.

For the reader interested in the very latest material by an author or on a subject, American publishers have produced some very valuable and useful tools. The standard American book-trade journal is *Publishers' Weekly* (*PW*), which contains a bibliographical list of new publications arranged alphabetically by author and main entry.[22] The *American Book Publishing Record* (*BPR*)[23] provides a subject approach to *PW* by cumulating the "Weekly Records" from *Publishers' Weekly* in Dewey Decimal Classification order with separate author and title indexes. *Forthcoming Books*[24] is an author and title index listing books to be published in the next five months. The *Subject Guide to Forthcoming Books*[25] provides a subject approach to the author and title lists in *Forthcoming Books*.

The *Publishers' Trade List Annual*[26] is a collection of major publishers' catalogs arranged alphabetically under the publisher's

[21] (New York, H. W. Wilson Co., 1898–). Published periodically since 1898, with cumulations to form supplements to the *United States Catalog*. In 1930 the subtitle, *A World List of Books in the English Language*, was added. Now published monthly, except July and August. Quinquennial cumulations from 1928 to 1956; biennial since 1957.

[22] (New York, R. R. Bowker Co., 1872–). Weekly.

[23] (New York, R. R. Bowker Co., 1961–). Monthly. *American Book Publishing Record* also has been published as an annual since 1966. The years 1960–64 have been cumulated in four volumes published in 1968, the years 1965–69, in five volumes published in 1970.

[24] (New York, R. R. Bowker Co., 1966–). Bimonthly.

[25] (New York, R. R. Bowker Co., 1967–). Bimonthly.

[26] (New York, R. R. Bowker Co., 1873–). Annual.

name with an index of authors and titles, called *Books in Print*,[27] and a subject index, called *Subject Guide to Books in Print*,[28] which follows basically the subject headings established by the Library of Congress. *Forthcoming Books*, beginning with its November, 1967, issue, serves as a continuing cumulative index to books published since the latest *Books in Print*.

With the ever growing number of paperbacks, *Paperbound Books in Print* has become increasingly important.[29] Paperbacks bring back into print some very important titles and present original titles.

Great Britain

For English books there are comparable tools, and they go back farther. The most important guide to books published before 1640 is Pollard and Redgrave's *Short-Title Catalogue*, often cited as *STC*.[30] This comprehensive record of English books is an author list of about 26,500 items with a location list of British and American libraries. Wing's *Short-Title Catalogue* continues Pollard and Redgrave down to 1700, and it locates copies in more than two hundred libraries in Great Britain and the United States.[31] For

[27] (New York, R. R. Bowker Co., 1948–). Annual.

[28] (New York, R. R. Bowker Co., 1957–). Annual.

[29] (New York, R. R. Bowker Co., 1955–). Issued monthly with quarterly cumulations.

[30] Alfred W. Pollard and G. R. Redgrave, *A Short-Title Catalogue of Books Printed in England, Scotland, and Ireland and of English Books Printed Abroad, 1475–1640* (London, Bibliographical Society, 1926). Paul G. Morrison has compiled an *Index of Printers, Publishers, and Booksellers in A. W. Pollard and G. R. Redgrave, "A Short-Title Catalogue"* (Charlottesville, Bibliographical Society of the University of Virginia, 1950). There are numerous titles which give other locations for *STC* books in the research libraries of the United States and Great Britain.

[31] Donald G. Wing, *Short-Title Catalogue of Books Printed in England, Scotland, Ireland, Wales, and British America, and of English Books Printed in Other Countries, 1641–1700*, 3 vols. (New York, printed for the Index Society by Columbia University Press, 1945–51). Paul G. Morrison has also compiled an *Index of Printers, Publishers, and Booksellers in Donald Wing's "Short-Title Catalogue"* (Charlottesville, University of Vir-

26

1700 to 1855 the only list available is the *London Catalogue of Books*,[32] which gives poor and incomplete coverage and has been superseded by the *Bibliotheca Britannica*,[33] *The Bibliographer's Manual of English Literature*,[34] and the *English Catalogue of Books*.[35] In the nineteenth century, things improved. The standard English trade list, the *English Catalogue of Books*, was based on the weekly lists in the *Publishers' Circular*, the English equivalent of the American *Publishers' Weekly*. From 1889 on, the *English Catalogue of Books* listed books under the author's name with added title and catchword subject entries. With the 1960–62 volume it changed its arrangement again and divided into sections: paperbacks, authors with full bibliographic information, titles, maps and atlases, and publishers.

In the late nineteenth century Joseph Whitaker began to issue the *Reference Catalogue of Current Literature*,[36] listing all the books in print at that time. It has changed its name and today is called *British Books in Print*.[37] It records in separate author and title lists the books in print at the end of the previous April and on sale in the United Kingdom. In the 1920's, *Whitaker's Cumulative*

---

ginia Press for the Bibliographical Society of Virginia, 1955). There are several other volumes that list additional locations for the Wing items.

[32] (London, publisher varies). Alfred Growoll gives a record of editions in his *Three Centuries of English Booktrade Bibliography* (New York, Dibdin Club, 1903).

[33] Robert Watt, *Bibliotheca Britannica: Or a General Index to British and Foreign Literature*, 4 vols. (Edinburgh, printed for A. Constable and Co., 1824).

[34] William Thomas Lowndes, *The Bibliographer's Manual of English Literature*, new ed., rev., corr., and enl. by H. G. Bohn, 6 vols. (London, Bell & Daldy, 1858–64).

[35] *English Catalogue of Books . . . Issued . . . in Great Britain and Ireland . . .* (London, S. Low, 1864–1901; Publishers' Circular, 1906–). The subject entries for 1837 to 1889 are in the *Index to the English Catalogue of Books, 1837–1889*, 4 vols. (London, S. Low, 1858–93).

[36] (London, J. Whitaker & Sons, 1874–). Irregular.

[37] (London, J. Whitaker & Sons, 1965–). With the 1967 edition, it is to become an annual. The R. R. Bowker Co., New York, distributes it in the United States and Mexico.

Book List,[38] based on records in the *Bookseller*, began to appear. It is a classified list; that is, arranged by subject with author and title indexes. Like the *English Catalogue of Books*, it provides comprehensive but not complete coverage.

While British books are included in the *CBI*, the best current British list is the *British National Bibliography*. Often referred to as the *BNB*, this official catalog of British publishing was established in 1950.[39] It is a subject list arranged by the Dewey Decimal Classification System, with an alphabetical author, title, and subject index. The lists are compiled from books and pamphlets received under the provisions of the Copyright Act at the British Museum. Full bibliographical information is given for every entry. The British also have a catalog of paperbacks, called *Paperbacks in Print*,[40] which corresponds to the American *Paperbound Books in Print*.

WORLD BIBLIOGRAPHIES

The student interested in countries other than the United States and Great Britain can find out about their national bibliographies from guides. The major guide to national bibliographies is *Current National Bibliographies*, compiled by Helen F. Conover.[41] It is an extension of "Current National Bibliographies," which appeared in the *Library of Congress Quarterly Journal of Current Acquisitions* from 1949 to 1953. Limited to the current records of the book trade in sixty-seven countries in mid-1954, the volume is arranged by broad political areas and individual countries and includes annotations and complete bibliographical descriptions. It lists books,

[38] (London, J. Whitaker & Sons, 1924–). Issued quarterly; cumulates annually and every four or five years.

[39] (London, Council of the British National Bibliography, British Museum, 1950–). Weekly with annual and five-year cumulations. *Cumulative Subject Catalog, 1950–1954*, 2 vols.; *1955–1959*, 3 vols.; *Cumulated Index, 1950–1954*; *1955–1959*.

[40] (London, J. Whitaker & Sons, 1960–). Semiannual.

[41] U.S., Library of Congress, General Reference and Bibliography Division (Washington, D.C., 1955).

28

periodicals, government documents, and directories. There is an index of titles and a directory of publishers.

Robert L. Collison has published two valuable guides to national bibliography: *Bibliographies, Subject and National: A Guide to Their Contents, Arrangement, and Use*[42] and *Bibliographical Services Throughout the World, 1950–1959.*[43] The first guide includes history titles, arranged by Dewey Decimal Classification, in its section on subject bibliographies and universal and national bibliographies for Great Britain, the United States, France, and Germany in its national section. Annotations are included for the titles in both sections. Collison's second title, *Bibliographical Services Throughout the World*, appears in two parts. Part 1 summarizes the bibliographic activities for each country and territory and part 2 summarizes the bibliographical activities of United Nations agencies and eighty-three other international organizations during the decade of the 1950's. He has emphasized the smaller countries and has given sketchy information on the larger countries. Listings in *Bibliography, Documentation, Terminology*[44] provide more recent information on national and international bibliographic activities.

The authoritative and monumental guide to all bibliographies—national, trade, and other—is Theodore A. Besterman's *A World Bibliography of Bibliographies and of Bibliographical Catalogs, Calendars, Abstracts, Digests, Indexes, and the Like.*[45] Almost 117,000 separately published bibliographies of books, manuscripts, and patent abridgments are listed under 16,000 subjects arranged alphabetically. The index in the fifth volume is a dictionary catalog of authors, editors, translators, titles of serials and anonymous works, libraries, and patents. An estimate of the number of items in a bibliography appears in parentheses.

[42] 2d ed., rev. and enl. (New York, Hafner Publishing Co., 1962).

[43] *UNESCO Bibliographical Handbooks* (Paris, UNESCO, 1961).

[44] *Bibliography, Documentation, Terminology* (Paris, UNESCO, 1961–). Bimonthly.

[45] 4th ed., 5 vols. (Lausanne, Societas Bibliographica, 1965–66).

While Besterman is universal in coverage, the *Bibliographic Index* emphasizes material published mainly in English in books, pamphlets, and periodicals since 1937.[46] It is arranged alphabetically by subject and lacks an author index; therefore, its approach is limited to subject. It is especially useful for minor subjects.

The student working on a topic should first find out what has been written on his subject. An appropriate bibliography will give him this information. He might find such a bibliography in the national library catalogs, the trade bibliographies, or one of the universal or world bibliographies.

[46] (New York, H. W. Wilson Co., 1938–). Published semiannually since 1951 with the December issue being the annual cumulation, which cumulates irregularly.

3
Guides, Manuals, and Bibliographies of History

General

The inexperienced student doing his first research will find many guides to help him. There are guides to techniques of research, guides to reference books, and guides to historical resources. Among the many books on research, Jacques Barzun and Henry G. Graff's *The Modern Researcher* is outstanding.[1] Although the book will be of use to anyone doing research in any field, history students will find it especially rewarding. The two authors, both Columbia University historians, have written about research methods, evaluation and interpretation of facts, and the mechanics of writing the paper, report, book, thesis, or dissertation. In the new enlarged edition they have again emphasized "how skillful expression is connected throughout with the technique of research and the art of thought."[2]

The big three reference guides are by Winchell, Walford, and Malclès. Although instruction in the use of these guides is often limited to library science students, the undergraduate, the graduate, and the faculty member in almost any field can profit from investigating their contents.

The reference librarian's bible is Constance Winchell's *Guide to Reference Books*.[3] The new eighth edition covers about 7,500

[1] (New York, Harcourt, Brace, 1957).
[2] (New York, Harcourt, Brace & World, 1970), xvii.

titles published before 1965. This standard guide to basic reference books began sixty-five years ago. Alice Kroeger compiled the first two editions; Isadore Mudge, the next four; and Constance Winchell, the seventh and eighth. International in scope with emphasis on English-language material, it is divided into five parts in this new edition: General Reference Works, Humanities, Social Sciences, History and Area Studies, and Pure and Applied Sciences. In each part reference books are grouped into and listed under the following categories: Guides and Manuals, Bibliographies, Indexes and Abstract Journals, Encyclopedias, Dictionaries of Special Terms, Handbooks, Annuals and Directories, Histories, Biographical Works, Atlases, and Serial Publications. The index includes entries for authors, subjects, and some titles.

The *First Supplement*, covering about one thousand reference books, includes new works, new editions, and new parts of continuations in all fields. Eugene P. Sheehy, editor of the *First Supplement* and head of the Reference Department in the Columbia University libraries, has introduced some new features, such as the Library of Congress card number and references to reviews in selected American Library Association periodicals. As in the earlier supplements to previous editions, prices and cross references to the basic volume are given. Succinct annotations and an author-title-subject index makes this *Supplement* especially useful. Semiannual supplements and semiannual annotated lists in the January and July issues of *College and Research Libraries* keep Winchell up to date.

Albert J. Walford's *Guide to Reference Material* represents the British viewpoint.[4] Emphasizing current British reference books,

[3] Constance M. Winchell, *The Guide to Reference Books*, 8th ed. (Chicago, American Library Association, 1967); Eugene P. Sheehy, ed., *First Supplement*, 1965–66 (Chicago, American Library Association, 1968); Eugene P. Sheehy, ed., *Second Supplement*, 1967–68 (Chicago, American Library Association, 1970).

[4] 2d ed. (London, Library Association, 1966–). Vol. 1, *Science and Technology* (1966); vol. 2, *Philosophy and Psychology, Religion, Social Sciences, Geography, Biography, and History* (1968); vol. 3, *Generalia, Language and Literature, the Arts*, forthcoming.

this volume is arranged by subject classification according to the 1957 abridgment of the Universal Decimal Classification, which puts history in class nine. Annotations and indexes are included in each volume. This reference aid is especially useful because it includes literature surveys and lists of subject materials published in scholarly serials.

Louise-Noëlle Malclès' *Les sources*,[5] which represents perhaps the most scholarly point of view of the three, was designed as a textbook and guide and has a great amount of introductory material. International in scope, it emphasizes French and European works. Although it includes basic works of earlier dates, it also emphasizes publications of the last twenty-five years, especially those of the 1940–50 decade. The first volume is concerned with bibliographies of bibliographies, printed library catalogs, and society publications; the second, with dictionaries, encyclopedias, periodicals, treatises, and bibliographies in the humanities and social sciences; and the third, with exact sciences and technology. There are author, title, and subject indexes in each volume, but no cumulative index for all the volumes.

Guides, manuals, and bibliographies can lead the history student to available materials and help him select the best for his subject. The American Historical Association's *Guide to Historical Literature*,[6] which is a revision of the old standard *Guide to Historical Literature*,[7] is the first source the student should consult. It is divided into nine sections: (1) Introduction and General History, (2) Historical Beginnings, (3) The Middle Period in Eurasia and North Africa, (4) Asia Since Early Times, (5) Modern Europe,

[5] *Les sources du travail bibliographique*, 3 vols. in 4 (Geneva, E. Droz, 1950–58).

[6] George Frederick Howe, Gray Cowan Boyce, Thomas Robert Shannon Broughton, Howard Francis Cline, Sidney Bradshaw Fay, Michael Kraus, Earl Hampton Pritchard, and Boyd Carlisle Shafer, eds. (New York, Macmillan Co., 1961).

[7] George M. Dutcher, William Henry Allison, Sidney Bradshaw Fay, Augustus Hunt Shearer, and Henry Robinson Shipman, eds. (New York, Macmillan Co., 1931). Hereafter cited as Dutcher's *Guide to Historical Literature*.

(6) The Americas, (7) Africa, (8) Australasia and Oceania, and (9) The World in Recent Times. Within each section the materials are arranged by form: bibliographies, libraries, and special museum collections; encyclopedias and works of reference; geographies, gazetteers, and atlases; anthropologic, demographic, and linguistic works; printed collections of sources; shorter and longer general histories; histories of periods, areas, and topics; biographies; government publications; publications of academies, universities, and learned societies; and periodicals. The emphasis is on English-language materials, and specialists have selected and briefly annotated the materials for their sections. An analytical index adds to the usefulness of this volume.

Lubomyr R. Wynar's *History: A Selective and Annotated Bibliographical Guide*,[8] one of a series in which Wynar discusses social sciences in general, sociology, and political science, is a guide to history that can be used to supplement the *Guide to Historical Literature*. The scope of this work is limited to basic historical references in the University of Colorado libraries; the arrangement is alphabetical by subject (general reference sources and general historical references) and by nation; and the annotations are brief and informative.

In his *Sources of Information on the Social Sciences: A Guide to the Literature*, Carl M. White has included a chapter on history.[9] An excellent introductory essay on historiography and a listing of the basic works in the major fields of history by James P. Shenton is followed by sections on the major guides to history, abstracts and digests, bibliographies, biography, dictionaries, encyclopedias, atlases, handbooks, compendia, yearbooks, and so on, with periodicals listed for each category of history. The annotations are excellent; they are descriptive and critical.

Edith M. Coulter and Melanie Gerstenfeld's *Historical Bibliog-*

[8] *Social Sciences General References: Selective and Annotated Bibliographical Guides*, no. 4 (Boulder, University of Colorado, Social Science Library, 1963).

[9] (Totowa, N.J., Bedminster Press, 1964), 62–120.

34

raphies: A Systematic and Annotated Guide is out of date in many sections, but is still valuable for certain basic bibliographies. It will direct the student "to the printed materials required for minute research in almost any special field."[10] The annotations are critical and evaluative.

United States

Research techniques and specialized historical resources useful to the student of American history are discussed in a number of guides. Homer C. Hockett's *The Critical Method in Historical Research and Writing,*[11] a rewritten and expanded edition of his *Introduction to Research in American History,* includes sections on research techniques, the principles of historical criticism, and American historiography, as well as an excellent bibliography. Methods of choosing a subject and writing a master's essay and doctoral dissertation are also discussed.

The guide of first importance to students of United States history is the *Harvard Guide to American History.*[12] The forerunner of this basic work is Albert Bushnell Hart and Edward Channing's *Guide to the Study of American History,*[13] which was revised by its two original authors and Frederick Jackson Turner under the title *Guide to the Study and Reading of American History.*[14] In the new *Harvard Guide* six Harvard professors, several of whom are Pulitzer Prize winners, have collaborated and "have attempted to construe American history in its widest sense, . . . to assimilate the findings of recent scholarship, . . . to remember that in many cases older books still retain their value, . . . [and] to maintain a balance

[10] Foreword by Herbert Eugene Bolton (Berkeley, University of California Press, 1935), iii. This is an expansion of Edith M. Coulter's *Guide to Historical Bibliographies,* which was published in 1927, by the University of California Press.

[11] (New York, Macmillan Co., 1955).

[12] Oscar Handlin, Arthur Meier Schlesinger, Samuel Eliot Morison, Frederick Merk, Arthur Meier Schlesinger, Jr., and Paul Herman Buck, eds. (Cambridge, Harvard University Press, Belknap Press, 1954).

[13] (Boston, Ginn & Co., 1897).

[14] Rev. ed. (Boston, Ginn & Co., 1912).

between useful sections of general works available in all libraries and learned monographs that will interest few except the specialist."[15] The *Harvard Guide*, which sets December 31, 1950, as the terminal date for publications, is divided into large parts: (1) Status, Methods, and Presentation; (2) Materials and Tools; (3) Colonial History and the Revolution; (4) National Growth, 1879–1863; (5) The Rise of Modern America; and (6) America in the Twentieth Century. An excellent author-title-subject index helps the user find the sections and items he needs.

Writings on American History, prepared and published by the American Historical Association, is a very important annual classified list of all books and important articles on American history that have appeared in the year.[16] Up to 1936 it includes all writings published during the year on Latin America, and up to 1940 all those on British North America. In addition to the author-title-subject index in each volume, there is a cumulated index for 1902–40. The biggest drawback is the slowness of publication of volumes. The volume for 1958 did not come out until 1966.

The General Reference and Bibliography Division of the Library of Congress has published *A Guide to the Study of the United States of America: Representative Books Reflecting the Development of American Life and Thought*.[17] Thirty-two chapters, covering some 6,400 items with annotations averaging one hundred words, include general, diplomatic, military, intellectual,

[15] Handlin et al., *Harvard Guide to American History*, viii.

[16] 1902, E. C. Richardson and A. R. Morse, comps. (Princeton, N.J., Library Book Store, 1904); 1903, A. C. McLaughlin, W. A. Slade, and E. D. Lewis, comps., 2 vols. (Washington, D.C., Carnegie Institute, 1905); 1906–39/40, Grace Gardner Griffin et al., comps., 33 vols. (New York, 1908–10, Washington, D.C., 1914–19, 1921–44). Publisher varies beginning with volume 13, published as supplements to or as volume 2 of the *Annual Report* of the American Historical Association. 1948– , comp. for the National Historical Publications Commission, James R. Masterson, ed. (Washington, D.C., U.S. Government Printing Office, 1952–). Annual. *Index, 1902–1940* (Washington, D.C., American Historical Association, 1956).

[17] Prepared under the direction of Roy P. Basler, by Donald R. Mugridge and Blanche P. McCrum (Washington, D.C., 1960).

and local history. The index includes authors, titles, and subjects.

The standard, though old, work on bibliographies of American history is Henry Putney Beers's *Bibliographies in American History: Guide to Materials for Research.*[18] It deals with general aids, bibliographies of the colonial, revolutionary, Confederation, and national periods of United States history and includes bibliographies of economic, constitutional, diplomatic, social, cultural, and scientific history as well as bibliographies for each of the states. Bibliographical entries are not annotated.

A new abstracting guide to periodical literature that provides a bibliographical review of articles in periodicals, transactions, proceedings, *Festschriften*, and *mélanges* of the United States and Canada from prehistory to the present is *America: History and Life: A Guide to Periodical Literature.*[19] Edited by Eric H. Boehm and modeled on *Historical Abstracts*, this new guide offers short summaries and annotated bibliographical citations of articles from more than five hundred United States and Canadian periodicals in a classified arrangement: (1) North America; (2) Canada; (3) United States of America to 1945; (4) United States of America: 1945 to Present; (5) United States of America: Regional, State, or Local History; and (6) Historiography and Methodology. Each abstract, signed by an abstracter who is identified in the list of abstracters for that issue, gives the author's full name and affiliation, the title of the article, the name of the periodical, the volume number, the date, pages, and CUES for that article. The CUES are subject headings or facets listed in abbreviated form; they serve as a subject index. Because *America: History and Life* appears fairly promptly, it makes up for the time lag in the appearance of *Writings on American History*. There are annual author and biographical indexes.

Besides these general guides to and bibliographies of United

---

[18] Rev. ed. (New York, H. W. Wilson Co., 1942). The first edition was published in 1938.

[19] (Santa Barbara, Calif., Clio Press for the American Bibliographical Center, 1964–). Quarterly.

States history, there are guides and bibliographies for special fields of United States history. The exhaustive *Guide to the Diplomatic History of the United States, 1775–1921*,[20] compiled by Samuel Flagg Bemis and Grace Gardner Griffin, is the authoritative work in its field. Part 1 consists of bibliographical chapters, topically and chronologically arranged, on the period from the Revolution to 1921. Part 2 concerns sources for diplomatic history: printed state papers of the United States and foreign governments, published records of international groups, and manuscripts. Excellent annotations and indexes make this guide invaluable.

A new guide in the field of diplomatic relations is David F. Trask, Michael C. Meyer, and Roger B. Trask's *A Bibliography of United States–Latin American Relations Since 1810: A Selected List of Eleven Thousand Published References*.[21] This guide is designed to provide the student with the literature of United States–Latin-American relations in one volume. The bibliography includes published materials of all kinds in many languages. The books, articles, pamphlets, and documents are in English, Spanish, Portuguese, French, German, Italian, Russian, and Japanese.

A Bibliography of United States–Latin American Relations Since 1810 is organized in two main sections, which are supplemented by several specialized chapters. Chapters 3–10 provide a chronological survey of United States–Latin-American relations from the beginning of the national independence movements in Latin America in 1810 up to the present. Chapters 13–24 offer a country-by-country survey. Chapter 1 includes an extensive list of guides and aids, chapter 2 covers general studies of the field, chapter 11 focuses on the course of the Pan-American movement since 1889, and chapter 12 lists works relating to certain Latin-American movements of a political, ideological, and cultural nature which have exerted significant influence on the course of

[20] Samuel Flagg Bemis and Grace Gardner Griffen, *Guide to the Diplomatic History of the United States, 1775–1921* (Washington, D.C., Government Printing Office, 1935).

[21] (Lincoln, University of Nebraska Press, 1968).

hemispheric relations, in particular, Pan-Hispanism, Yankee-phobia, and Aprismo. Each item is cited in full only once, but cross references are provided for other relevant sections of the bibliography. All citations are alphabetized by author, or by title if no author is given, within sections and subsections. The index lists only items with identifiable authors; the detailed table of contents, therefore, serves as an aid in locating information on specific topics.

Also available are bibliographies on special subjects, such as Elizabeth W. Miller's *The Negro in America: A Bibliography* and Dorothy B. Porter's *The Negro in the United States: A Selected Bibliography.*[22] There are guides for special regions, such as Thomas D. Clark's two collections on travels in the South[23] and Henry Raup Wagner's bibliography on the West, *The Plains and the Rockies: A Bibliography of Original Narratives of Travel and Adventure, 1800–1865.*[24] There are guides for special periods, such as Allan Nevins' *Civil War Books: A Critical Bibliography.*[25]

Guides to autobiographies, diaries, and manuscripts are described in chapters 8 and 9.

Americans are inveterate indexers, arrangers, and bibliographers, and the many excellent indexes, guides, and bibliographies to their history reflect these interests.

Ancient

There is no separate guide in English to Greek and Roman

[22] Comp. for the American Academy of Arts and Sciences (Cambridge, Harvard University Press, 1966); comp. from the Library of Congress holdings (Washington, D.C., for sale by the Superintendent of Documents, Government Printing Office, 1970).

[23] *Travels in the Old South: A Bibliography*, 3 vols. (Norman, University of Oklahoma Press, 1956–59); *Travels in the New South: A Bibliography*, 2 vols. (Norman, University of Oklahoma Press, 1962).

[24] Rev. by Charles L. Camp, 3d ed. (Columbus, Ohio, Long's College Book Co., 1953).

[25] James I. Robertson, Jr., and Bell I. Wiley, 2 vols. (Baton Rouge, printed for the U.S. Civil War Centennial Commission by the Louisiana State University Press, 1967–68).

history;[26] therefore, the undergraduate student will need to use Dutcher's *Guide to Historical Literature* and the revised *Guide to Historical Literature*. Donald McFayden and Arthur Edward Romilly Boak compiled the sections on "Ancient Greece and the Hellenistic World" and "Rome: The Republic and the Empire" in the Dutcher volume, while Carl A. Roebuck and T. Robert S. Broughton edited these sections in the latter volume. All agree that the student will need to turn to the annual bibliographies for much of his bibliography.

L'Année philologique[27] and *The Year's Work in Classical Studies*[28] are two annual bibliographies for ancient history. *L'Année philologique*, the standard bibliographical work for classical studies, has sections on Greek and Roman history for the specialist. The nonspecialist can use *The Year's Work in Classical Studies*, which contains brief annual bibliographies up to 1950 and the current listing of books and articles on ancient history in the *American Historical Review*.[29]

Both the Dutcher and the revised *Guide to Historical Literature* also emphasize that extensive and reliable bibliographies can be found in the *Cambridge Ancient History* volumes.[30] Planned by J. B. Bury, this standard work is the most exhaustive work in English on the problems and periods in Greek and Roman history. Each volume has been written by a specialist. Both guides also list and annotate shorter general histories and histories of the special

[26] Paul Petit has written a guide in French, *Guide de l'étudiant en histoire ancienne*, new ed. (Paris, Presses Universitaires de France, 1962).

[27] *L'Année philologique: Bibliographie critique et analytique de l'antiquité gréco-latine*, 1924/1926– (Paris, Société d'Éditions "Les Belles-Lettres," 1928–). Annual. It was published under the direction of Jules Marouzeau et al. and is a continuation of Marouzeau's *Dix années de bibliographie classique de l'antiquité gréco-latine pour la période 1914–1924*, 2 vols. (Paris, Société d'Éditions, "Les Belles-Lettres," 1927–28).

[28] Ed. for the Classical Journals Board, 34 vols. (London, J. Murray, 1907–50). Annual that has ceased publication.

[29] (New York, Macmillan Co., 1895–). Quarterly.

[30] 12 vols. and 5 vols. of plates (Cambridge, At the University Press, 1923–39).

40

periods and special areas of ancient history which provide more retrospective bibliography.

Medieval and Renaissance

There are several guides available for the study of medieval history. The best, though outdated, is Louis J. Paetow's *A Guide to the Study of Medieval History*.[31] It is comprehensive, scholarly, and critical. Part 1, General Books, covers bibliographical works, reference works, source auxiliaries to the study of medieval history, general modern historical works, and large collections of original sources; part 2 concerns the general history of the Middle Ages; and part 3 covers medieval culture.

From Paetow, the student will learn about three great bibliographies for medieval history. The first, Cyr Ulysse Joseph Chevalier's *Repertoire des sources historiques du Moyen Age*, is the best guide to the literature of the Middle Ages.[32] The first two volumes, "Bibliographie," are devoted to people. Listed alphabetically under the French form of the name are people who lived in the first fifteen centuries after Christ, with references to works about them. Many obscure medieval figures appear in this list, which makes no critical appraisal of the titles given. The last two volumes concern places, institutions, and topics.

The second important bibliography for medieval history is *Quellenkunde der deutschen Geschichte* by Friedrich Christoph Dahlmann and Georg Waitz.[33] First published in 1830, this standard bibliography of German history is now in its tenth edition. The tenth edition is being issued in sections. It is expected to consist of eight volumes and to continue through 1945. Previous

[31] Dana C. Munroe and Gray C. Boyce, eds., rev. ed., prepared under the auspices of the Mediaeval Academy of America (New York, F. S. Crofts & Co., 1931).

[32] Cyr Ulysse Joseph Chevalier, *Repertoire des sources historiques du Moyen Age: Biobibliographie*, new rev., corr., and enl. ed., 2 vols. in 4 (Paris, Picard, 1894–1907).

[33] Ed. at the Max-Planck Institute for History by H. Heimpel and H. Geuss, 10 vols. (Stuttgart, Hiersemann, 1965–).

editions include virtually all works of any importance on German history in the German language, though lists of non-German works are less complete. The only indication of the importance of the publications is the small type used for the less important titles.

Finally, *The Sources and Literature of English History*, by Charles Gross, is the basic bibliographical guide for English medieval history.[34] It is a systematic and critical bibliography of the sources and secondary works for English history from its beginning to 1485.

August Potthast's *Bibliotheca Historica Medii Aevi* is primarily a bibliography of medieval chronicles and biographies.[35] It analyzes the collections of sources and lists the chronicles chronologically by countries. An international committee of medievalists is bringing out a new edition of this standard work which will contain sets that Potthast omitted and sets published since 1896.[36]

Because Paetow's *Guide to the Study of Medieval History* is over thirty years old, the student will find more recent references in the *Guide to Historical Literature*, a bibliography, and several new serial titles. From the *Guide to Historical Literature*, for example, comes Harry F. Williams' *An Index of Mediaeval Studies Published in Festschriften, 1865–1946*.[37] It lists material from five hundred *Festschrift* volumes dealing with the culture and art of the Middle Ages.

Medieval and Renaissance Studies[38] can be used as a biblio-

---

[34] *The Sources and Literature of English History from the Earliest Times to About 1485*, 2d rev. and enl. ed. (1915; reprint ed., New York, Peter Smith, 1951).

[35] *Bibliotheca historica Medii Aevi: Wegweiser durch die Geschichtswerke des europaischen Mittelallers bis 1500*, 2d corr. and limited ed., 2 vols. (Berlin, W. Weber, 1896).

[36] *Repertorium fontium historiae Medii Aevi: Primum ab Auguste Potthast Digestum*, now in the care of the Colleges of History, amended and authored by many nations, 2 vols. (Rome, Instituto Storico Italiano per il Medio Evo, 1962–). Vol. 1 (1962); Vol. 2 (1967).

[37] *An Index of Mediaeval Studies Published in Festschriften: 1865–1946 with Special Reference to Romantic Material* (Berkeley, University of California Press, 1951).

[38] North Carolina University Library, Humanities Division. *Medieval*

graphic guide, although it was written as a guide for the students using the Duke University and the University of North Carolina libraries.

Several new serials serve as guides to studies of the Middle Ages. The *International Guide to Medieval Studies: A Quarterly Index to Periodical Literature*[39] lists articles by author, with cumulative author and subject indexes. *Progress of Medieval and Renaissance Studies in the United States and Canada*,[40] an annual survey which ceased publication in 1960, lists papers, projects, publications, and doctoral dissertations as well as lists of medieval and Renaissance specialists with their publications. The *International Medieval Bibliography*[41] lists periodical articles from 160 journals and *Festschriften* concerning the history and civilization of Europe from the accession of Diocletian to the end of the fifteenth century. It is arranged by subject, with indexes of authors and personal and place names. A very new index is the *Bibliographie internationale de l'Humanisme et de la Renaissance*.[42] It covers literature, philosophy, history, religion, the arts, economics, political science, law, science, and technology. Although the emphasis is on the fifteenth and sixteenth centuries, this new index extends back to the humanists of the fourteenth century and forward to Renaissance influence on the seventeenth century. It is compiled from lists supplied by scholarly associations in European countries, the United States, and Latin America, and it includes journals, congresses, and *Festschriften*, with an index of persons, places, and subjects.

---

and Renaissance Studies: A Location Guide to Selected Works and Source Collections in the Libraries of the University of North Carolina at Chapel Hill and Duke University (Chapel Hill, University of North Carolina, 1967).

[39] (Darien, Conn., American Bibliographic Service, 1961–). Quarterly.

[40] (Boulder, University of Colorado, 1923–60). Bulletin nos. 1–25.

[41] *International Medieval Bibliography*, 1967– (Minneapolis: Department of History, University of Minnesota, 1968–). Semi-annual. R. S. Hoyt and P. H. Sawyer are the directors. Originally issued in card form, volume 1 reproduced the cards issued during 1967. Beginning with 1968, the bound volumes appear semi-annually.

Great Britain

Students of English history will find a variety of guides available: a guide to resources for Commonwealth studies,[43] excellent bibliographies for specific periods of English history, and a current bibliography of writings on British history.

The remarkable *Bibliography of British History* has volumes covering the Tudor periods,[44] the Stuart periods,[45] and the eighteenth century.[46] A continuation of Gross's *Sources and Literature of English History*, these volumes are arranged by subject and cover the social, cultural, political, economic, colonial, and military aspects of English history. Each volume has its own author index.

Writings on British History[47] is a comprehensive bibliography of books and articles on British history from A.D. 450 to 1914. Volume 1 covers publications for the years 1934–45 and includes a select list of publications in those years on British history since 1914. This comprehensive bibliography emphasizes English-language materials, and entries are arranged under general works and periods of English history. Although there are no annotations,

[42] (Geneva, E. Droz, 1966–). Vol. 1, *Travaux parus en 1965*.

[43] A. R. Hewitt, *Guide to Resources for Commonwealth Studies in London, Oxford, and Cambridge, with Bibliographical and Other Information* (London, Athlone Press for the Institute of Commonwealth Studies, University of London, 1957).

[44] Conyers Read, ed., *Bibliography of British History: Tudor Period, 1485–1603*, 2d ed. (Oxford, Clarendon Press, 1959). First published in 1933.

[45] Godfrey Davies, ed., *Bibliography of British History: Stuart Period, 1603–1714*, (Oxford, Clarendon Press, 1928).

[46] Stanley Pargellis and D. J. Medley, eds., *Bibliography of British History: The Eighteenth Century, 1714–1789*, (Oxford, Clarendon Press, 1951).

[47] *Writings on British History: A Bibliography of Books and Articles on the History of Great Britain from About 450 A.D. to 1914* (London, J. C. Cape, 1937–). Annual. Volumes published for the years 1935–39 have an appendix containing a select list of publications in 1934–39 on British history since 1914. *1940–1945*, 2 vols. (London, J. C. Cape, 1960). *1901–1933*, ed. by H. H. Bellot, 5 vols. (London, J. C. Cape, 1968–).

44

there are references to reviews. Each volume has an author-subject index.

More recent references can be found in Louis Benson Frewer's *Bibliography of Historical Writings Published in Great Britain and the Empire, 1940–1945*,[48] Joan C. Lancaster's *Bibliography of Historical Works Issued in the United Kingdom, 1946–1956*,[49] and William Kellaway's *Bibliography of Historical Works Issued in the United Kingdom, 1957–1960*,[50] and *1961–1965*.[51] Though not limited to English history, these works contain strong sections on English history. Frewer compiled his work for the British National Committee of the International Committee of the Historical Sciences. The books, pamphlets, and periodicals listed are arranged by areas and periods, with indexes of persons and places. Lancaster and Kellaway continued the listing for books and pamphlets.

Besides *Progress of Medieval and Renaissance Studies in the United States and Canada*, which has ceased publication, there is a new index: the *Bibliographie internationale de l'Humanisme et de la Renaissance* published by the Federation internationale des sociétés et instituts pour l'étude de la Renaissance.[52] It covers literature, philosophy, history, religion, the arts, economics, political science, law, science, and technology. Although the emphasis is on the fifteenth and sixteenth centuries, this new index extends back to the humanists of the fourteenth century and forward to Renaissance influence on the seventeenth century. It is compiled from lists supplied by scholarly associations in European countries, the United States, and Latin America, and it includes journals,

[48] Ed. for the British National Committee of the Historical Sciences (Oxford, B. Blackwell, 1947).

[49] (London, University of London, Institute of Historical Research, 1957).

[50] (London, University of London, Institute of Historical Research, 1962).

[51] (London, University of London, Institute of Historical Research, 1967).

[52] (Geneva, E. Droz, 1966–). Vol. 1, *Travaux parus en 1965*.

congresses, and *Festschriften*, with an index of persons, places, and subjects.

Russia

For Russian history, library catalogs as well as bibliographies are available. The Library of Congress *Cyrillic Union Catalog in Microprint* consists of entries in Russian, Ukrainian, Belorussian, Bulgarian, and Serbian for material in and reported to the Library of Congress by 185 major research libraries. The first part is arranged by author and added entry; the second, by title; and the third, by subject. The entries are transliterated into the Roman alphabet, and titles for the post-1917 publications, except for belles-lettres, are translated into English.[53] The *Cyrillic Union Catalog* was prepared by Readex Microprint Corporation at the initiative of the Coordinating Committee for Slavic and Eastern European Library Resources and in co-operation with the American Library Association's Committee on Resources and the Library of Congress.

Another important catalog for Russian history is *The Dictionary Catalog of the Slavonic Collection* of the New York Public Library Reference Department.[54] This catalog lists by author and subject materials in or translated from the Slavic languages and material in any language about Slavic affairs. It covers periodical articles as well as books. The Library of Congress has, in addition to its regular catalogs for books which include Russian-language works, an accessions list for Russian-language monographs and periodicals received currently in the Library of Congress and a group of co-operating libraries.[55] This union list is divided into three parts: Part A, Monographs; Part B, Periodicals, with their tables of con-

[53] 1244 cards in 7 boxes (New York, Readex Microprint Corp., 1963).

[54] 26 vols. (Boston, G. K. Hall & Co., 1959).

[55] U.S. Library of Congress, Processing Department, *Monthly Index of Russian Accessions*, vol. 1– , 1942– . From 1948 to 1957, it was called the *Monthly List of Russian Accessions*.

46

tents translated into English; Part C, Alphabetical Subject Index to Parts A and B, under subject headings.

In addition to the section by Fritz T. Epstein in the *Guide to Historical Literature*, there are several excellent bibliographic aids relating to Russian history. The Hoover Institution on War, Revolution, and Peace has published a multivolume *Guide to Russian Reference Books*.[56] It consists of six volumes and lists more than 3,500 titles of "reference tools pertaining to the historical, political, economic, social, scientific, technical, and intellectual life of the Russian people." Not limited to holdings at the Institution, the series includes the following titles: volume 1, General Bibliographies and Reference Books; volume 2, Historical Sciences; volume 3, Social Sciences, Religion, and Philosophy; volume 4, Humanities; and volume 5, Science, Technology, and Medicine. The sixth volume will include supplementary materials and contain a cumulative index to the entire work.

The Hoover Institution's *Guide to Russian Reference Books* is the first general guide to Russian bibliographies and reference books. It is selective, it covers reference works listing materials from the eleventh century to the end of 1960, and it is restricted to materials in Russian and Western European languages. The first volume, after covering bibliographies of bibliographies, takes up Russian national bibliographies, lists of bibliographies for each Soviet republic, bibliographies of Russian publications published outside Russia, bibliographies of non-Russian publications relating to Russia, library catalogs, rare and illustrated books, catalogs of manuscripts, bibliographies of dissertations, translations, congresses, periodicals, newspapers, indexes, and abstracts. Chapters also cover general encyclopedias, biographical dictionaries, dictionaries of anonyms and pseudonyms, dictionaries of abbreviations, language dictionaries, and handbooks. The second volume of the *Guide to Russian Reference Books* surveys bibliographies of

[56] Karol Maichel, *Guide to Russian Reference Books,* ed. by J. S. G. Simmons, 6 vols. (Stanford, The Hoover Institution on War, Revolution, and Peace, Stanford University, 1962–).

Russian history in general and by special period and subject and treats bibliographies of world history, auxiliary historical sciences, ethnography, geography, and geology. The index is an alphabetical index of authors, titles, and subjects. Annotations explain the form, content, scope, and function of each title.

Paul L. Horecky has edited two basic and selective bibliographic guides. The first, *Basic Russian Publications: A Selected and Annotated Bibliography on Russia and the Soviet Union*, contains titles limited to works in political and social science published in Russian in Tsarist Russia, the Soviet Union, and other countries.[57] A few non-Russian-language materials representing bibliographic references to or partial texts of Russian works were also included. The major sections in this volume are: General Reference Aids and Bibliographies, The Land, The People, History, The State, The Economic and Social Structure, Society and Intellectual Life.

Perhaps of more use to the undergraduate is Horecky's companion volume on Western-language publications, *Russia and the Soviet Union: A Bibliographic Guide to Western-language Publications*.[58] Its organization is the same as *Basic Russian Publications*. In his introduction, Horecky comments: "Together, the two [publications] represent a rigorously pruned inventory of Russian and Western publications in the field of studies on Russia and the USSR. As area bibliographies they do not cover communism *per se*, but only its Russian brand." The annotations are accurate and informative.

Rosemary Neiswender's *Guide to Russian Reference and Language Aids* is a highly selective and practical guide to current Russian linguistic and reference aids.[59] This annotated guide to over two hundred current textbooks, language records, dictionaries, glossaries, encyclopedias, geographical reference works, bibliographies, indexes, and other reference sources also gives information

---

[57] (Chicago, University of Chicago Press, 1962).

[58] (Chicago, University of Chicago Press, 1965).

[59] Special Libraries Association Bibliography, no. 4 (New York, Special Libraries Association, 1962).

48

on transliteration systems and bibliographic terminology. Although it slights the humanities and social sciences intentionally, it does complement Maichel's *Guide to Russian Reference Books* and the Horecky volumes.

A selective bibliography of works in English on Russian history is David Shapiro's *A Select Bibliography of Works in English on Russian History, 1801–1917*.[60] This classified bibliography of 1,070 books and articles in English has a critique at the beginning of each section, references to reviews listed under title, and an author index.

The annual *American Bibliography of Slavic and East European Studies* made its initial appearance in 1957.[61] The first volume covers books and articles in the humanities published in 1956; later volumes added the social sciences and history.

Latin America

Michael R. Martin and Gabriel H. Lovett's *Encyclopedia of Latin-American History*[62] is a convenient reference volume on Latin-American history from the earliest times to the 1960's. Its entries cover major pre-Columbian civilizations; European colonies in the region; political, social, and economic development of Latin-American nations; inter-American relations and Latin-American relations with other leading world powers; principal cities and geographical features; major wars and battles; governmental institutions; developments in agriculture, industry, and labor; and biographies of notable political, military, and cultural figures. Definitions of Spanish and Portuguese words and phrases are given if they have a special significance in Latin-American history. Entries are arranged alphabetically, and the use of small capitals or italics for names, words, and phrases indicates that the particular term appears elsewhere as a separate entry.

Cecil Knight Jones was the pioneer figure with respect to bib-

[60] (Oxford, Blackwell, 1962).
[61] (Bloomington, Indiana University Press, 1957–). Annual.
[62] Rev. ed. by Robert Hughes (Indianapolis, Bobbs-Merrill Co., 1968).

liography concerning Latin America. Arthur E. Gropp, the librarian of the Columbus Memorial Library, Pan American Union, has updated Jones's second edition of *Bibliography of Latin American Bibliographies*. The new edition comprises 2,900 items retained from the Jones edition and 4,000 new references to publications of a monographic nature.[63] Gropp has changed Jones's arrangement from a geographic one to a subject one with geographic subdivisions. The detailed index includes names of persons, corporate bodies, government offices, titles of series, and subject entries. If no location is given for an entry, it is to be assumed that it is available from the Columbus Memorial Library and/or the Library of Congress. Other locations are indicated by symbols, which are identified in a separate list.

Robin Arthur Humphreys has written the valuable annotated guide *Latin American History: A Guide to the Literature in English*. Issued under the auspices of the Royal Institute of International Affairs, it is an expansion of the author's 1949 book, *Latin America: A Selective Guide to Publications in English*. Organized by topic, period, and geographical area, *Latin American History* covers economics, politics, and sociology but omits archaeology and ethnology in its 2,089 references to books and periodical articles.[64]

The *Handbook of Latin American Studies*, the standard, authoritative bibliography of current material, supplements these two

[63] *A Bibliography of Latin American Bibliographies*, an updating of the 2d ed., comp. by C. K. Jones (Metuchen, N.J., Scarecrow Press, 1968). C. K. Jones, *A Bibliography of Latin American Bibliographies*, 2d ed. rev. and enl. by the author with the assistance of James A. Granier (Washington, D.C., 1942). See also Benito Sanchez Alonso in footnote 114 for Spanish bibliography.

[64] (London, Oxford University Press, 1958). For John P. Harrison's *Guide to Materials on Latin America in the National Archives*, see note 31 in chapter 9. Charles Gibson's *The Colonial Period in Latin American History* (Washington, D.C., American Historical Association, 1958) is a brief, authoritative summary guide to recent research with much bibliographical insight, according to the American Historical Association's *Guide to Historical Literature*, 667.

titles.[65] It is an excellent selected, annotated bibliography of all kinds of material on all aspects, including the history of Latin America, with author and subject indexes.

An expansion of his 1961 *Latin America: A Bibliographical Guide to Economy, History, Law, Politics, and Society* is Stojan A. Bayitch's *Latin America and the Caribbean: A Bibliographical Guide to Works in English*.[66] This selective, unannotated bibliography contains over 32,000 references to books and articles in English dealing with some aspect of the social sciences of Latin America and the Caribbean. It includes six parts: (1) Bibliographies and Reference Works, (2) General Information, (3) Fundamentals and Backgrounds, (4) Guide by Countries, and (6) The Caribbean. Comprehensive in its coverage of articles and books dealing with politics, history, economy, and society, it has a subject index but lacks an author approach. Because entries in *Latin America and the Caribbean* are restricted to English-language materials only and because this volume is aimed at the general public, it is less selective than the *Handbook of Latin American Studies*.

There are two extremely important periodicals dealing with Latin-American history. The first, *Hispanic American Historical Review*,[67] publishes documented articles on any phase of Latin-American history. R. L. Butler's *Guide to the Hispanic American Historical Review, 1918–1945* is an invaluable guide to its contents for the first twenty-odd years.[68] The second important periodical for Latin-American history is *Latin American Research Review: A Journal for the Communication of Research Among*

[65] (Gainesville, University of Florida Press, 1936–). Annual. With the 1964 issue it divided into two sections: Humanities, which includes history, and Social Sciences. Published in alternate years.

[66] University of Miami School of Law, Interamerican Legal Studies, vol. 10 (Coral Gables, University of Miami Press, 1967).

[67] (Baltimore, Williams & Wilkins Co., 1918–22; Durham, N.C., Duke University Press, 1926–).

[68] (Durham, N.C., Duke University Press, 1950).

Individuals and Institutions Concerned with Studies in Latin America,[69] which contains articles in both English and Spanish.

Latin-American history has an outstanding index to periodical literature, the Pan American Union's *Index to Latin American Periodical Literature, 1929–1960.*[70] It cites articles from over three thousand different periodicals indexed at the Columbus Memorial Library of the Pan American Union. Another retrospective Latin-American periodical index is Sturgis E. Leavitt's *Revistas hispanoamericanas: Índice bibliográfico, 1843–1935.*[71] It contains a classified listing of 30,107 articles from fifty-six journals with a separate section for translations, an index of names, and a list of libraries having complete sets of the fifty-six journals. It emphasizes literature, linguistics, and folklore.

A new and current index to 331 periodicals published in Latin America is the *Index to Latin American Periodicals: Humanities and Social Sciences.*[72] Prepared by the Columbus Memorial Library of the Pan American Union, it offers both an author and subject approach in its index.

For the latest books in Spanish, besides those listed in the *National Union Catalog*, there are two important reference tools. The first is *Libros en venta en Hispanoamérica y España,*[73] a "books in print" for books written in Spanish. Volumes contain author, title, and subject classification sections arranged by the Dewey decimal system, plus a subject index. More than 87,000 books are listed, representing the output of more than eight hundred publishers in nineteen countries.

[69] (Austin, University of Texas, Latin American Research Review Board, 1966–).

[70] 8 vols. (Boston, G. K. Hall & Co., 1962).

[71] (Santiago de Chile, Fondo Histórico y Bibliográfico José Turibio Medina, 1960).

[72] (Boston, G. K. Hall & Co., 1962–). Annual.

[73] (New York, R. R. Bowker Co., 1964–). *Suplemento, 1964–1966* (Buenos Aires, Bowker Editores, 1967); *Suplemento, 1967/1968* (Buenos Aires, Bowker Editores, 1969).

The second important title is *Fichero bibliográfico Hispano-americano*.[74] Issued quarterly, this publication is a classified bibliography of new books in Spanish published in the Spanish-speaking part of Latin America, as well as works in Spanish published in Canada, Brazil, the European possessions in the Caribbean area, and the United States. Unlike *Libros en venta*, this bibliography does not include books in Spanish published in Spain. There is an author-title index.

Martin Sable's *A Guide to Latin American Studies*[75] continues the work begun by the *Latin American in Periodical Literature*,[76] a quarterly publication of the Latin American Center. Sable's *Guide to Latin American Studies* is a guidebook to basic and advanced textbooks, standard reference sources, conference proceedings, periodicals, documents, and pamphlet material. It is selective and has approximately five thousand annotations in all fields of knowledge related to Latin America. There are author and subject indexes to the materials which are arranged alphabetically by broad subject divisions.

The Far East

J. D. Pearson's *Oriental and Asian Bibliography: An Introduction with Some Reference to Africa*, a pioneer attempt at compiling Oriental and Asian bibliography, is "intended to be an introduction to the subject of Oriental and Asian bibliography as a whole and is, therefore, primarily concerned with institutions, books, and libraries which relate to the whole of, or substantial parts of the Asian continent."[77] The author expects to publish volumes of a more specialized nature on Africa, the Islamic Near East, the non- and pre-Islamic Near East, South Asia, Southeast Asia and

[74] (New York, R. R. Bowker Co., 1964–). Quarterly.

[75] University of California, Los Angeles, Latin American Center, *Reference Series*, no. 4, 2 vols. (Los Angeles, University of California, Latin American Center, 1967).

[76] 2 vols. (Los Angeles, University of California, Latin American Center, January, 1962–June, 1963).

[77] (Hamden, Conn., Archon Books, 1966), ix.

Oceania, and Central Asia and the Far East. The present volume is divided into three parts: (1) institutions producing literature, (2) the bibliographical apparatus available for control and use of this literature, and (3) libraries and archives where the literature is stored together with the special problems affecting them. The section on the literature and its controls deals with European manuscripts relating to Asia, including catalogs and indexes; and bibliographies, including general bibliographies, those concerned with parts of Asia, and selective bibliographies. Appendix B has a list, arranged alphabetically by author, of the works referred to in the text with page references.

The brief but authoritative *Select List of Books on the Orient*[78] lists books, written mostly in English, about Egypt, the Middle East, India, Southeast Asia, and the Far East, from ancient to modern times. This publication is the result of a conference held by the Association of British Orientalists, which selected 870 reliable and readable books about Asia from the great mass of specialized writings. The books are arranged in four main divisions dealing with the civilizations of Ancient Egypt and the Ancient Near East and Middle East, Islam, India and Further India, and the Far East. Brief introductions on the scope and range of the subjects preface each section and terse annotations illuminate many of the titles listed.

Another selective bibliography is the American Universities Field Staff's *Select Bibliography: Asia, Africa, Eastern Europe, Latin America.*[79] It was compiled by a large group of scholars who listed some six thousand of what they regarded as the most useful books and journals available for college study and general reading about the civilizations of these areas. The titles, 2,747 of which are on Asia, are arranged by regional and cultural sections within the major geographical area and are subdivided by subject. There are supplements for 1961 and 1963.

The *Bibliography of Asian Studies*, formerly the *Bulletin of Far*

[78] W. A. C. H. Dobson, ed. (Oxford, Clarendon Press, 1955).
[79] (New York, American Universities Field Staff, Inc., 1960).

54

Eastern Bibliography, provides the best coverage for Eastern Asia.[80] In 1955 it began to include items on India and the remaining parts of South Asia (although Southeast Asia has been included from the very beginning). It is a comprehensive, classified list of all types of material on Asia in English, with an author index.

Two older guides to Far Eastern history are available. John K. Fairbank and Kwang Ching Liu's *Modern China: A Bibliographical Guide to Chinese Works, 1898–1937* is an annotated bibliography to Chinese-language works concerning affairs in China since the Reform Movement of 1898.[81] Emphasis is on works of reference, government, law, economics, foreign affairs, and social problems. The annotations are in English, and the authors and title entries are given in Chinese characters and in the Wade-Giles romanization with an English translation. The second guide, Robert J. Kerner's *Northeastern Asia: A Selected Bibliography*, contains nearly fourteen thousand titles in Far Eastern and Western languages.[82] There is a table of contents and a subject index.

John F. Embree and Lillian O. Dotson's *Bibliography of the Peoples and Cultures of Mainland Southeast Asia* is an essential bibliography covering Burma, Indochina, and Thailand.[83] This

[80] In *Journal of Asian Studies* (Ann Arbor, Mich., Association for Asian Studies, 1957–). Annual. From 1936 through 1955, it was called, with slight variations, "Far Eastern Bibliography" in the *Far Eastern Quarterly*. G. K. Hall & Co. recently published a four-volume author catalog, *Cumulative Bibliography of Asian Studies, 1941–1965*, which is a cumulation in one alphabet of the entries published for twenty-five years in the *Bibliography of Asian Studies* and the *Far Eastern Quarterly*. In 1970, G. K. Hall & Co. published a four-volume subject catalog for those twenty-five years.

[81] Harvard-Yenching Institute Studies, vol. 1 (Cambridge, Harvard University Press, 1950).

[82] 2 vols. (Berkeley, University of California Press, 1939).

[83] Yale University Southeast Asia Studies (New Haven, Conn., Yale University Press, 1950). Maureen L. P. Patterson and Ronald B. Inden have edited *Introduction to the Civilization of India, South Asia: An Introductory Bibliography* (Chicago, University of Chicago Press, 1962). This classified bibliography lists more than 4,300 works, primarily in English, on India, Pakistan, Ceylon, and Nepal. There is an author and title index to the entries which are grouped into the following classes: general, history;

extensive bibliography refers to about twelve thousand books and periodical articles in Western languages on archaeology, ethnology, cultural history, social organization, and law. Arranged by country and topic with occasional brief annotations, it lacks an author index. The three latest bibliographical guides on this area are: Stephen N. Hay and Margaret H. Case's *Southeast Asian History: A Bibliographical Guide*,[84] a selected, annotated guide to 632 books, periodical articles, and dissertations, mostly in English but with a few in French; James K. Irikura's *Southeast Asia: Selected, Annotated Bibliography of Japanese Publications*,[85] a valuable guide for specialists with 965 entries; and Cecil Hobbs's *Southeast Asia: An Annotated Bibliography of Selected Reference Sources in Western Languages*, a useful listing of 535 items.[86]

Among the guides to reference works, P. K. Garde's *Directory of Reference Works Published in Asia* applies to these areas.[87] Garde has listed 1,619 ready reference books and bibliographies published in India, Pakistan, Afghanistan, the countries of East and Southeast Asia, Indonesia, and the Philippines. The entries are arranged by Universal Decimal Classification and then by country. Titles in Asian languages are transliterated and given English translations. There are indexes of authors, subjects, and language dictionaries.

Henri Cordier has compiled the standard bibliography for nineteenth-century China. His *Bibliotheca Sinica* is the basic bibliography of books and articles in Western languages on China.[88] The East Asiatic Library, Columbia University libraries, has com-

social structure and organization; political and economic structure; religion and philosophy; and literature, science, and the arts.

[84] (New York, Praeger, 1962).

[85] Yale University Southeast Asia Studies in association with the Human Relations Files (New Haven, Conn., Yale University Press, 1956).

[86] 2d rev. and enl. ed. (Washington, D.C., Library of Congress, Reference Department, Orientalia Division, 1964).

[87] (Paris, UNESCO, 1956).

[88] *Bibliotheca Sinica: Dictionnaire bibliographique des ouvràges relatifs à l'Empire Chinois*, 2d. ed., rev., corr., and greatly enl., 4 vols. (Paris, Guilmoto, 1904–1908). *Supplément* (Paris, Geunthner, 1922–24).

56

piled and issued an index to it.[89] Yüan T'ung-li's *China in Western Literature: A Continuation of Cordier's "Bibliotheca Sinica"* is an indispensable list of almost all books concerning China published in English, French, and German between 1921 and 1957.[90] It is the best comprehensive guide for its period. C. O. Hucker's *China: A Critical Bibliography* is the best short guide to works on China in Western languages, especially English.[91]

Peter Berton and Eugene Wu's *Contemporary China: A Research Guide* is a new guide for modern China.[92] It covers bibliographical and reference works, documentary materials, and selective serial publications in the social sciences and humanities for post-1949 Mainland China and post-1945 Taiwan. Entries have descriptive and evaluative annotations. There are detailed author-title and subject indexes and two appendices: one on publications devoted to the resources of research libraries and institutions and one listing dissertations and theses on contemporary China accepted by American universities.

Herschel Webb and Marleigh Ryan have compiled the most comprehensive work in English on Japanese history, *Research in Japanese Sources: A Guide*.[93] It steers the reader to basic bibliographies, research guides, and standard works in the field.

In addition to *Research in Japanese Sources*, there is a comprehensive guide to Japanese-language reference books. The *Guide to Japanese Reference Books* is an English version of the second edition of the Japanese *Nihon no sankotosho*.[94] Over two thousand

[89] East Asiatic Library, Columbia University Libraries, comp. *Author Index to the "Bibliotheca Sinica"* (New York, East Asiatic Library, Columbia University Libraries, 1953).

[90] *Far Eastern Publications* (New Haven, Conn., Yale University Press, 1958).

[91] (Tucson, University of Arizona Press, 1962).

[92] Howard Koch, Jr., ed., *Hoover Institution Bibliographical Series*, no. 3 (Stanford, Calif., Hoover Institution on War, Revolution, and Peace, 1967).

[93] (New York, published for the East Asian Institute, Columbia University, 1965).

[94] International House Library, trans. and ed. (Chicago, American Library Association, 1966).

entries are arranged in four major divisions (general works, humanities, social sciences, and science and technology) which have been broken down into nineteen specific sections. Entries are listed, for the most part, by author, editor, or issuing body; yearbooks, handbooks, and catalogs are usually listed under title. Each entry includes the author's name, first in roman type, then in Japanese; the title, first in roman type, then in Japanese with an English translation; the place of publication if other than Tokyo; the publisher in roman type; the date of publication according to the Western calendar; and the number of pages or volumes. A concise description, explaining the work's coverage, importance, or usefulness, is given in smaller type. An excellent index lists personal and corporate authors, titles, and subject and topical headings.

The older standard bibliographies of works in European languages on Japan are Friedrich von Wenckstern's *A Bibliography of the Japanese Empire*,[95] which covers the years 1859–1906, and Oskar Nachod's *Bibliographie von Japan*, which covers 1906–37.[96] Hugh Borton has continued the coverage up to 1952 in *A Selected List of Books and Articles on Japan in English, French, and German*.[97]

Modern

For history since 1775 there is the abstract index *Historical Abstracts, 1775–1945: Bibliography of the World's Periodical Literature*, edited by Eric H. Boehm.[98] Covering all kinds of modern history, *Historical Abstracts* is divided into three main parts: (1) General (general bibliography, methodology and re-

---

[95] *A Bibliography of the Japanese Empire: Being a Classified List of All Books, Essays, and Maps in European Languages Relating to Dai Nihon Published in Europe, America, and in the East*, 2 vols. (London, Kegan Paul, 1895–1907).

[96] 6 vols. (Leipzig, Hiersemann, 1928–40).

[97] Rev. and enl. ed. (Cambridge, Harvard University Press for the Harvard-Yenching Institute, 1954).

[98] (Santa Barbara, Calif., Clio Press with the International Social Science Institute, 1955–). Quarterly.

58

search methods, historiography, philosophy and interpretations of history, archives, libraries and institutions, meetings, and pedagogy); (2) Topics (international relations, wars and military history, World Wars I and II, political history, social and cultural history, economic history, religion and churches, sciences and technology); and (3) Area or Country (sections on Africa, Asia and the Pacific, Latin America, and North America).

Each abstract includes the full name of the author and his affiliation, the title of the article, the name of the periodical, the volume number, date, and pages, and the abstract with the abstracter's name. CUES (subject headings listed in abbreviated form) have been assigned to each abstract since 1964 when Boehm used them in *America: History and Life.* In addition to the annual subject-name index, there are two five-year indexes, for volumes 1–5 (1955–59), which was published in 1963, and for volumes 6–10 (1960–64), which was published in 1965.

The *International Bibliography of Historical Sciences,*[99] begun in 1926 and edited for the International Committee of Historical Sciences, is a current bibliography covering events from prehistory through modern history. Since 1947 it has been edited with the assistance of UNESCO. This selected, classified list of books and periodical articles from various countries is concerned with political, constitutional, religious, cultural, economic, and social history. There is an author-proper name index.

The closest thing to a general bibliography of modern European history is *A Bibliography of Modern History.*[100] The old *Cambridge Modern History* volumes are noted for their extensive bibliographies. When *A New Cambridge Modern History* was published, the bibliographies were omitted.[101] The contributors to the *New Cambridge Modern History* contributed the annotations to *A Bibliography of Modern History,* which is arranged by sections which can be used with volumes of the *New Cambridge*

[99] (Oxford, University Press, 1926–).
[100] John Roach, ed. (Cambridge, At the University Press, 1968).
[101] (Cambridge, At the University Press, 1957–).

Modern History. It emphasizes books in English published before 1961. There is an analytical subject index to the 6,040 entries.

There are also bibliographies for different periods, for different areas, and for different subjects in European history. Two bibliographies that take 1815 as their starting point are L. C. Bullock and A. J. P. Taylor's *A Select List of Books on European History, 1815–1914*[102] and Lowell J. Ragatz's *A Bibliography for the Study of European History, 1815–1939*.[103] The first is a selective list of secondary works in English and common Western European languages. The second is arranged in three sections: (1) Europe as a Whole, (2) Individual Countries, and (3) Europe. The section on Europe is divided topically into social, political, economic, and cultural history, imperialism, science, and government. Each country has the same subdivisions, with an added section on biography. The section on international relations is arranged according to major issues and periods. Examples of a bibliography on a special topic are John S. Bromley and Albert Goodwin's *A Select List of Works on Europe and Europe Overseas, 1715–1815*[104] and Roland H. Bainton's *Bibliography of the Continental Reformation: Materials Available in English*.[105] Some of the best bibliographies on a special topic are found in authoritative books on the topic, such as Carlton J. H. Hayes's *Essays on Nationalism*[106] and Parker T. Moon's *Imperialism and World Politics*.[107]

R. J. Kerner's *Slavic Europe: A Selected Bibliography in the Western European Languages: Comprising History, Languages, and Literature*,[108] a selected list of basic works in Western European languages on all phases of life in Slavic Europe, is an example of a bibliography on a region. For each country or area there are special tools available. Bibliographies for France include Pierre

---

[102] 2d ed. (Oxford, Clarendon Press, 1957).
[103] (Ann Arbor, Mich., Edwards Bros., 1942).
[104] (Oxford, Clarendon Press, 1956).
[105] (Chicago, American Society of Church History, 1935).
[106] (New York, Macmillan Co., 1926).
[107] (New York, Macmillan Co., 1926).
[108] (Cambridge, Harvard University Press, 1918).

60

Caron's bibliographies,[109] Eugene Saulnier and A. Martin's *Bibliographie des travaux publiés de 1866 à 1897 sur l'histoire de la France de 1500 à 1789*,[110] Pierre Caron and Henri Stein's *Répertoire bibliographique de l'histoire de France*,[111] the *Répertoire méthodique de l'histoire moderne et contemporaine de la France, pour les années 1898–1913*,[112] and *Bibliographie annuelle de l'histoire de France du cinquième siècle à 1939*.[113] Benito Sanchez Alonso's *Fuentes de la historia española e hispanoamericana*,[114] Raymond Foulché-Delbosc and Louis Barrau-Dihigo's *Manuel de l'hispanisant*,[115] and *Indice histórico español*[116] cover Spain. Jean Sauvaget's *Introduction to the History of the Muslim East: A Bibliographical Guide*,[117] concerns the Muslim East, and Friedrich Christoph Dahlmann and Georg Waitz's *Quellenkunde der deutschen Geschichte*,[118] Gunther Franz's *Bucherkunde zur deutschen Geschichte*,[119] and *Bibliographie zur deutschen Geschichte . . . 1888–1927*[120] focus on Germany. These are only a few of the more important titles.

[109] *Manuel pratique pour l'étude de la Révolution Française*, new ed. (Paris, A. et J. Picard, 1947); *Bibliographie des travaux publié de 1866 à 1897 sur l'histoire de la France depuis 1789* (Paris, E. Cornely et cie, 1912).

[110] 2 vols. (Paris, Les Presses Universitaires de France, 1932–38).

[111] 6 vols. (Paris, A. et J. Picard, 1923–38).

[112] Vols. 1–7, vols. 9–11 (Paris, Rieder, 1899–1932).

[113] (Paris, issued by the Comité Français des Sciences Historiques and the Centre National de la Recherche Scientifique, 1956–). Annual.

[114] Benito Sanchez Alonso, *Fuentes de la historia española e hispanoamericana*, 3d rev. and corr. ed., 3 vols. (Madrid, Consejo Superior de Investigaciones Cientificas, 1952).

[115] Raymond Foulché-Delbosc, *Manuel de l'hispanisant*, 2 vols. (New York, G. P. Putnam, 1920; Hispanic Society of America, 1925).

[116] (Barcelona, Editorial Teide, 1953–). Quarterly.

[117] Based on the 2d ed., as recast by Claude Cahen (Berkeley, University of California Press, 1965).

[118] Ed. at the Max-Planck Institute for History by H. Heimpel and H. Geuss, 10 vols. (Stuttgart, Hiersemann, 1965–).

[119] (Munich, R. Oldenbourg, 1951).

[120] (Leipzig, B. G. Teubner, 1889–1918; Dresden, Baensch, 1920–31). Annual. Issued as a supplement to *Historische Vierteljahrschrift*; no longer published.

4
Encyclopedias
and Dictionaries

In approaching an unfamiliar subject, the student should begin with a general source of information, such as an encyclopedia, dictionary, handbook, or textbook. From these general sources he can obtain an overview of his subject and find several avenues of approach. The articles in an encyclopedia are usually written by experts. They usually contain objective summaries of man's knowledge of a subject down to the time of writing and often have excellent bibliographies which serve as guides to original and selected secondary sources.

ENCYCLOPEDIAS

English Language

English-language encyclopedias often contain the exact information a student needs. Some, of course, are more valuable than others for historical data. Two extremely useful titles for history students are the *Encyclopaedia Britannica* and the *Encyclopedia Americana*. The ninth[1] and eleventh[2] editions of the *Encyclopaedia Britannica* are still quite valuable from the historical point

[1] 25 vols. (Edinburgh, A. C. Black, 1875–89).
[2] 29 vols. (Cambridge, At the University Press, 1910–11). Supplemented by two sets of supplementary volumes: 3 vols. (1922) and 3 vols. (1926).

of view. They contain long, monographic articles on general subjects written by specialists and accompanied by good bibliographies and illustrations. More specific subjects are treated as parts of general subjects and can be found through the index.

Since the fourteenth edition in 1936, the *Britannica* has stopped numbering its editions. Instead, it turns out annual printings, produced in accordance with a policy of continuous revision. Under this system the *Britannica* is divided into a number of classes, which periodically are revised as a whole, although any article may be revised at any time. Since 1938, to keep a basic set up to date, the *Britannica* has published the *Britannica Book of the Year*. The yearbooks for the decade leading up to and including World War II have been cumulated as *10 Eventful Years*.[3]

The *Encyclopedia Americana* consists of many small articles and is especially good for quick reference to American items. For example, it provides a list of states in order of their admission to the Union, with the date of their organization as territories, and includes a summary of historical events by century. Special items of value to history students in the index volume of the set are the latest census figures for the population of the United States, by state and places of more than three thousand; the latest census figures for the population of Canada, by province and places of more than fifteen hundred; a list of Indian reservations, arranged alphabetically by name, with the names of the tribes living on the reservation; and an illustrated chronology of world events for the five years preceding the publication date of the edition. Like the *Britannica*, the *Americana* follows the policy of continuous revision and has an annual to keep its basic set up to date.

There are many other general English-language encyclopedias available. S. Padraig Walsh has compiled *General Encyclopedias in Print: A Comparative Analysis*,[4] which gives information about

---

[3] *10 Eventful Years: A Record of Events of the Years Preceding, Including, and Following World War II, 1937 Through 1946*, prepared under the editorial direction of Walter Yust, 4 vols. (Chicago, Encyclopaedia Britannica, 1947).

[4] (New York, R. R. Bowker Co., 1957).

the coverage, accuracy, contributors, illustrations and maps, bibliographies, and indexing for the encyclopedias of today. He also has compiled *Anglo-American General Encyclopedias*,[5] an in-depth evaluation of the historical value of over four hundred encyclopedias published in the United States, Canada, and England from the *Universal, Historical, Geographical, Chronological and Classical Dictionary* in 1703, to *Chambers's Encyclopaedia* in 1967. The student can use *General Encyclopedias in Print* and *Anglo-American General Encyclopedias* as guides to the encyclopedias he will need to consult.

Foreign Language

Like English-language encyclopedias, the major foreign-language encyclopedias contain valuable information about persons, places, and events. There are two major French encyclopedias. The first, *La Grande Encyclopédia*,[6] is still of major importance for Europe if recent data is not essential. The second, the *Grand Larousse Encyclopédique*,[7] the latest Larousse encyclopedia, in most respects supersedes the *Nouveau Larousse illustré*[8] and the *Grand Dictionnaire universel du XIXéme siècle français*.[9] Like them, the *Grand Larousse Encyclopédique* combines the features of a dictionary and encyclopedia. It gives definitions and etymology for many words and has very brief entries of one or two lines on many small subjects.

The standard German encyclopedia is *Der grosse Brockhaus*.[10] Its brief and excellent articles are trustworthy and especially sound for German history. The beautiful Italian encyclopedia is the *Enciclopedia italiana di scienze, lettere ed arti*.[11] It has excellent

[5] (New York, R. R. Bowker Co., 1967).
[6] 31 vols. (Paris, H. Lamirault et cie, 1886–1902).
[7] 10 vols. (Paris, Librairie Larousse, 1960–64).
[8] 8 vols. (Paris, Librairie Larousse, 1898–1907).
[9] 17 vols. (Paris, Librairie Larousse, 1965–90?).
[10] 12 vols. (Wiesbaden, E. Brockhaus, 1952–60). *Ergänzungaband*, 2 vols.
[11] 35 vols. (Rome, Instit. della Enciclopedia Italiana, fondata da Giov-

long, signed articles with bibliographies and is noted for its many beautiful art and travel illustrations. The great Spanish encyclopedia, *Enciclopedia universal ilustrada europeo-americana*, often referred to as *Espasa*, is invaluable not only for Spain but also for Latin America.[12] Its maps and plans of cities are a unique feature. Russia, too, has several encyclopedias reflecting its viewpoints. The official one and the most extensive is *Bol'shaia sovetskaia entsiklopediia*.[13] The second edition is supposed to be "purged of the gross theoretical and political errors of the earlier edition"; hence, amid other changes, the article on Lavrenti P. Beria has been excised and the article on Stalin changed.

ENCYCLOPEDIAS AND DICTIONARIES OF THE SOCIAL SCIENCES

Of the subject encyclopedias, the *Encyclopedia of the Social Sciences*, edited by Edwin R. A. Seligman, has been the comprehensive work for the whole field for forty years.[14] Prepared under the auspices of ten learned societies, including the American Historical Association, it deals with history "only to the extent that historical episodes or methods are of especial importance to the student of society."[15] Its long, signed articles by specialists have excellent bibliographies. About fifty per cent of the articles are biographical, many of deceased persons. Today the *Encyclopedia of the Social Sciences* is out of date in many respects, but it is still an excellent place to begin a search.

---

anni Treccani, 1929–37). *Index*, vol. 23 (1939); *Appendice 1* (1938); *Appendice 2, 1938–1948*, 2 vols. (1948–49); *Appendice 3, 1949–1960*, 2 vols. (1961).

[12] 80 vols. in 81 (Barcelona, J. Espasa é hijos, 1905–33). *Apéndice*, 10 vols. (Madrid, Espasa-Calpe Gropp, 1930–33). *Suplemento anual*, 1934– (Madrid, Espasa-Calpe, 1935–).

[13] 53 vols. (Moscow, Sovetskaia Entsiklopediia, 1949–60).

[14] Alvin Johnson, assoc. ed., 15 vols. (New York, Macmillan Co., 1930–35).

[15] *Ibid.*, 1, xix.

The new *International Encyclopedia of the Social Sciences*[16] is designed to complement, not to supplant, its predecessor. The work of fifteen hundred contributors and two hundred advisory editors from thirty countries, it consists of fairly lengthy, signed articles with bibliographies on topics and people in anthropology, economics, education, geography, history, law, political science, psychology, and sociology. Unlike its predecessor the *Encyclopedia of the Social Sciences*, which emphasizes the concrete and descriptive, the *International Encyclopedia of the Social Sciences* emphasizes the abstract and conceptual. Also, it omits many of the valuable historical and evaluative accounts of events, institutions, and people which appear in the *Encyclopedia of the Social Sciences*. The *International Encyclopedia of the Social Sciences* has fewer biographical articles than its predecessor (which has about four thousand), though a greater proportion of its six hundred biographical articles concern academic social scientists about whom information is not easily found elsewhere. Living persons born after 1890 are excluded.

The new *International Encyclopedia of the Social Sciences* is organized alphabetically with extensive cross references. Many specific articles that share the same general subject matter are grouped under one title. Most of the articles are followed by a list of four or five references to other articles in the encyclopedia. The subject index refers the reader to articles by title, volume, and page. This is the comprehensive encyclopedia on the social sciences of today.

There is a need in the social sciences for an encyclopedia or dictionary to bring together the terms used by the constituent disciplines and to define these terms in concise and clear language. There are two such dictionaries for the social sciences that are very important, though they do not consider history as one of their disciplines. Under the auspices of UNESCO Julius Gould and

[16] David L. Sills, ed., 17 vols. (New York, Macmillan Co. and the Free Press, 1968).

W. L. Kolb have compiled *A Dictionary of the Social Sciences*,[17] which defines one thousand general concepts and terms in political science, social anthropology, economics, social psychology, and sociology. The *Dictionary of Social Sciences*, compiled by John T. Zadrozny, takes most of its entries from sociology, political science, and economics and a fair sprinkling of terms from the fields of population studies, psychology, physical anthropology, prehistory, jurisprudence, and statistics.[18] The history student often is working in an area where he will need to know some of the technical terms in these fields, especially political science.

Dictionaries of political science; bibliographies, such as the *London Bibliography of the Social Sciences*[19] and the computerized bibliographies of the Universal Reference System's *Political Science Series*;[20] and guides, such as J. K. Zawodny's *Guide to the Study of International Relations*,[21] are especially valuable for history students. Some of the major political science dictionaries are Harry Back, Horst Cirullies, and Gunter Marquard's *POLEC: Dictionary of Politics and Economics*;[22] Florence Elliott and Michael Summerskill's *A Dictionary of Politics*;[23] Walter Theimer's *Encyclopedia of Modern World Politics*;[24] and W. W. White's

[17] (New York, Free Press of Glencoe, 1964).

[18] Introduction by William F. Ogburn (Washington, D.C., Public Affairs Press, 1959).

[19] B. M. Headicar and Clifford Fuller, comps., introduction by Sidney Webb (London, London School of Economics, 1931–32). *Supplements*: 1st and 2d, covering 1929–31, vols. 5–6 (1934–37); vols. 7–9, covering 1936–50 (1952–55); vols. 10–11, covering 1950–55 (1958–60); vols. 12–14, covering 1956–62 (1966–68).

[20] Alfred de Grazia, ed., 10 vols. (Princeton, N.J., Universal Reference System, 1965–66). *Annual Supplements*, 1967– (1968–). Vol. 1, *International Affairs*, of the basic set and the section on international affairs in the *Annual Supplement* will be of special interest to the history student in foreign affairs.

[21] (San Francisco, Chandler Publishing Co., 1966).

[22] 2d ed. (Berlin, Walter de Gruyter & Co., 1967).

[23] 4th rev. ed. (London, Penguin Books, 1964).

[24] (New York, Rinehart, 1950).

Political Dictionary.[25] Dictionaries of American political science terms are extremely useful to American history students. Some of the more important ones are Eugene McCarthy's *The Crescent Dictionary of American Politics,*[26] Jack C. Plano and Milton Greenberg's *The American Political Dictionary,*[27] Edward C. Smith and Arthur J. Zurcher's *Dictionary of American Politics,*[28] and Hans Sperber and Travis Trittschuh's *Dictionary of American Political Terms.*[29]

CHRONOLOGIES

Books of dates or outlines of chronology can be extremely helpful to all students of history. They tell when something happened or when somebody lived, what other things were happening, and who else was alive at that time. Sigfrid Henry Steinberg's *Historical Tables* is invaluable although it lacks an index.[30] Steinberg gives a slight emphasis to British and United States history. He has presented the life of man as a whole by showing what was going on in a given age in various parts of the world in different fields of activity. Except for the sections on the period up to Charlemagne, the beginning of England, and the World War I period, there are usually six columns for each time period. For most of the book the three columns on the left deal chiefly with the relations of the major powers. The three columns on the right deal with ecclesiastical history, constitutional and economic history, and cultural life.

[25] Wilbur Wallace White (New York, World Publishing Co., 1947).

[26] (New York, Macmillan Co., 1962).

[27] Rev. and expanded ed. (New York, Holt, Rinehart and Winston, 1967).

[28] 2d ed. (New York, Barnes & Noble, c.1968).

[29] (Detroit, Wayne State University Press, 1964).

[30] *Historical Tables: 58 B.C.–A.D. 1963,* foreword by G. P. Gooch, 7th ed. (London, Macmillan, 1964). An older timetable is Margaret C. Morison's *Time Table of Modern History: A.D. 400–1870,* 2d ed. (London, Archibald Constable & Co., 1908). The French equivalent of Steinberg's *Historical Tables* is Jean Delorme's *Chronologie des civilisations* (Paris, Les Presses Universitaires de France, 1949), which consists of tables from 3000 B.C. to A.D. 1945, with an alphabetical index.

Neville Williams' *Chronology of the Modern World*,[31] like Steinberg's *Historical Tables*, is arranged by year. It begins with 1763, the year the Treaty of Paris ended the Seven Years' War, and continues through 1964. The left-hand page covers political and international events, which are arranged first by year and then by month; the right-hand page deals with achievements in arts and science, under classified headings. An index of persons, places, subjects, and book titles directs the user to the page on which he can find the date and other contemporary events and people mentioned.

Alfred Mayer's *Annals of European Civilization* presents the principal events of European cultural history from 1500 to 1900 in a year-by-year chronological order.[32] Events are arranged by country under the date. There is an index of names and summaries by major topics in chronological order: academies; aesthetics; architecture; astronomy; biology, botany, and zoology; chemistry; physics; church; colonization; economics, politics, and sociology; history; literature; mathematics; medicine; music; painting; pedagogics; philology; philosophy; poetics; and theatre. The *Annals of European Civilization* will be of most help to a student interested in cultural history.

Some books on chronology are really dictionaries arranged alphabetically by entry. *Everyman's Dictionary of Dates*[33] and Robert Collison's *Dictionary of Dates*[34] are two examples. The first gives a slight emphasis to Great Britain's history but also deals with other countries, institutions, dynasties, families, the arts, science, philosophy, religion, inventions, and a miscellany of notorious and interesting items. Prefacing this dictionary are Jewish, Roman, and Orthodox calendars as well as a calendar of secular (mainly political) anniversaries and a table reconciling the Jewish and Gregorian calendars. *Everyman's Dictionary of Dates*

---

[31] *Chronology of the Modern World: 1763 to the Present Time* (New York, David McKay, 1966).

[32] Foreword by G. P. Gooch (London, Cassell, 1949).

[33] 4th ed. (London, Dent, 1964).

[34] (New York, Philosophical Library, 1962).

has narrative entries for countries, long lists for classified entries, and many small entries of interest but not of great historical value for British history.

Collison's *Dictionary of Dates* is concerned more with scientific and technological achievements and with cultural and sociological leaders than it is with military history or leaders. It contains a small section, arranged by month and day, which lists a few important events and the births and deaths of famous people.

There are whole books on day-by-day chronology; Stanford M. Mirkin's *What Happened When* is a modern example.[35] When Mirkin was a member of the program staff at Columbia Broadcasting System, he put together a chronology of the rise of the National Socialist Party in Germany for President Franklin D. Roosevelt. Eighteen years later his *When Did It Happen*[36] appeared. Later this book was updated and retitled *What Happened When*. In selecting material, Mirkin has emphasized the major events of the nineteenth and twentieth centuries and incidents of human interest.

Some chronologies are arranged alphabetically by country and then by date. Helen Rex Keller uses this arrangement in her *Dictionary of Dates*, a history of the world from earliest times through 1930.[37] The first volume, which is based on Joseph Haydn's *Dictionary of Dates*,[38] deals with the Old World, World War I, the Paris Peace Conference, the League of Nations, the International Labor Organization, the Permanent Court of International Justice, and other international affairs. The second volume covers the New World. A brief summary of a country's history appears in para-

[35] *What Happened When: A Noted Researcher's Almanac of Yesterdays* (New York, Ives Washburn, 1966).

[36] Stanford M. Mirkin (New York, Washburn, 1957).

[37] 2 vols. (New York, Macmillan Co., 1934).

[38] *Dictionary of Dates and Universal Information Relating to All Ages and Nations*, 25th ed. (London, Ward, Locke, & Co., 1910). The first edition appeared in 1841 and the last in 1910. This old standard dictionary of miscellaneous subjects is arranged alphabetically and treated chronologically.

graph form, and outstanding events of its history are arranged by year.

Some chronologies by country are concerned with only one country. *The Encyclopedia of American Facts and Dates*[39] is a chronology for the United States. It is arranged chronologically, with every pair of facing pages divided into four columns, each of which deals with certain historical topics listed at the top of that column. Column one, for example, is concerned with politics and government, war, vital statistics, treaties, immigration, westward expansion, Indian affairs, slavery, and trade agreements; column two, with books and periodicals, painting, architecture, sculpture, music, and thought and comment; column three, with economics, science, industry, education, religion, philosophy, medicine, business, finance, technology, colleges and universities, and communications; and column four, with sports, fashion, popular entertainment, and society. The index covers all items listed and refers to them by column and page. Christopher Robert Cheney has compiled a similar volume for English history, a *Handbook of Dates for Students of English History*.[40] It reprints sections revised from Frederick Maurice Powicke's *Handbook of British Chronology*.[41]

In addition to the chronologies and outlines discussed, there are encyclopedias and dictionaries of history that also give chronology, such as William L. Langer's *An Encyclopedia of World History* and Richard Morris' *Encyclopedia of American History*. These are treated in the next sections.

Besides the regular chronologies, which often list famous people and give tables of rulers, there are several other types of reference aids which list people at specified times. Miriam Allen de Ford's *Who Was When?* is probably unique in naming the contemporaries of any celebrated person from 500 B.C. to 1938 A.D.[42] The time

---

[39] Gorton Carruth, ed., 4th ed. (New York, Thomas Y. Crowell, 1966).

[40] Royal Historical Society Guides and Handbooks no. 4 (London, Royal Historical Society, 1945).

[41] Royal Historical Society Guides and Handbooks no. 2, 2d ed. (London, Royal Historical Society, 1961).

period is listed in the first column, and people for that date are listed under columns labeled Government and Law; Military and Naval Affairs; Industry, Commerce, Economics, Finance, Invention, and Labor; Travel and Exploration; Philosophy and Religion; Science and Medicine; Education, Scholarship and History; Literature; Painting and Sculpture; Music; and Miscellaneous.

Regenten und Regierungen der Welt,[43] compiled by Bertold Spuler, lists the names of sovereigns of the great powers since 1492 and the names of ministers from the beginning of their offices. He has emphasized Germany, and he uses the German form of the Christian name of people and topographical features in the text. Special lists give various forms of Christian names, a list of countries in five languages, and a list of various ministerial departments (approximately translated).

White's Conspectus of Biography[44] carries out a similar function for United States history by listing important American men and women in a chronological and classified arrangement. A revised edition of *White's Conspectus* includes part of the conspectus and index volume of the *National Cyclopaedia of American Biography* as well as a subject index to its biographies. The *National Cyclopaedia of American Biography* may be regarded as the most comprehensive listing of American notables, living and dead, available in any one source.[45]

[42] *Who Was When? A Dictionary of Contemporaries*, 2d ed. (New York, H. W. Wilson Co., 1930).

[43] *Regenten und Regierungen der Welt: Sovereigns and Governments of the World*, 4 vols. (Wurzberg, A. G. Ploetz, 1962). *Supplement*, 1964–65 (1966).

[44] *White's Conspectus of American Biography: A Tabulated Record of American History and Biography*, 2d rev. and enl. ed. (New York, J. T. White & Co., 1937).

[45] John Dickson, ed., *National Cyclopaedia of American Biography*, 47 vols. (New York, J. T. White & Co., 1892–). *Current Volumes*, A– (1930–). *Indexes* (1945–), loose-leaf: pt. 1, vols. 1–30; pt. 2, vol. 31 and subsequent volumes; pt. 3, current volumes. Parts 2 and 3 are revised as new volumes appear.

72

ENCYCLOPEDIAS AND DICTIONARIES OF HISTORY

One very valuable type of encyclopedia or dictionary is that dealing with periods in history. The one important encyclopedia attempting to cover all history from prehistoric to modern times is William L. Langer's *An Encyclopedia of World History*.[46] Chronologically arranged in narrative form and dealing mainly with political, military, and diplomatic events, this handbook is a new version of Karl Ploetz's *Manual of Universal History*.[47] Outline maps and genealogical tables are scattered through the text. Lists of Roman emperors, Byzantine emperors, caliphs up to 1256, Roman popes, Holy Roman emperors, British ministries since Walpole, French ministries from 1815 to 1870, presidents and prime ministers of the Third French Republic, and Italian ministries since 1860 appear in the appendices.

An older example of an alphabetical historical dictionary covering all history is Ebenezer Brewer's *The Historic Notebook*. This dictionary contains brief entries for historic events, acts of Parliament, treaties, customs, terms, and phrases.[48] It is more concerned with odd bits of information than with universal coverage of standard historical events.

Some dictionaries treat only one aspect of universal history. For example, two dictionaries devoted exclusively to battles are Thomas Harbottle's *Dictionary of Battles from the Earliest Date to the Present Time*[49] and David Eggenberger's *Dictionary of Battles*.[50] Both are alphabetically arranged by the name of the battle. Harbottle deals with battles from ancient times to 1904,

[46] *An Encyclopedia of World History: Ancient, Medieval, and Modern, Chronologically Arranged*, 4th rev. and enl. ed. (Boston, Houghton Mifflin, 1968).

[47] W. H. Tillinghast, trans., Harry Elmer Barnes, ed., with the collaboration of A. H. Imlah, T. P. Peardon, and J. H. Wuorinen (Boston, Houghton Mifflin Co., 1925).

[48] *The Historic Notebook with an Appendix of Battles* (Philadelphia, J. B. Lippincott Co., 1907).

[49] (New York, Dutton, 1905).

[50] (New York, Crowell, 1967).

with emphasis on British history; Eggenberger covers battles from ancient times to 1966. Eggenberger has broadened the concept of battles to include cases in twentieth-century warfare where entire countries have become battlefields and the fighting has gone on for weeks or months. Both Harbottle and Eggenberger identify the war in which the battle was fought, the date of the combat, the commander, the number of troups involved, and the outcome.

United States

United States history is covered by many dictionaries, encyclopedias, and handbooks. The most comprehensive reference work for American history is the *Dictionary of American History*.[51] The basic set consists of over six thousand entries dealing with all aspects of United States history, except biographical, from 1600 to 1940. Articles are arranged in alphabetical order and have been signed with the full name of the specialist who compiled them. Articles generally are brief. However, there are "covering articles" which deal with the subjects in orderly sequence and which send the reader to related articles where individual phases of the subject are treated in more detail. The reader who wants to know a general succession of events can find it in one article; the reader who wants information on only one aspect of the subject can find it through the index. Usually a short bibliography at the end of the article gives the student the basic book, document, or periodical for the topic.

There are two major one-volume encyclopedias covering American history. The first, the *Encyclopedia of American History*, is a chronological manual beginning with 1763.[52] It lacks a bibliography and references to the sources of its information. Part 1 is a basic chronology of the major political and military events in

[51] James Truslow Adams, ed., 2d rev. ed., 5 vols. and index (New York, C. Scribner's Sons, 1942–61). 1st ed. (1940). J. G. Hopkins and Wayne Andrews, eds., vol. 6, *Supplement One* (1961).

[52] Richard B. Morris, ed., updated and rev. ed. (New York, Harper & Row, 1965).

American history. Part 2 is a topical chronology of constitutional development, American expansion, and demographic, economic, scientific, and cultural trends. Part 3 consists of biographies of four hundred notable Americans. The second major one-volume encyclopedia of American history is *The Oxford Companion to American History*.[53] This volume covers people, places, and events significant in United States history. Because it is a companion volume to *The Oxford Companion to American Literature*, this encyclopedia emphasizes the historical rather than the literary importance of writers. The text of the Constitution is at the end of the volume, and lists of officials are scattered throughout under the name of the office, such as secretaries of state under *State, U.S. Department of*. Arranged alphabetically, *The Oxford Companion to American History* lacks an index, and bibliographic information is given only for the longer articles.

Two other one-volume dictionaries of lesser importance are Solomon Holt's *The Dictionary of American History*[54] and Michael Martin and Leonard Gelber's *The New Dictionary of American History*.[55] Both include important people, places, and events. A chronology from 1492 to 1962 precedes the main dictionary section in Holt's *Dictionary of American History*.

Joseph Kane is the author of two books on facts about United States history: *Famous First Facts*[56] and *Facts About the Presidents*.[57] *Famous First Facts* is arranged alphabetically by subject, with a chronological approach in its index-by-year and its index-by-day. Part 1 of *Facts About the Presidents* presents genealogical facts; data on elections, congress, the president's cabinet and the

[53] Thomas H. Johnson in consultation with Harvey Wish (New York, Oxford University Press, 1966).

[54] (Dobbs Ferry, New York, Oceana Publications, 1963).

[55] (New York, Philosophical Library, 1952).

[56] *Famous First Facts: A Record of First Happenings, Discoveries, and Inventions in the United States*, 3d ed. (New York, H. W. Wilson Co., 1964).

[57] *Facts About the Presidents: A Compilation of Biographical and Historical Data* (New York, H. W. Wilson Co., 1959).

vice president; and the highlights of each administration in chronological order. Part 2 presents the material in comparative form, with data and statistics on the presidents as individuals and on the office of the presidency.

There are dictionaries on specific periods of American history. For example, the *Encyclopedia of the American Revolution*, compiled by Mark M. Boatner III, deals primarily with the period 1763–83—from the Treaty of Paris ending the Seven Year's War to the Treaty of Paris ending the American Revolution.[58] Articles are arranged alphabetically, and maps and sketches are scattered throughout the book with a separate index. The British, French, and German participation in the Revolution, as well as the American, is included. The *Encyclopedia of the American Revolution* is especially strong for biographical and military material.

The Civil War Dictionary, also compiled by Mark Boatner, emphasizes inclusiveness by covering the maximum number of important subjects.[59] Major personalities and events are treated briefly, while minor characters, battles, and events are more fully identified. Over half the dictionary is devoted to people; all the full generals and outstanding officers of lower rank on both sides are covered. Military operations are next in the number of entries. The author, a lieutenant colonel in the United States Army, has included the campaigns, military organization, weapons, tactics and strategy, military terms, naval matters, and political issues. Special maps enable the reader to follow the campaigns.

Three American presidents are the subjects of encyclopedias. Thomas Jefferson is the subject of *The Jeffersonian Cyclopedia*. As Julian Boyd says in his introduction, those who quote Jefferson have found "Foley's *Jeffersonian Cyclopedia* to be the most inclusive, reliable, and convenient single guide to his utterances on a multitude of subjects."[60] *The Theodore Roosevelt Cyclopedia* is a

[58] (New York, David McKay Co., 1966).

[59] (New York, David McKay Co., 1959).

[60] John Foley, ed. (New York, Funk, 1900); reprinted with an introduction by Julian Boyd, 2 vols. (New York, Russell & Russell, 1967). Vol. 1, introduction, unpaged.

76

collection of four thousand quotations from the writings, letters, and speeches of this president.[61] *The Lincoln Encyclopedia* consists of Lincoln quotations arranged alphabetically by subject.[62] Each quotation is identified as to exact time, place, and circumstances, with reference to the title of the volume where the quote can be found. *The Lincoln Encyclopedia* must be used with great care, however, because it contains inaccuracies and a number of known forgeries.

These three presidents, who have been quoted and misquoted, enunciate the basic political tenets of our democracy in their writings and speeches; thus these encyclopedias are invaluable as sources for their actual words.

Ancient

There are many handbooks, English and foreign, which supply background information on the ancient world. One of the new handbooks is the *New Century Classical Handbook*.[63] Defining the Classical Age as the period running from prehistoric times to the last of the Julian emperors of Rome, the book includes mythological and legendary figures, authors, artists, philosophers, political and military leaders, "lost ladies and scoundrels," résumés of the classics, and places of mythological, historical, and archaeological interest.

Another extremely useful volume is the *Oxford Classical Dictionary*.[64] Modeled on the eighth edition of Lübker's *Reallexikon*[65]

[61] Albert Bushnell Hart and Herbert R. Ferleger, eds.; foreword by William Allen White, introduction by David C. Mearns (New York, Roosevelt Memorial Association, 1941).

[62] Archer H. Shaw, comp. and ed., *The Lincoln Encyclopedia: The Spoken and Written Words of A. Lincoln Arranged for Ready Reference* (New York, Macmillan Co., 1950).

[63] Catherine B. Avery, ed. (New York, Appleton-Century-Crofts, 1962).

[64] Max Cary et al., eds. (Oxford, Clarendon Press, 1949).

[65] Lübker, Friedrich, *Reallexikon das klassischen Altertums*, 8th completely rev. ed., ed. by J. Feffcken and E. Ziebarth (Leipzig, Teubner, 1914).

and designed to cover the same ground on a different scale as Sir William Smith's older dictionaries,[66] this comprehensive and scholarly work deals with antiquities, biography, literature, and geography from the beginning of history to the death of Constantine in 337. A special feature is the inclusion of longer articles surveying main subjects and placing minor characters, places, and events in their appropriate literary or historical context.

The *Praeger Encyclopedia of Ancient Greek Civilization* is the newest title in the area.[67] It is the work of archaeologist Pierre Devambez in collaboration with literary historian Robert Flacelière, philosopher Pierre-Maxime Schuhl, and Roland Martin, a professor of Greek. There are over 750 brief entries, each signed with the author's initials, and illustrations.

There are several older guides to the classics. *Harper's Dictionary of Classical Literature and Antiquities*, compiled by Harry Peck, is a popular work with concise articles and brief bibliographies on many topics in the classical world.[68] *The Dictionary of Greek and Roman Antiquities*, by William Wayte and G. E. Marindin, is an older, standard work.[69] More valuable is Charles Daremberg and Edmond Saglio's *Dictionnaire des antiquitiés grecques et romaines*,[70] the authoritative French dictionary. This publication has long signed articles by specialists, with detailed bibliographies on manners, customs, institutions, the arts, science, religion, and military affairs. It does not cover biography and literature. The indexes, to authors, Greek words, Latin words, and subjects, are helpful. Another valuable guide is *Pauly's Real-Encyclopädie der Classischen Altertumswissenschaft*, often re-

[66] *Dictionary of Greek and Roman Biography and Mythology*, 3 vols. (London, Murray, 1880). *Dictionary of Greek and Roman Geography*, 2 vols. (London, Murray, 1873–78). Smith's more recent work is the *New Classical Dictionary of Greek and Roman Biography, Mythology, and Geography*, rev. with corrections and additions by C. Anton (New York, Harper, 1932).

[67] Pierre Devambez, ed. (New York, Frederick A. Praeger, 1967).

[68] (New York, Harper & Brothers, 1897).

[69] 3d rev. and enl. ed., 2 vols. (London, J. Murray, 1890–91).

[70] 5 vols. (Paris, Hachette, 1877–1919).

ferred to as *Pauly's Wissowa or R.E.*[71] This standard German work covers classical literature, history, biography, antiquities, and other subjects. The long signed articles, with detailed bibliographies, have been written by specialists. Extensive corrections ("berichtingungen") and appendices ("nachtrage") make this volume somewhat difficult for the student to use.

Modern

In modern history, Alan W. Palmer's *A Dictionary of Modern History, 1789–1945*, emphasizes British affairs but includes entries for the United States, Slavonic countries, Latin America, the Far East, and Western Europe.[72] Palmer summarizes the histories of individual states only when there are few biographical or topical entries. Political and historical personages are emphasized at the expense of literary figures, artists, and museums.

A new authoritative and comprehensive volume covering much the same period as Palmer's *Dictionary of Modern History, 1789–1945* is the *Harper Encyclopedia of the Modern World.*[73] This work covers essential facts and includes many charts, tables, and maps.

There are various dictionaries, encyclopedias, and handbooks which are compilations of miscellaneous information important for reference purposes for the history of various countries and continents. In the next few pages some of the more important

[71] New revision started by G. Wissowa, continued by W. Kroll and K. Mittelhaus, with the co-operation of many colleagues, ed. by K. Ziegler, 23 vols. in 24 (Stuttgart, A. Metzler, 1894–1962). *Supplement,* vol. 1– (1903–).

[72] (London, Cresset Press, 1962). There are several Philosophic Library dictionaries covering premodern history: Percival G. Woodcock's *A Concise Dictionary of Ancient History* (1955); William S. Roeder's *Dictionary of European History* (1954), which begins with A.D. 500 and covers the Middle Ages, the Renaissance, and modern Europe to the 1950's; and *Dictionary of the Renaissance,* edited by Frederick M. Schweitzer and Harry E. Wedeck (1967).

[73] Richard B. Morris and Graham W. Irwin, eds. (New York, Harper & Row, 1970).

references will be listed for Great Britain, Europe, Russia, the Near East, Africa, the Far East, and Latin America.

Great Britain

While most general chronologies, dictionaries, and encyclopedias give special emphasis to Great Britain, there are several dictionaries which are devoted exclusively to British history. The newest is Sigfrid H. Steinberg's *A New Dictionary of British History*,[74] a successor to John Brendon's *A Dictionary of British History*.[75] Steinberg has excluded the purely biographical entries, which were half the entries in Brendon's dictionary, and has extended the scope to include countries which have at some time been a part of England, her overseas possessions, the British Empire, or the Commonwealth of Nations. Steinberg has tried to include political, constitutional, administrative, legal, ecclesiastical, and economic events and to exclude histories of literature, music, the arts, architecture, philosophy, and science. He has treated Scotland and Ireland mostly in terms of their relations with England, but he has treated Wales, which has been associated closely with England from Roman times, more fully. The articles, signed with the initials of the contributors listed in the preface, have bibliographic references only if there is a monograph on the topic.

Europe

Western Europe: A Handbook[76] provides background information with statistical tables and maps on an area stretching from Iceland to Turkey and including twenty-seven European, non-

[74] (London, St. Martin's Press, 1963).
[75] John Adams Brendon, ed. (New York, Longmans, Green & Co., 1937). Another old dictionary of English history, which is more for the layman than for the scholar, is Sir Sidney J. Low and F. S. Pulling's *The Dictionary of English History*, rev. and enl. by F. J. C. Hearnshaw, H. M. Chew, and A. C. F. Beales, new ed. (London, Cassell and Co., 1928).
[76] John Calmann, ed. (New York, Praeger, 1967).

80

Communist states. Part 1, arranged alphabetically by country, gives geographic, historical, political, and economic facts and cultural and social patterns for each country. Part 2 consists of excellent essays by specialists, with bibliographies on European defense, agriculture, income, prices, immigrant labor, education, churches, and the arts. Part 3 deals with the institutions of Western European integration, such as the Common Market (EEC) and the European Free Trade Association (EFTA); it analyzes their structures, objectives, and potentials. This book will be most useful to the student of current history. It provides in one place much of the information that the student usually can obtain only from checking yearbooks and government sources.

The more advanced student of French, German, and Spanish history will find older dictionaries written in French, German, and Spanish listed in Winchell's *Guide to Reference Books*[77] and *The Guide to Historical Literature*.[78] The student interested in Spanish history will find two works in English that should help him. Edgar A. Peer's *Spain: A Companion to Spanish Studies*[79] offers helpful background information. Specialists have written chapters on the peoples, languages, and country of Spain, its literature, arts, architecture, music, and history. Bibliographies appended to each chapter refer the student to a list of carefully selected books. *The Handbook of Hispanic Source Materials*[80] covers not only Spain; but also Portugal; Latin America of the pre- and post-Columbian periods; and Florida, Texas, the Southwest, and California before their annexation by the United States. It surveys materials in the humanities, social sciences, fine arts, and the natural sciences in some exceptional collections. Collections are described by state and locality. The student needing a particular item can refer to the index.

[77] Pp. 491–92, 494, 504.
[78] Pp. 465, 551, 504–505.
[79] Rev. and enl. by R. F. Brown, 5th ed. (London, Methuen, 1956).
[80] Ronald Hilton, ed., *The Handbook of Hispanic Source Materials and Research Organizations in the United States*, 2d ed. (Stanford, Calif., Stanford University Press, 1956).

Russia

Russia, occupying one-sixth of the earth's land surface with a population over 230 million, is the subject of three handbooks of information. Robert Maxwell's *Information U.S.S.R.*[81] reflects the Soviet viewpoint, in fact, the first 763 pages were translated by J. T. McDermott from volume 50 of the *Great Soviet Encyclopaedia*. The *McGraw-Hill Encyclopedia of Russia and the Soviet Union*[82] is a comprehensive volume with many articles written by specialists, who are named in the list of contributors and who have signed their articles with their initials. In addition to the many brief entries on people, places, and events, there are some longer articles on the Russian government, economic system, history, culture, and science. Sergej Utechin, with the aid of specialists, has compiled *Everyman's Concise Encyclopaedia of Russia*, an alphabetical arrangement of the principal people, places, and events in Russian history.[83]

Africa

The standard reference book on Africa is *Africa: A Handbook of the Continent*.[84] Part 1 of this comprehensive handbook is made up of a series of chapters on individual countries grouped either by geographic area or by colonial ties. Part 2 deals with politics, art, literature, cultural patterns, religion, economics, and attitudes of the United States, Russia, Great Britain, and France toward Africa, the press, trade unions, the African Development Bank, and the Institute for Economic Development and Planning.

Two older handbooks which still might be of use are *A Handbook of African Affairs*[85] and *The Handbook of Africa*.[86] This

[81] (New York, Pergamon Press for the Macmillan Co., 1962).

[82] Michael T. Florinsky, ed. (New York, McGraw-Hill, 1961).

[83] (London, Dent, 1961).

[84] Colin Legum, ed., rev. and enl. ed. (New York, Praeger, 1966).

[85] Helen Kitchen, ed. (New York, published for the African American Institute by Praeger, 1964).

[86] Violaine I. Junod, comp. and ed., with assistance of Idrain N. Resnick (New York, New York University Press, 1963).

82

second title was the first book to provide factual information on each of the fifty-odd political units of Africa. From the facts and figures the reader can get a picture of the social, political, and economic life of each country and a basis for comparison. For example, the following information is given for Ghana: figures for population, area, and density; a short geographic sketch; a short historical sketch; a short sketch of the government (status, statement about the constitution, franchise, types of local government, political parties); a population breakdown (urban distribution, rural distribution, ethnic distribution, religious affiliation, languages, sex distribution, age distribution); social data (education, health and social services); economy (transportation and communication, resources and trade, marketing and co-operative societies, and livestock); industry (manufactures, mining, power); finance (currency, banking, budget, development plan, labor); and notes at the end giving sources of information.

Another reference book on Africa, *The New Africans*, has been compiled by British journalists.[87] It summarizes Africa's change from a colonial status to a series of independent countries, the struggles for power, and the movement toward African unity through the Organization of African Unity (OAU). The African states are listed alphabetically, and for each there is a map, a historical sketch, an account of the social, economic, and cultural development, and biographies and pictures of leaders. Because the authors believe that the lives of the African leaders tell the story of Africa's struggle for independence, they have put strong emphasis on the biographical sections, with a separate index to all of the biographies.

There also are encyclopedias concerned with only parts of Africa. *The Encyclopaedia of Southern Africa* covers the Republic of South Africa, Rhodesia, Zambia, Malawi, South-West Africa, Mozambique, Basutoland, Swaziland, and Bechuanaland.[88] Over

[87] Sidney Taylor, ed., *The New Africans: A Guide to the Contemporary History of Emergent Africa and Its Leaders* (New York, Putnam, 1967).
[88] Eric Rosenthal, comp. and ed., 5th ed. (London, Warne, 1970).

five thousand items concerning history, biography, literature, geography, geology, natural history, sports, shipwrecks, local customs, political organizations, costumes, and so on are arranged alphabetically in the form of a dictionary. The main articles, listed by title and author in the front of the book, are incorporated into this dictionary arrangement. Walter Causton and E. Lois Martin are responsible for the illustrations, maps, and plates. The newest statistics and a table of battles are important features of this new edition. There are many entries for specific historical events.

The Middle East and North Africa[89] covers Algeria, Chad, Ethiopia, French Somaliland, Libya, Mali, Mauritania, Morocco, Niger, Somalia, Spanish North Africa, the Sudan, Tunisia, the United Arab Republic (Egypt), Aden (South Arabia), Cyprus, Iran, Iraq, Israel, Jordan, Kuwait, Lebanon, Masqat and Oman, the Persian Gulf States, Saudi Arabia, the Syrian Arab Republic, Turkey, and Yemen. *The Middle East and North Africa* was originally published in 1948 as *The Middle East*; North Africa was not included until the eleventh edition in 1964. Part 1 is a general survey of developments in the Arab world and Africa, including regional organization efforts. Part 2 provides tables and maps on the geography, history, economics, government, political parties, judicial system, religion, press, radio, television, finance, trade and industry, transport, tourism, and education in each of the countries. Part 3 consists of a "Who's Who" section of prominent people from the Middle East and North Africa, bibliographies, and research institutions. This volume is valuable for students interested in the current problems of this part of the world.

Stephan and Nandy Ronart have compiled a two-volume encyclopedia which will be useful to students interested in the Arab countries, the *Concise Encyclopedia of Arabic Civilization*.[90] Entries, arranged alphabetically in both volumes, provide information on the social, political, and religious structure of the Arab countries and prominent figures in Arab culture and history.

[89] 14th ed. (London, Europa Publications, 1967).
[90] 2 vols. (New York, Frederick A. Praeger, Inc., 1960–66).

84

The outstanding reference work on Islamic civilization is *The Encyclopedia of Islam*.[91] The first edition was published in four volumes, with a supplement in 1938–41. This authoritative, scholarly work contains signed articles with bibliographies on history, geography, religion, institutions, customs, manners, biography, tribes, industry, the sciences, and the arts. The student interested in any topic concerning Islam will find this work indispensable.

The Far East

Guy Wint's *Asia: A Handbook* provides the most up-to-date information on China, Japan, and the new Asian nations.[92] Like other handbooks, it gives basic information for each country, surveys the political, social, economic, and religious aspects of Asia, and reproduces extracts from treaties and agreements signed since World War II. There are several older works in English on China and Japan which the student will find still useful. Samuel Couling's *Encyclopaedia Sinica*[93] gives information on the history, geography, literature, art, religions, institutions, botany, zoology, and famous people of old China. Edmond Papinot's *Historical and Geographical Dictionary of Japan* contains short, descriptive articles about important people, places, and events in old Japan from legendary times to 1906.[94] The valuable appendices include an alphabetical index of English names, which refer to articles in the dictionary; an alphabetical list of forenames, which refer to family names where biographical material is given; provinces, departments, and districts; generations of mythological terms; lists

---

[91] H. A. R. Gibb et al., eds., under the patronage of the International Union of Academies, new ed. to be in 5 vols. (Leiden, E. J. Brill, Ltd., 1954–).

[92] (New York, Praeger, 1966).

[93] (Shanghai, Kelly and Walsh, Ltd., 1917).

[94] (Ann Arbor, Mich., Overbeck Co., 1948). The *Historical and Geographical Dictionary of Japan* originally was published in French in Tokyo in 1906 and then was translated into English and published in Yokohama in 1910. It was reprinted in two volumes in 1964 by the F. Ungar Publishing Company, New York.

of emperors, shoguns, and ministries since 1885; the Japanese calendar; and tables of weights and measures. Reference aids which will aid the study of recent Japanese history are *Things Japanese*,[95] *Maku Jaya's Things Japanese*,[96] and *Japan: Its Land, People, and Culture*.[97]

Australia and New Zealand

The Modern Encyclopaedia of Australia and New Zealand[98] is an authoritative reference work which provides in one volume a wealth of information on the history, people, geography, flora, fauna, arts, industry, sports, and so on, of Australia, New Zealand, and Papua-New Guinea. No previously published work has attempted to encompass in an integrated form such a breadth of information about these countries. A unique feature is the presentation of a concise history of Australia, New Zealand, and Papua-New Guinea in the form of a combined chronology of the principal events which have occurred in each country to 1963. The appendix, or "quick reference section," provides valuable tabulated information on subjects ranging from horse racing to the decimal currency, wool and wheat production, and lists of prime ministers and state premiers.

[95] Basil Hall Chamberlain, *Things Japanese: Being Notes on Various Subjects Connected with Japan, for the Use of Travellers and Others*, 6th rev. ed. (London, Kegan Paul & Co., 1939).

[96] Maku Jaya (Tokyo, Tokyo News Service, 1958).

[97] Japanese National Commission for UNESCO, rev. ed. (Tokyo, Printing Bureau, Ministry of Finance, 1964).

[98] (Sydney, Horwitz-Grahame, 1964).

5

Almanacs, Yearbooks, Statistical Handbooks, and Current Surveys

The almanacs, yearbooks, and handbooks discussed in this chapter contain bits and pieces of information—miscellaneous facts about all kinds of subjects. These books can often answer questions concerning current trends and developments and the events, progress, and conditions of the year covered. They are particularly valuable for historical research because they reflect contemporary opinion; they are edited and published soon after the events they discuss have occurred.

According to the *A.L.A. Glossary of Library Terms*, an annual is a "yearly publication that reviews events or developments during a year,"[1] and a yearbook is "an annual volume of current information in descriptive and/or statistical form, sometimes limited to a special field."[2] There are three groups of annual publications: encyclopedia supplements, almanacs, and subject records of progress. Yearbooks that are supplements to encyclopedias include information relating to the year covered and are more up to date than general encyclopedias.[3]

---

[1] American Library Association, Committee on Library Terminology, *A.L.A. Glossary of Library Terms, with a Selection of Terms in Related Fields*, prepared by Elizabeth H. Thompson (Chicago, American Library Association, 1943), 5.

[2] *Ibid.*, 150.

[3] See the section on encyclopedias in chapter 4.

ALMANACS AND OTHER YEARBOOKS

An almanac is defined by the *A.L.A. Glossary of Library Terms* as "an annual publication containing a calendar, frequently accompanied by astronomical data and other information" or as "an annual yearbook of statistics and other information sometimes in a particular field."[4] Originally related to the calendar, the almanac has evolved into an annual compendium of statistics and facts, some retrospective and others current. Newspaper publishers produce almanacs as by-products of the requirements of daily news reporting. The newspaper almanac is a systematic selection from the newspaper's morgue of facts and figures of interest to the public. Because these almanacs are not associated with encyclopedias, they furnish retrospective as well as current information. The best almanacs can be as indispensable reference tools as dictionaries and encyclopedias.[5]

Since its publication in 1868 by the *New York World*, the *World Almanac* has been the standard American reference almanac.[6] Joseph Pulitzer, publisher of the *St. Louis Post-Dispatch*, acquired the *World Almanac* when he bought the *New York World* from Jay Gould. He saw this almanac as a handbook making facts available to his reporters. "Accuracy, accuracy, accuracy!" Pulitzer's credo, became the watchword of the *World Almanac* from 1886 on. In 1966, Newspaper Enterprise Association, the oldest and largest newspaper feature service in the world, acquired the *World Almanac* from Scripps-Howard when the *New York World-Telegram & Sun* folded. The centennial edition in 1968 was the first produced entirely under NEA management. President Lyndon B. Johnson wrote the foreword for this edition. He describes the *World Almanac* as an "indispensable reference work."[7] So inclu-

---

[4] P. 4.

[5] Louis Shores, *Basic Reference Sources: An Introduction to Materials and Methods* (Chicago, American Library Association, 1954), 92–93.

[6] *World Almanac and Book of Facts* (New York, 1968–). Annual. Various publishers.

[7] P. 36. *World Almanac*, 36.

sive that it might be called an encyclopedia of current events, the *World Almanac* is strongest in matters pertaining to the United States, though it covers other countries as well. The centennial edition of the *World Almanac* contains a chronology of the year with maps; a history of the world; a million facts pertaining to the social, industrial, political, financial, religious, educational, and historical subjects and statistics; an index; and a special article, "The Next 100 Years," by Isaac Asimov.

A new almanac, *Information Please Almanac*,[8] appeared on the scene in 1947, edited by John Kieran, a sports columnist for the *New York Times* and the "Information Please" radio expert. *Information Please Almanac* is a readable collection of miscellaneous information similar in content to the *World Almanac*, though it contains many items not in that older compilation. Each edition has a special introductory article on some topic.

A third United States almanac, the *Reader's Digest Almanac*, started publication in 1966.[9] It contains over 75,000 facts, figures, names, and dates, and three hundred photographs, maps, charts, and illustrations. Like the other two United States almanacs, it has calendars, chronologies, surveys, and an excellent index.

An outstanding reference work published in 1969 by the *New York Times* is *The New York Times Encyclopedic Almanac, 1970*, edited by Seymour Kurtz. Based on the resources of that newspaper, it includes the usual almanac features, Rand McNally and *New York Times* maps, and authoritative background articles on news stories. A detailed index enables the reader to find the information readily.

The best almanac for the British Isles is *Whitaker's Almanack*,[10] the English counterpart of the *World Almanac*. All three editions (the complete edition with maps, the complete edition without

---

[8] *Information Please Almanac, Atlas, and Yearbook*, 1947– . Planned and supervised by Dan Golenpaul Associates (New York, Simon and Schuster, 1947–). Annual.

[9] *Reader's Digest Almanac and Yearbook* (New York, Reader's Digest Association, 1966–). Annual.

[10] (London, J. Whitaker & Sons, Ltd., 1869–). Annual.

maps, and the shorter edition) contain a section of miscellaneous information, a calendar section, a section on the world, and a section on the United Kingdom. The complete edition contains sections on the United Nations and foreign countries, reviews of the year in science, literature, drama, films, and sports, data on religion and education, and lists of important people. *Whitaker's Almanack* is especially strong on information about Great Britain and the Commonwealth countries. It gives lists of royalty, nobility, clergy, members of Parliaments, and so on, thus serving as a condensed version of Burke's *Peerage*. The index, though omitting most personal names, is still invaluable for locating other information.

Almanacs do not always duplicate information, for some give material which others do not contain. Also, their coverage varies from year to year. Thus it may be necessary to consult more than one almanac to find the information desired.

There are almanacs for different countries, such as the *Canadian Almanac and Directory*[11] and the *Sociological Almanac for the United States*.[12] There are almanacs for regions, for example, *The Comparative International Almanac* presents facts and figures for 214 countries.[13] The editors have given each country equal space regardless of the status and importance of the country, and they have tried to tell each nation's story through meaningful figures obtained from the United Nations and its collateral agencies.

There are almanacs dealing with special subjects, such as *The Negro Almanac*, a reference book with over one thousand entries on the Negro in American life.[14] The first section is a chronology of major events in Negro history (1492–1954), a review of the civil rights movement (1954–64), important events (1965–67),

[11] (Toronto, Copp Clark Co., 1847–). Annual.
[12] Murray Gendell and Hans L. Zeherberg, eds. (Totowa, N.J., Bedminster Press, 1961–). Biennial.
[13] Morris L. Ernst and Judith A. Posner, eds. (New York, Macmillan, 1967).
[14] Harry A. Ploski and Roscoe C. Brown, Jr., comps. and eds. (New York, Bellwether Publishing Co., 1967).

and deaths of prominent Negroes (1965–66). Other sections are concerned with documents affecting the Negro; landmarks, monuments, and shrines of Negro America; the legal status of the Negro; the Negro population, family, employment, and education; the Negro in the federal government and the fine arts and Negro inventors and scientists; the Negro in jazz, the judiciary, literature, the performing arts, sports, and the United Nations; Negro women; and Negro organizations. This volume complements two other reference books on the Negro: *The Negro Handbook*[15] and *The American Negro Reference Book.*[16]

The *Congressional Quarterly Almanac* is another example of an almanac dealing with one subject, the United States Congress.[17] It presents a complete, concise, and unbiased record of congressional activity for the calendar year. Based on the *CQ Weekly Report*, a weekly service with a quarterly index, the *Congressional Quarterly Almanac* gives a summary of the sessions; lists members of Congress with their seniority, the members of the cabinet, and the governors of states; gives key votes of the year, Supreme Court highlights, and the president's legislative record; summarizes major legislation for agriculture, appropriations, education and welfare, foreign policy, general government, national security, public works and resources, taxes and economic policy; supplies roll-call vote charts and records of individual performances, public laws, presidential messages, action on nominations, investigations, and political background.

As in the case of almanacs, there are many yearbooks with inter-

[15] Editors of *Ebony*, comps. (Chicago, Johnson Publishing Co., 1966).
[16] John P. Davis, ed. (Englewood Cliffs, N.J., Prentice Hall, 1966).
[17] *Congressional Quarterly Almanac: A Service for Editors and Commentators* (Washington, D.C., Congressional News Features, 1945–). Annual. *CQ Weekly Report* (1943–). *Congress and the Nation* is a series based on abridgements of the *Congressional Quarterly Almanac.* Vol. 1, *Congress and the Nation, 1945–1964: A Review of Government and Politics in the Postwar Years* (Washington, D.C., Congressional Quarterly Service, 1965); vol. 2, *Congress and the Nation, 1965–1968: A Review of Government and Politics* (Washington, D.C., Congressional Quarterly Service, 1969).

national coverage. For example, there is the *Annual Register,* an outstanding yearbook which has been published for two centuries.[18] Edmund Burke, its first editor, originated the idea of using essays written by specialists to present a broad grouping of the main subjects of each year. International in scope but British in emphasis, the first part of the *Annual Register* covers the history of the United Kingdom; the second, the Commonwealth; the third, international organizations; and the next sections, the Americas, the Soviet Union and eastern Europe, western and central Europe, the Middle East, Africa, and East and Southeast Asia. The later sections include documents, obituaries, reviews of developments in religion, science, law, and the arts, and a chronicle of principal events of the year. Maps, sketches, graphs, and an index add to the usefulness of this yearbook.

The *Statesman's Year-Book* is another essential statistical and historical annual of the world.[19] This manual, a one-volume encyclopedia of all nations, combines information from official and unofficial sources and covers countries from Afghanistan to Yugoslavia, including great powers like Russia, tiny principalities like Andorra, and countries not in the United Nations. It is divided into four major parts: International Organizations, The British Commonwealth, The United States, and The Rest of the World. The *Statesman's Year-Book* is independent of official approval and can use facts and figures that are fully authenticated but not necessarily agreeable to certain governments. Next to the *World Almanac,* the *Statesman's Year-Book* is probably the most widely used yearbook.

Two yearbooks provide information on international organizations and countries of the world. The *International Yearbook and Statesmen's Who's Who* gives political, statistical, and directory information about each country of the world and biographical

[18] *Annual Register of World Events: A Review of the Year* (London, 1758–). Annual. Various publishers.

[19] *The Statesman's Year-Book: Statistical and Historical Annual of the States of the World for the Year* (London, Macmillan & Co., 1864–). Annual.

sketches of world leaders.[20] *Europa Year Book* offers information about international organizations and European countries in its first volume and African and Asian countries in its second volume.[21] Information for each country includes an introductory survey, a statistical survey, a summary of the constitution, names and positions of government officials, the composition of the legislative body, and data on political parties, the legal system, religion, the press and publishers, radio and television, finance, trade and industry, transportation and tourism, and atomic energy. Since 1963 the *Europa Year Book* has provided only a brief list of universities because its publishers have transferred detailed information on universities to their *World of Learning*.[22] The condensation of so much material into two volumes makes *Europa Year Book* an indispensable reference volume.

A student investigating these yearbooks will find that yearbooks, like almanacs, duplicate some information and that some give information not contained in others.

There are annuals or yearbooks for certain types of information. The *Political Handbook and Atlas of the World* gives the student information valuable for political history.[23] It lists the chief government officials, party programs and leaders, political events, and the names of newspapers with their political affiliations, owner or editor, and, sometimes, the circulation.

An extremely valuable reference annual for international organizations, governmental and nongovernmental, is the *Yearbook of International Organizations*.[24] The eleventh edition of this title

[20] (London, Burke's Peerage, 1953–). Annual.

[21] (London, Europa Publications, 1959–). Annual. This supersedes the old *Europa Year Book* (1926–29), the *Encyclopedia of Europe* (1930–58), and *Orbis, Encyclopedia of Extra-European Countries* (1938–59).

[22] (London, Europa Publications, 1947–). Annual.

[23] *Political Handbook and Atlas of the World: Parliament, Parties, and Press* (New York, Council on Foreign Relations, 1927–). Annual.

[24] *Yearbook of International Organizations: The Encyclopaedic Dictionary of International Organizations, Their Officers, Their Abbreviations* (Brussels, Union of International Associations, 1948–). Annual, 1948–50; biennial beginning with 1951–52.

(1966–67) now offers data on more than three thousand international organizations—old, new, and very new. In this new edition all currently active organizations are arranged alphabetically by their English title in a dictionary arrangement. The following information is given for each organization: name, initials or acronyms, officers, history, aims, finance, relations with other international organizations, activities, meetings, and publications. New features in this edition are the inclusion of short entries on recently established bodies for which copies of constitutions and lists of members are not available and classified lists of the organizations based on the status and subject division of the organization.

The *Yearbook of the United Nations*[25] is a yearbook presenting an authoritative account of the organization of the United Nations, its activities and proceedings, and the political, economic, financial, and legal questions facing it. Texts of documents, lists of publications, and bibliographies are also included. The first part of the volume concerns the United Nations; the second, the intergovernmental organizations related to it.

There are several yearbooks dealing with regions. For the United States in general there is the *American Yearbook: A Record of Events and Progress*,[26] which has ceased publication. It provides long survey articles with bibliographies by specialists on developments in politics, government, economics, business, social conditions, science, and the humanities in the United States for the year. It gives a clearly focused picture of events and achievements in the United States and in the area of American influence for that time.

The *Book of the States*,[27] an authoritative source of information on the structure, working methods, financing, and functional activities of the state governments, is concerned with the legislative, executive, and judicial branches of the government of each state,

[25] United Nations (New York, United Nations, Department of Public Information, 1947–). Annual.

[26] *American Yearbook, A Record of Events and Progress, 1910–1919*, 36 vols. (New York, D. Appleton and Co., 1911–50).

[27] (Chicago, Council of State Government, 1935–). Biennial.

with the governmental relations between states, and with their public services. Two *Supplements* list state officials and members of state legislatures. Only state manuals give more details for each state.

The *Municipal Year Book* is a reference source for information on current activities and practices of cities in the United States.[28] Although the emphasis is on statistics for individual cities, some attention is given to developments in metropolitan areas and urban counties. Many sections are revised and brought up to date for each edition, such as the comprehensive directories of officials. Other sections, reflecting contemporary problems, are published in one edition, for example, the 1967 yearbook gives considerable attention to fire and police manpower.

The *British Commonwealth Yearbook* contains general and statistical information about the British Empire and Commonwealth nations.[29] For the Middle East there is the *Middle East and North Africa* (see chapter 4). For Latin America there is the *South American Handbook*,[30] an invaluable guide to the countries of South America, Central America, Mexico, the Caribbean, and the West Indies. Based on information drawn from government sources, the Royal Mail Lines, and the Pacific Steam Navigation Company, the *South American Handbook* provides information on each country, including a general geographic description, a summary of its history, a directory of cities and towns (with travel information on restaurants, travel agents, and excursions), a discussion of the economy, and maps and indexes of places, names, and products.

Practically every country has a yearbook; there are *"The Times*

[28] *Municipal Year Book: The Authoritative Résumé of Activities and Statistical Data of American Cities* (Chicago, International City Managers' Association, 1934–). Annual.

[29] 10 vols. (London, Newman Neame, 1952–59; MacGibbon and Kee, 1960–63). Title varies: *Commonwealth Co-operation: The Empire and Commonwealth Year Book*, 1952/53; *The Empire and Commonwealth Year Book*, 1953/54–1959/60.

[30] (London, Trade and Travel Publications, Ltd., 1924–). Annual.

of India" Directory and Year Book,[31] the *China Yearbook,*[32] the *Communist China Yearbook,*[33] and the *Israel Yearbook.*[34] The student should also investigate Winchell's *Guide to Reference Books,* the *Guide to Historical Literature,* and guides and bibliographies of specific countries or subjects.

STATISTICAL GUIDES AND HANDBOOKS

Statistical information, whether it concerns population, agriculture, manufactures, transportation, education, religion, employment, sex, age, health, or income, offers the history student basic data for his hypotheses and interpretations of historical facts. For example, Frederick Jackson Turner's famous frontier hypothesis was based on his study of the statistical and geographical publications of the United States Census Bureau,[35] and Charles A. Beard used statistical records to support his controversial economic interpretation of the Constitution.[36]

To locate current statistical data, a student should consult

[31] *"The Times of India" Directory and Year Book, Including Who's Who* (London, Bennett, Coleman, 1914–). Annual. Title varies: *Indian Year Book,* 1914–47; *The Indian and Pakistan Year Book and Who's Who,* 1949–1952/53.

[32] 1937/43– (Taipei, Taiwan, China Publishing Co., 1943–). Irregular. Title varies, *China Handbook,* 1937/43–1957. Imprint varies.

[33] 1962– (Hong Kong, China Research Associates, 1963?–). Annual.

[34] In co-operation with the Economic Department of the Jewish Agency (Tel Aviv, Israel, Israel Yearbook Publications, Ltd., 1951–). Annual. Succeeds the *Anglo-Palestine Yearbook* (1946, 1947–48) and the *Palestine-Yearbook and Israeli Annual.*

[35] Frederick Jackson Turner, "The Significance of the Frontier in American History," in *The Frontier in American History,* with a foreword by Ray Allen Billington (c. 1920; reprint ed., New York, Holt, Rinehart and Winston, 1962), 1–38. For a scholarly discussion of Turner and his celebrated hypothesis, see Ray Allen Billington, *America's Frontier Heritage* (New York, Holt, Rinehart and Winston, 1966).

[36] Charles A. Beard, *An Economic Interpretation of the Constitution of the United States,* with a new introduction (New York, Macmillan Co., 1941). Originally published in 1913.

Statistical Sources.[37] This publication includes statistical sources on international activities and statistical compilations for each of the countries of the world. It emphasizes American publications and national rather than regional or local sources. Entries are arranged alphabetically by subject.

There are other guides to statistics. *Statistical Bulletins,*[38] compiled by the Library of Congress, lists periodicals issued more frequently than once a year. *Statistical Yearbooks,*[39] also compiled by the Library of Congress, lists periodicals issued each year. Both guides to statistics are arranged first by continent and then by country.

The *Guide to U.S. Government Statistics*[40] provides a handy subject listing of statistical sources and a comprehensive guide to the statistical contents of the voluminous output of the federal government. This guide is arranged alphabetically under the following headings: Departments and Agencies, Executive Office of the President, Judicial Branch, and Legislative Branch. It lists various government publications, the statistical data of each (with appropriate bibliographical information), and concise annotations of the statistical content. The index is a detailed subject index with each entry coded to show the frequency and type of data.

The United Nations puts out two important statistical yearbooks which are international in coverage. The *Demographic Yearbook*[41] is a source for statistics on the area, population, economic activity,

[37] Paul Wasserman, Eleanor Allen, and Charlotte Georgi, eds., 2d ed. (Detroit, Gale Research Co., 1965).

[38] U.S., Library of Congress, *Statistical Bulletins: An Annotated Bibliography of the General Statistical Bulletins of Major Political Subdivisions of the World,* prepared by Phyllis G. Carter (Washington, D.C., Government Printing Office, 1954).

[39] U.S., Library of Congress, *Statistical Yearbooks: An Annotated Bibliography of General Statistical Yearbooks of Major Political Subdivisions of the World,* prepared by Phyllis G. Carter (Washington, D.C., Government Printing Office, 1953).

[40] John Androit, ed., 3d ed. (Arlington, Va., Documents Index, 1961).

[41] United Nations, Statistical Office (New York, United Nations, 1949–). Annual. The 1963 yearbook has a cumulative subject index covering all previous issues.

international migration, nationality, mortality, diseases, marriages, and divorces of about 250 geographic areas of the world. The *Statistical Yearbook*,[42] which continues the *Statistical Year-Book of the League of Nations*,[43] covers world-wide statistics on agriculture and industrial production, population, manpower, manufacturing, transportation, public finance, education and culture, communications, and social conditions. It is supplemented by the *Monthly Bulletin of Statistics*.[44]

There is an excellent guide to statistics for foreign countries, *Foreign Statistical Documents: A Bibliography of General International Trade and Agricultural Statistics, Including Holdings of the Stanford University Libraries*.[45]

Many countries issue compilations of historical statistics as well as annual statistical yearbooks. For example, there is *Annuaire statistique de la France* for France,[46] the *Statistisches Jahrbuch für die Bundesrepublik Deutschland* for Germany,[47] and *Sommario statistico delle regioni d'Italia*[48] and *Annuario statistico italiano*[49] for Italy. Only the statistical compilations for the United States, Great Britain, and Latin America will be discussed in detail.

There are a great number of statistical yearbooks for the United

[42] United Nations, Statistical Office, *Statistical Yearbook: Annuaire statistique* (New York, United Nations, 1949–). Annual.

[43] *Statistical Year-Book of the League of Nations*, 1926–1942/44, Publications of the League of Nations, II, Economic and Financial, 17 vols. (Geneva, League of Nations, 1927–45). Annual.

[44] United Nations, Statistical Office, no. 1, August, 1946– (New York, United Nations, 1947–). Monthly.

[45] Roberta Gardella, comp., Joyce Ball, ed., Hoover Institution on War, Revolution and Peace, Bibliographical Series 28 (Stanford, Hoover Institution, Stanford University, 1967).

[46] National Institute of Statistics and Economic Studies, 1877– , 56 vols. (Paris, Imprimerie nationale, 1878–1950/55). Title and publisher vary.

[47] (Federal Republic, 1949–), Federal Statistical Office, Wiesbaden, 1952– (Stuttgart-Mainz, Kohlhammer, 1952–). Annual. Continues the *Statistisches Jahrbuch für das deutsche Reich*, 57 vols.

[48] Central Institute of Statistics (Roma, 1947).

[49] Central Institute of Statistics (Roma, Instit. Poligrafico dello Stato, 1878–).

States. The *Statistical Abstract of the United States*,[50] published annually since 1878, is the standard summary of statistics on the social, political, and economic organization of the United States. The statistics, arranged in thirty-three broad subject fields, such as population, finance, railroads, and commerce, emphasize national data, but many tables give information for individual states. Each table or chart notes its source; thus the student can update his material by checking that source for the latest figures. *Statistical Abstract of the United States* is supplemented by the *County and City Data Book*,[51] which includes data on population, area, labor force, housing, retail trade, manufacturing, bank deposits, agriculture, and education.

The Statistical History of the United States from Colonial Times to the Present,[52] is two volumes in one. It combines *Historical Statistics of the United States, Colonial Times to 1957*[53] and the *Continuation to 1962, and Revisions*,[54] both compiled by the Bureau of the Census with the co-operation of the Social Science Research Council. *Historical Statistics* presents statistics on every major aspect of the nation's social and economic development in over eight thousand statistical time series (1610–1957), with text notes giving sources of the data and evaluating their reliability. Colonial statistics are a separate chapter. The *Continuation* updates *Historical Statistics*, and the *Statistical Abstract* keeps both up to date. There is a subject index. The *Statistical Abstract* keeps *The Statistical History* up to date.

[50] U.S., Bureau of the Census, 1878– (Washington, D.C., Government Printing Office, 1879–). Annual.

[51] U.S., Bureau of the Census, 1949– (Washington, D.C., Government Printing Office, 1942–). Irregular. It combines two earlier publications, *Cities Supplement* (1949) and the *County Data Book* (1947).

[52] U.S., Bureau of the Census, issued under the direction of the U.S. Bureau of the Census with the co-operation of the Social Sciences Research Council (Stamford, Conn., Fairfield Publication, 1965).

[53] U.S., Bureau of the Census (Washington, D.C., Government Printing Office, 1960).

[54] U.S., Bureau of the Census, *Historical Statistics of the United States,*

There are several nongovernmental compilations of statistics which are most useful. *The Economic Almanac*,[55] published by the National Industrial Conference Board, is a quick reference source for United States economic and business statistics. Arranged by topics, it includes special sections on Canadian statistics and international economics. Much of its statistical material is based on research by the Conference Board and cannot be found in other sources. *Economic Almanac* always cites the source of its figures and often points out limitations or qualification of the material.

Profile of the U.S. Economy[56] is an interpretive survey of economic factors, geographical features, population, health, education, and government. Tables of historical and current statistics and, sometimes, estimates of future statistics back up the text.

Election returns are easily available for the years after 1900. Edgar E. Robinson has published the figures from 1896 to 1932 in *The Presidential Vote*[57] and from 1934 through 1944 in *They Voted for Roosevelt*.[58] *America Votes*[59] covers the years from 1948, giving national statistics by state for presidential elections. For each state *America Votes* provides an information profile sheet with state, city, and congressional district maps and county and

Colonial Times to 1959: Continuation to 1962 and Revisions (Washington, D.C., Government Printing Office, 1965).

[55] 1940– (New York, National Industrial Conference Board, 1940–).

[56] Emma S. Woytinsky, *Profile of the U.S. Economy: A Survey of Growth and Change* (New York, Praeger, 1967).

[57] (Stanford, Calif., Stanford University Press, 1934).

[58] (Stanford, Calif., Stanford University Press, 1947).

[59] Richard M. Scammon, comp. and ed., *America Votes: A Handbook of Contemporary American Election Statistics*, 1954/55– . (Pittsburgh, University of Pittsburgh Press, 1956–). Biennial. Publisher varies. With volume 6 the Government Affairs Institute, in co-operation with the *Congressional Quarterly*, took over publication. Vol. 1 covers the elections of 1952 and 1954; vol. 2, 1954 and 1956; vol. 3, 1956 and 1958; vol. 4, 1958 and 1960; vol. 5, 1962; vol. 6, 1964; and vol. 7, 1968. See also, *America at the Polls: A Handbook of American Presidential Election Statistics, 1920–1964*, comp. and ed. by Richard M. Scammon (Pittsburgh: University of Pittsburgh Press, 1956).

ward breakdowns of the most recent voting for president, governor, and senator.

The British have comparable statistical tools. The *Annual Abstract of Statistics*[60] is comparable to the *Statistical Abstract of the United States*, and the *Abstract of British Historical Statistics*[61] is somewhat comparable to *Historical Statistics of the United States*. *Abstract of British Historical Statistics* is restricted to economic statistics, which are arranged in sixteen sections: Population and Vital Statistics; The Labour Force; Agriculture; Coal; Iron and Steel; Tin, Copper, and Lead; Textile Industries; Transport; Building; Miscellaneous Production Statistics; Overseas Trade; Wages and the Standard of Living; National Income and Expenditure; Public Finance; Banking and Insurance; and Prices. The beginning date of these sections varies; some go back to 1199; others, to the eighteenth century; and most, only to the nineteenth century. All end in 1938 before World War II. Each section is prefaced with a commentary and concluded with a bibliography which lists the major publications referred to in the text and tables. The bibliography refers the user to works in which the statistics are discussed and criticized and suggests main sources of additional statistics. The *Annual Abstract of Statistics* continues most of the series.[62]

British Parliament Election Results, 1950–1964[63] and *British Parliamentary Election Statistics, 1918–1968*[64] are comparable to *America Votes*. A student hunting British election statistics will

[60] Great Britain, Central Statistical Office (London, H. M. Stationery Office, 1854–). Annual. Numbers 1–83 were issued by the Board of Trade as the *Statistical Abstract of the United Kingdom*, and each contained statistics for the preceding fifteen years. It now covers ten-year periods.

[61] Brian R. Mitchell, with the collaboration of Phyllis Deane (Cambridge, Cambridge University Press, 1962).

[62] Judith B. William's *Guide to the Printed Materials for English Social and Economic History, 1750–1850*, 2 vols. (New York, Columbia University Press, 1926) offers help to those who want less specialized statistics.

[63] Brian R. Mitchell and Klaus Boehm (Cambridge, Cambridge University Press, 1965).

[64] F. W. S. Craig (Glasgow, Political Reference Publications, 1968).

run into trouble unless the statistics he wants are in the period covered in these compilations. *British Parliament Election Results* was the first statistical compilation to give the following information for each by-election and election by constituency: the size of the electorate, the turnout, the percentage of votes cast for each candidate, and detailed maps showing the location of constituencies. *British Parliamentary Election Statistics* is an authoritative compendium of election statistics for the past fifty years in Great Britain. Its cumulative tables are based upon the preparation of a definitive text of general election and by-election contests in Britain since 1918. The data is not yet in print but is in the course of being put on magnetic tape for computer analysis at the Survey Research Center of the University of Strathclyde, Glasgow. *British Parliamentary Election Statistics* is one volume in a series. F. W. S. Craig expects to publish two more volumes in 1969: *British Parliamentary Elections: Constituency Results*, volume 1, *1918–1949*; volume 2, *1950–1969*.

The Latin American Center of the University of California at Los Angeles has been publishing a *Statistical Abstract of Latin America*[65] since 1956 when its first volume, which covered the year 1955, appeared. It provides a single, easily accessible source for comparative statistical data on Latin America for the following topics: area and land use, population, social organization, and economy and finance. Sources for each table and a bibliography of statistical sources for Latin America help to guide the student to other statistical references.

CURRENT SURVEYS

Annuals and almanacs supplement the encyclopedias in pro-

[65] University of California at Los Angeles, Committee on Latin American Studies (Los Angeles, University of California at Los Angeles, Committee on Latin American Studies, 1956–). Biennial beginning with 1964–65; previously published annually. Since 1964 the United Nations Economic Commission for Latin America has been publishing a *Boletin estadistico de American, Statistical Bulletin for Latin America* (New York, United Nations, 1964–).

viding current information, but sometimes the information needed is too recent to be included in these yearbooks. In this case periodical indexes, newspaper indexes, and weekly and fortnightly news service publications can be extremely useful.

The *African Recorder*[66] and the *Asian Recorder*[67] are concerned with the cultural, economic, and political events on their respective continents. The first is a selective biweekly; the second, a selective weekly. Both are arranged alphabetically by country, and both have indexes. The *Current Digest of the Soviet Press* is the weekly condensation of the news from Russian newspapers and periodicals.[68] Each article is translated into English and the source is given with full details on date, paging, number of words, and a notation as to whether it is a complete translation or a condensation. Each issue has a weekly index to the contents of *Pravda* and *Izvestia*. Arranged by subject with quarterly indexes, the *Current Digest of the Soviet Press* is indispensable to those working in Russian history and diplomatic history.

Facts on File[69] is a weekly digest of news arranged by subjects such as world affairs, national affairs, foreign affairs, Latin America, finance, economy, arts, science, education, religion, sports, and obituaries. It is really an encyclopedia of current events. Because it is weekly, *Facts on File* fills in the gap between the time something happened and the time the twice-monthly *New York Times Index* appears. *Facts on File* is less detailed and more popular than *Keesing's Contemporary Archives*,[70] which is its British counter-

[66] M. Henry Samuel, ed., *African Recorder: A Fortnightly Record of African Events with Index*, 1962– (New Delhi, 6 Dr. Rajendra Prasas Rd., 1962–). Fortnightly with semiannual and annual indexes. Loose-leaf.

[67] M. Henry Samuel, ed., *Asian Recorder: A Weekly Digest of Outstanding Asian Events with an Index* (New Delhi, Asian Recorder, 1955–). Weekly.

[68] (New York, Joint Committee on Slavic Studies, 1949–). Weekly.

[69] *Facts on File: A Weekly World News Digest with Cumulative Index* (New York, Facts on File, 1940–). Weekly, with annual bound volumes. Indexes are published twice monthly and cumulative throughout the year. *Five-Year Index: The Index to World Events* (New York, Facts on File, 1957–). 1946–50 (1958); 1951–55 (1957); 1956–60 (1961).

part with a British emphasis. Published weekly since 1931, *Keesing's Contemporary Archives* covers the day-to-day developments in national and international politics, economics, industry, commerce, finance, defense, sports, education, and religion. It presents extensive summaries or verbatim accounts of all important international treaties, charters, and conferences, as well as the major statements of world leaders. It is authoritative, objective, and reliable.

[70] *Keesing's Contemporary Archives: Weekly Diary of World Events, with Index Continually Kept Up-to-date* (London, Keesing's, 1931–), vol. 1– . Issued weekly with detailed indexes, cumulating fortnightly, quarterly, annually, and biennially. It is also issued in German, *Archiv der genewart.*

6

Serials
and Newspapers

SERIALS

Much of the important work in history is reported in specialized history serials. For example, Frederick Jackson Turner's frontier hypothesis first appeared in a serial publication when his essay "The Significance of the Frontier in American History," which he had read at a meeting of the American Historical Association on July 12, 1893, was first printed in the *Proceedings* of the State Historical Society of Wisconsin for 1893 and reprinted in the *Annual Report* of the American Historical Association for 1893.

To make the best use of periodical literature, the history researcher needs three kinds of reference aids: a bibliography or catalog of periodicals, a union list of periodicals, and an index to periodicals.

The following definitions may help to clear up confusion about what serials, periodicals, and continuations are.

A serial is:

A publication issued in successive parts, usually at regular intervals, and, as a rule, intended to be continued indefinitely. Serials include periodicals, newspapers, annuals (reports, yearbooks, etc.), memoirs, proceedings, transactions of societies, and many include monographic series and publishers' series.[1]

A periodical is:

A serial issued in parts which are not monographs and which usually contain articles by several contributors. It generally has a distinctive title and the successive numbers or parts are intended to appear at stated or regular intervals, and, as a rule, for an indefinite period.[2]

A continuation is:

A work issued as a supplement to one previously issued. A part issued in continuance of a book, a serial, or a series.[3]

Directories

A bibliography or catalog of periodicals provides directory information: the current title, subject, publisher, address, price, and so on. One of the major current works listing periodicals is *Ulrich's International Periodicals Directory*.[4] The first edition of *Ulrich's International* appeared in 1932.[5] The thirteenth edition, published in 1969, lists 40,000 in-print periodicals published throughout the world in one alphabet of major subject headings. History periodicals are listed in volume 1 on pages 627–52. The thirteenth edition also has an index to new periodicals and a list of periodicals that have ceased publication.

Each entry includes the title and subtitle of a periodical, the date of origin (if known), frequency of publication, the price, the

[1] Emory Koltay, ed., *Irregular Serials and Annuals: An International Directory, A Classified Guide to Current Foreign and Domestic Serials, Excepting Periodicals Issued More Frequently Than Once a Year* (New York, R. R. Bowker Co., 1967), ix.

[2] *Ibid.*

[3] *Ibid.*

[4] *Ulrich's International Periodical Directory: A Classified Guide to Current Periodicals, Foreign and Domestic*, 13th ed., 2 vols. (New York, R. R. Bowker Co., 1969–70). Vol. 1, A–L. Vol. 2, M–Z.

[5] The earlier editions are useful for lists of periodicals no longer published and for special lists, such as "A List of Clandestine Periodicals of World War II," edited by Adrienne Florence Mussy, in the 5th edition (1947).

publisher's name and address, the editor's name, information on any annual or cumulative indexes, circulation figures, and items characteristic of each periodical, such as whether book reviews are carried or advertisements accepted. *Ulrich's International* also notes whether there is a yearbook, directory, or special number, whether the text is in more than one language, and whether there are summaries in various languages. A unique feature, and an especially valuable one, is the practice of indicating in the individual entry the indexes and abstracts which include that particular title.

A second important current work which lists periodicals is *Irregular Serials and Annuals*.[6] It covers some 14,500 of the most important titles which appear irregularly. Planned as a companion volume to *Ulrich's International Periodicals Directory, Irregular Serials and Annuals* follows *Ulrich's* in general format. It is international in coverage, attempting to include material in languages using the roman alphabet or having abstracts, subtitles, or some information in English; it is arranged by subject with indexes by title and subject and a cross index to subjects; and it excludes most national, state, and municipal documents. Each entry gives the title, subtitle or annotation, language or languages of the text, year of first publication, frequency, price, name and address of the publisher, the editor or editors, information about an index or cumulative index, and the Dewey classification number.

Another comprehensive directory listing current periodicals is the *Standard Periodical Directory*.[7] It is a guide to more than 39,000 United States and Canadian periodicals in all fields including history. Because this directory defines a periodical as "any publication with a regular frequency of at least once every two years," it includes many newsletters, governmental publications, house organs, advisory services, directories, transactions and proceedings of professional societies, yearbooks, and other serials

[6] For full bibliographic information, see note 1.

[7] (New York, Oxbridge Publishing Co., 1964–). Annual. The second issue was published in 1967.

not found in other periodical directories. Arranged by subject with an author index and subject guide, entries include the title, the publisher and his address, a thumbnail description of editorial contents, the year the publication was founded, frequency, subscription rate, and circulation.

Entries for microfilms of serials appear in a number of lists and guides. There is the *Union List of Microfilms*, which stopped publication with its *Cumulation*[8] because of the flood of microfilm accessions, the growing number of catalogs of microfilm by types or by subject, the demand for inclusion of all kinds of photographic reproductions (microprint, microcard, and microfiche), and the necessity for application of technological apparatus to place microform entries on reproducible records. The *Union List* and its *Cumulation* have omitted newspapers, which are recorded in *Newspapers on Microfilm*,[9] and American theses and American doctoral dissertations, which are listed in *Dissertation Abstracts*.[10] The *Union List* and its *Cumulation* do list microfilmed theses from books, foreign universities, serials from the *American Periodical Series, 1800–1850* and *English Literary Periodicals, 17th, 18th, and 19th Centuries*, and some manuscripts. Each entry includes all the bibliographical detail available as well as the locations of the master negative, negative and positive microfilms, and the original when available. The material is arranged alphabetically by main entry.

[8] Philadelphia Bibliographic Center and Union Library Catalogue, Committee on Microphotography, *Union List of Microfilms*, ed. by Eleanor Este Campion, rev., enl., and cum. ed. (Ann Arbor, Mich., Edwards Bros., 1951). *Cumulation*, 1949–59, 2 vols. (Ann Arbor, Mich., J. W. Edwards, 1961).

[9] See the section on "Directories" in this chapter.

[10] *Dissertation Abstracts: A Guide to Dissertations and Monographs* (Ann Arbor, Mich., University Microfilms, 1952–). Monthly. Published under the title *Microfilm Abstracts*, 1935–51. Beginning with volume 27 (July, 1966), the index appears in two sections: A, Humanities and the Social Sciences; B, Science and Engineering. Volume 13 lists dissertations submitted at all American universities.

The *Guide to Microforms in Print*[11] is an annual cumulative guide to books, journals, and other materials available in microform (microfilm, microcard, and microfiche) from United States publishers. It is arranged alphabetically by main entry. Books are entered under the author's name and include the title and date of publication of the work in its original form. Journals and sets are entered by title, and the entries include the title and date of publication of the work in its original form. Newspapers are entered by state, then by city, and lastly by name. Archival materials and manuscripts are entered under the form listed by the publishing company. The price and publisher are given for each entry. The *Subject Guide to Microforms in Print*[12] gives a subject approach to the materials in *The Guide to Microforms in Print.*

The *National Register of Microform Masters*[13] is a companion volume to *Newspapers on Microfilm.* It has a description and the location of master negatives of monographs, serials, pamphlets, foreign and domestic books, and foreign doctoral dissertations. It does not include technical reports, typescript translations, foreign or domestic archival or manuscript collections, or United States theses and dissertations.

Historical Periodicals is an annotated directory of serials with at least twenty per cent of its articles on history.[14] Arranged geographically, it has indexes of titles and the issuing bodies. Each entry includes the title of the periodical, frequency, the issuing body with its address, price, and, sometimes, editors. A content note touches on the subject matter, period and area concentra-

---

[11] (Washington, D.C., Microcard Edition, 1961–). Annual.

[12] (Washington, D.C., Microcard Editions, 1962–63–). Annual.

[13] Comp. by the Library Association and the Association of Research Libraries (Washington, D.C., Library of Congress, 1967). The first edition came out in 1965; it is irregular.

[14] Eric H. Boehm and Lalit Adolphus, *Historical Periodicals: An Annotated World List of Historical and Related Serial Publications* (Santa Barbara, Calif., Clio Press, 1961). For current titles this publication supersedes Pierre Caron and Marc Jaryc's *World List of Historical Periodicals* (New York, H. W. Wilson Co., 1939), which remains valuable for discontinued titles.

tions, book reviews, documents, bibliographies, and professional news.

The American Association for State and Local History issues *Directory: Historical Societies and Agencies in the United States and Canada*, a biennial directory to help people find the organization working with the local material in which they are interested.[15] The basic organization of this directory is alphabetical, first by state and then by city or town, and lastly by the name of the society or association.

Union Lists

The union lists of periodicals contain bibliographical data and supply information as to where the periodicals included in them might be found. Union lists facilitate interlibrary loans and the procurement of photocopies.

Ruth S. Freitag compiled the *Union List of Serials*,[16] which defines serials in the broadest sense to include newspapers, periodicals, annuals, services, government publications, proceedings of conferences and congresses, the publication of learned societies, and so on, and records 1,218 union lists. These union lists are arranged geographically by region or country and alphabetically within each section. There are three indexes: geographical, name (author, editor, compiler, or corporate body connected with the title), and subject. The *Union List of Serials* lists publications that indicate the location of serials in more than one library and gives the following information for each: the arrangement of the entries, the number and location of co-operating libraries, the number of serials included, whether or not the extent of library holdings is

[15] (Madison, Wis., American Association for State and Local History, 1956–). The 1965–66 edition was published in Nashville, Tenn., for the Association.

[16] U.S., Library of Congress, General Reference and Bibliography Division (Washington, D.C., Government Printing Office, 1964). This publication should not be confused with the *Union List of Serials in the Libraries of the United States and Canada.*

shown, and the presence of any indexes. This rather technical list can be of value to the history student.

The *Union List of Serials in Libraries of the United States* is the outstanding example of a union list.[17] The first edition (1927), edited by Winifred Gregory, has entries for 75,000 serial titles and located holdings in 225 libraries. The second edition (1943), also edited by Winifred Gregory, contains entries for 115,000 titles and locates holdings in 650 libraries. Both editions have two supplements. The third and last edition locates files of 157,000 journals in 956 United States and Canadian libraries. It incorporates into one alphabet the titles and holdings in the second edition and its two supplements with a number of new titles which began publication before January 1, 1950. This revision notes major additions and changes in the holdings of co-operating libraries, corrects earlier entries, and adds new titles.

The *Union List of Serials* is kept up to date and is supplemented by *New Serial Titles*.[18] In 1951 the Library of Congress started *Serial Titles Newly Received*. Initially confined to listing serials which had commenced publication on or after January 1, 1950, and which had been acquired by the Library of Congress, in 1953, with the support and co-operation of the Joint Committee on the *Union List of Serials*, *Serial Titles Newly Received* was expanded to include the acquisitions of other libraries and was renamed *New Serial Titles*. In 1955 a subject approach was added with the publication of *New Serial Titles—Classed Subject Arrangement*, which is arranged by Dewey Decimal Classification.[19]

[17] Edna Brown Titus, ed., *Union List of Serials in the Libraries of the United States and Canada*, 5 vols. (New York, H. W. Wilson Co., 1965).

[18] U.S., Library of Congress (Washington, D.C., Library of Congress, 1953–). Monthly with annual cumulations. *New Serial Titles: 1950–1960: Supplement to the Union List of Serials*, 3d ed., prepared under the sponsorship of the Joint Committee on the Union List of Serials, 2 vols. (Washington, D.C., Library of Congress, 1961) supersedes the earlier annual volumes. All the cumulations contain a section listing changes in serials.

[19] (Washington, D.C., Library of Congress, Card Division, 1955–). Monthly. *Subject Index to New Serials Titles, 1950–1965* (Ann Arbor,

Half a Century of Soviet Serials, 1917–1968[20] is a bibliography and union list of serials published in the USSR. All known serial publications appearing in the Soviet Union since 1917 in all except Oriental languages are included. Those in the Oriental languages, such as Armenian, Georgian, and Kirghiz, are included only if they have a Russian-language title page and some contributions in Russian. The language of a serial other than Russian is specified in parentheses following the title. There are 29,761 entries with more than 28,000 cross references. Serials without distinctive titles which are published by a society, institution, or government agency are grouped under the name of the organization responsible for their publication. Serials with distinctive titles are entered under the title. The compiler has used the Library of Congress transliteration system and the Library of Congress forms of entry. All titles of serial publications are capitalized and corporate headings are given in lower-case type. The title is followed by the place of publication, the year that the serial began publication (if known), the name of the issuing body (for title entries), the frequency of publication, and miscellaneous remarks regarding changes in title, suspension of publication for certain periods, and so on. The various changes in the publishers of a serial are not indicated; thus only the latest known issuing body is specified. If the publication ceased and the date is known, this date is indicated together with the first year of publication. Symbols of libraries in the United States and Canada in which the title can be found are given for each entry. A second list of symbols of the libraries gives the full name and location of the library.

Mich., Pierian Press, 1968) provides a subject approach to more than 200,000 serials.

[20] Rudolf Smits, comp., *Half A Century of Soviet Serials, 1917–1968: A Bibliography and Union List of Serials Published in the USSR*, 2 vols. (Washington, D.C., Library of Congress, 1968). A companion volume, although it does not give locations for titles, is *Half a Century of Russian Serials, 1917–1968: Cumulative Index of Serials Published Outside of the U.S.S.R.*, pt. 1, A–M (New York, Russian Book Chamber Abroad, 1970) by Michael Schatoff. Edited by N. A. Hale, it lists over one thousand serials published outside of the Soviet Union in Russian.

112

The standard union list for Great Britain is the *British Union-Catalogue of Periodicals*, a record of the periodicals of the world from the seventeenth century to the present in any language and on any subject.[21] This publication lists more than 140,000 titles and their holdings in about 440 British libraries. It includes many periodicals not in the *Union List* and enters periodicals under their earliest known names, with cross references from all later names to the original name. It also enters all academies, societies, and organizations under their original names with cross references. *New Periodical Titles*,[22] which lists all periodicals and serials which began publication in 1960 or later and records changes in or suspension of title, keeps the *British Union-Catalogue* up to date.

Indexes

Periodical indexes do for articles in magazines what the card catalog does for books. William Frederick Poole compiled *Poole's Index to Periodical Literature*, the first periodical index and the only index to nineteenth-century periodicals to 1890.[23] This subject index lists 590,000 articles in 479 American and English periodicals. Because entries in *Poole's Index to Periodical Literature* do not contain dates for articles, the student will need to use *Poole's Index, Date and Key Volume*.[24] This index contains an

[21] *British Union-Catalogue of Periodicals: A Record of the Periodicals of the World, from the Seventeenth Century to the Present Day, in British Libraries*, ed. for the Council of the British Union Catalogue of Periodicals by James D. Stewart, with Muriel E. Hammond and Erwin Saenger, 4 vols. (London, Butterworths Scientific Publications, 1955–58). The *Supplement to 1960* (1962) includes entries for new periodicals appearing since the publication of the main volumes, plus corrections and additions to the set.

[22] *British Union-Catalogue of Periodicals, Incorporating World List of Scientific Periodicals: New Periodical Titles* (London, Butterworths Scientific Publications, 1964–). Quarterly. Annual cumulations. It also lists library holdings in British libraries.

[23] *Poole's Index to Periodical Literature, 1802–1907*, 7 vols. (Boston, Houghton Mifflin and Company, 1882–1908).

[24] Marion V. Bell and Jean C. Bacon, *Poole's Index, Date and Volume*

alphabetical listing of the 479 periodicals in *Poole's Index to Periodical Literature* and gives the date for each volume number in a table. These two reference tools have been very important and will become even more so. University Microfilms has undertaken the project of microfilming the American and British serials indexed by Poole; thus, by using *Poole's Index to Periodical Literature* as a key, the student will have access to these periodicals.

The Nineteenth Century Readers' Guide to Periodical Literature,[25] one of the periodical indexes published by H. W. Wilson Company, is an author and subject index to fifty-one periodicals in the 1890's. From 1900 to 1922 this title indexed fourteen periodicals, which were carried on by the Wilson indexes, such as the *Readers' Guide to Periodical Literature* and the *International Index to Periodical Literature*.

The *Readers' Guide to Periodical Literature* began in 1900.[26] This most-used guide to about 130 popular, general magazines is an author, subject, and title index. Initially it covered only fifteen of the most popular periodicals. In 1903 it absorbed the *Cumulative Index* and in 1911, the *Annual Library Index*.[27] Each entry

Key, ACRL Monograph no. 19 (Chicago, Association of College and Reference Libraries, 1957).

[25] Helen Grant Cushing and Adah V. Morris, eds., *Nineteenth Century Readers' Guide to Periodical Literature*, 2 vols. (New York, H. W. Wilson Co., 1944–).

[26] (New York, H. W. Wilson Co., 1905–). A cumulated index including: permanent cumulated volumes (since 1935, two years to a volume; previous volumes varied from three to five years); annual volumes issued; published semimonthly, September to June; monthly July–August, cumulating at intervals.

[27] *Cumulative Index to a Selected List of Periodicals*, 8 vols. (Cleveland, Ohio, Public Library, 1896–1903). *Annual Library Index, 1905–1910: Including Periodicals, American and English: Essays, Book-Chapters, etc.*, 6 vols. (New York, Publishers' Weekly, 1906–11). The *Annual Magazine Subject Index, 1907–1949: A Subject Index to a Selected List of American and British Periodicals and Society Publications*, 43 vols. (Boston, F. W. Faxon Co., 1908–52) was intended as a supplement to other indexes; it indexes periodicals not indexed elsewhere. While it indexed general periodicals, over half was concerned with history, especially local history. It indexed many local history titles, such as transactions of local history societies

114

includes the author's name, the title, the name of the magazine, the volume number, the full date, paging, and information on illustrations, portraits, and maps.

The *Social Sciences and Humanities Index*[28] covers the well-known scholarly journals in anthropology, archaeology and classical studies, area studies, economics, folklore, geography, history, languages and literature, music, philosophy, political science, religion and theology, sociology, and theatre arts. It has good coverage of English-language periodicals published in the United States and England, but it does not index foreign-language periodicals. This author-subject index excludes book reviews but includes review articles; it also contains entries showing the contents of special issues or symposia with entries for individual authors and subjects. The *Social Sciences and Humanities Index*, which covers about 215 titles, is probably the first periodical index a history student should consult.

Another important selective but comprehensive American index is the *Public Affairs Information Service Bulletin* (PAIS).[29] It is a subject index, not only to periodicals and books, but also to pamphlets, documents, society publications, and mimeographed material on economics, social conditions, politics, government, international relations, and public administration. This

which Appleton Prentiss Clark Griffin had indexed in his *Bibliography of American Historical Societies* (the United States and the Dominion of Canada) 2d rev. and enl. ed. (Washington, D.C., Government Printing Office, 1907); hence, it is an informal continuation of Griffin. The G. K. Hall Co., Boston, has cumulated these forty-three volumes into one alphabet in two volumes, *The Cumulated Magazine Subject Index, 1907–1949: A Cumulation of the F. W. Faxon Company's "Annual Magazine Subject Index."*

[28] *Social Sciences and Humanities Index* (New York: H. W. Wilson Co., 1907–15–). Title varies: *Readers' Guide to Periodical Literature Supplement* (1907–1915–1916/19); *International Index to Periodicals* (1920–1923–1952/55); *International Index* (1955/59–March 1, 1965). Cumulative index including permanent cumulated volumes covering four, three, or two years; annual volumes; and current numbers are quarterly.

[29] (New York, Public Affairs Information Service, 1915–). Weekly. Cumulated five times a year; the fifth cumulation is the annual volume.

weekly bulletin cumulates five times a year and the fifth cumulated issue becomes a permanent volume for the year. The key to periodical references, a directory of publishers and organizations, and a list of publications analyzed are listed at the beginning of this annual volume. PAIS is limited to materials in the English language and is probably the major index in English in its field.

The *British Humanities Index*[30] is a new index which supersedes the *Subject Index to Periodicals.*[31] It indexes some 310 serials concerned with the arts and politics. There is very little duplication of titles in the *Social Sciences and Humanities Index* and this British index. The material in the *British Humanities Index* is arranged by subject with an author index in the annual volume.

According to Carl White, the *Internationale Bibliographie der Zeitschriftenliteratur* (IBZ),[32] is "the most extensive of periodical

[30] (London, Library Association, 1963–). Quarterly with annual cumulations.

[31] (London, Library Association, 1915–61). Quarterly with annual cumulations. Confined to British periodicals since 1947. It is useful for its inclusion of the publications of local antiquarian societies.

[32] (Osnabruck, F. Dietrich, 1897–). Pt. A, *A Bibliographie der deutschen Zeitschriftenliteratur,* 1896–1964, 128 vols. (1897–1964), semiannual; Pt. B, *Bibliographie der fremdsprachigen Zeitschriftenliteratur: Repertoire bibliographique international des revues; International Index to Periodicals,* 1911–19, 1925/26–1962/64, nF. vols. 1–52 (1911–64), semiannual; Pt. C, *Bibliographie der Rezension und Referate,* 77 vols. (1912– 43). Pt. A (1965) and Pt. B (1964) merged into *Internationale Bibliographie der Zeitschriftenliteratur allen Gebieten des Wissens,* ed. by Otto Zeller, 1963/64– (Osnabruck, Felix Dietrich, 1965–). Semiannual. With the end of the German *Bibliographie der Rezension* there has been a gap in book review guides. The *Book Review Digest* (New York, H. W. Wilson Co., 1905–) is an index to reviews of English-language books and is selective in that at least two reviews of a nonfiction title must be found in the indexed journals before any are cited. The *Index to Book Reviews in the Humanities,* which started in 1960 and the *Book Review Index,* which has been published by Gale Research, Inc. since 1965, have brought about an improvement in the indexing of book reviews of books in the English language. There are still difficulties in locating reviews of books published in foreign languages, of books published in the nineteenth century and earlier, and of books in highly specialized subject fields. *A Guide to Book Review Citations: A Bibliography of Sources,* compiled by Richard A. Gray

116

indexes."[33] Part A, *Bibliographie der deutschen Zeitschriften-literatur mit Einschluss von Sammelwerken*, is an alphabetical subject index to some 3,600 German-language periodicals and forty-five newspapers. Part B, *Bibliographie der fremdsprachigen Zeitschriftenliteratur: Répertoire bibliographique international des revues*, is an alphabetical subject index to some 3,200 periodicals and general works in the principal non-German languages. Part C, *Bibliographie der Rezensionen und Referate*, is a comprehensive listing of book reviews. From 1900 through 1911 Part C indexed only German reviews. From 1912 through 1943 there were two series numbered alternately. One indexed book reviews in 3,000 German periodicals; the other, book reviews in 2,000 non-German periodicals.

Other indexes on special historical topics are discussed in chapter 3. These include the guides on special areas or topics which list books, periodicals, and specific indexes to serials. An example of a guide to periodical articles on one facet of the history of a specific country is Oscar O. Winther's *A Classified Bibliography of the Periodical Literature of the Trans-Mississippi West, 1811–1957*.[34]

While the field of history does not yet have a reference aid which lists the advance bibliography of contents of serials, the history student interested in foreign affairs can profitably use the *A(dvance) B(ibliography) of C(ontents): Political Science and Government*,[35] which reproduces the tables of contents of 260

(Columbus, Ohio, Ohio State University Press, 1968) directs the readers to those indexes and bibliographies which will provide the largest number of reviews for any book regardless of its date, language, or subject. Arranged by classification, with a subject and personal name index, the entries have two annotations each: one giving the scope of the bibliography or index and the second describing its organization and the way the reviews are cited. A Chronology Index lists entries which cite reviews of books published during the nineteenth century and earlier, and a Country-of-Origin Index refers to those sources which either list books published exclusively in one country or sources which cite reviews appearing in the journals of only one country.

[33] White, *Sources of Information in the Social Sciences*, 31.

[34] (Bloomington, Indiana University Press, 1961).

[35] (Santa Barbara, Calif., published for the Bibliographic Center by the Clio Press, March, 1969–).

journals. Eight issues a year are published. There is an author index in each issue, a cumulated author index in the fourth and eighth issues, and an annual index for every eight issues.

NEWSPAPERS

Newspapers constitute one of the most important primary sources available to the historian. By recording contemporary events, opinion, and advertising, newspapers provide a basic source for the student of local, national, political, economic, or social history. The student can find what he needs in periodicals and newspapers by learning how to use the reference aids common to both: bibliographies and catalogs, union lists, and indexes.

Directories

In addition to the lists of newspapers in various encyclopedias, handbooks, almanacs, and other yearbooks, there are directories of newspapers and of newspapers and periodicals.

The *Editor and Publisher International Yearbook*[36] lists the daily papers of the United States (arranged alphabetically by state and city), the daily papers of Canada (arranged alphabetically by province and city), the weekly newspapers of the United States (by state), Negro newspapers of the United States, college-professional-business and special service daily newspapers of the United States (by subject), the principal foreign-language newspapers of the United States (by state), and the daily newspapers of Great Britain and Ireland. It also lists alphabetically by country the daily newspapers of Europe, Latin America, Australasia, Africa, the Near and Middle East, and Asia and the Far East. In addition, there are lists of groups of daily newspapers in the United States under common ownership; United States printing equipment manufacturers, suppliers, and services; United States advertising agencies; the United States Congressional Gallery; the foreign

[36] *Editor and Publisher International Yearbook Number* (New York, Editor and Publisher, 1920–). Annual.

press and radio and television correspondents in the United States, the Foreign Press Association, and the United Nations Correspondence Association; and a feature news and picture syndicate directory.

N. W. Ayer and Son's Directory of Newspapers and Periodicals,[37] a listing of newspapers and periodicals printed in the United States, Canada, Bermuda, Panama, and the Philippines, is the standard American list. It absorbed *Rowell's American Newspaper Directory* in 1910.[38] The main catalog of newspapers in the *Ayer and Son's Directory* covers over 1,200 pages in the 1967 edition and is arranged alphabetically by state and city. For each state there is a map and thumbnail sketch including figures on population, agriculture, manufactures, minerals, newspapers, and periodicals. There is a similar sketch for each city in which a newspaper listed is published. The following information is included: date of establishment, political preference, width and depth, cost of subscription, and circulation. Besides this main list, there are maps and statistics for the United States and classified lists of agricultural, college, foreign language, Negro, religious, trade and technical, and labor publications.

Documents from the underground press are and will be invaluable for historians, political scientists, sociologists, and other social scientists who are or will be interpreting the American scene of the latter half of the twentieth century. William D. Lutz has compiled a directory to these publications, *Underground Press Directory*.[39] The Bell and Howell Company of Wooster, Ohio, with the cooperation of the Underground Press Syndicate and the commendation of the American Library Association, has initiated a program for the microproduction of these newspapers. The basic collection covers these papers from 1965 to 1968, and there is an annual cumulation to keep the collection up to date.

[37] (Philadelphia, N. W. Ayer & Sons, Inc., 1880–). Annual.

[38] *Rowell's American Newspaper Directory*, 40 vols. (New York. G. P. Rowell & Co., 1869–1908).

[39] 3d ed. (Stevens Point, Wis., Counterpoint, 1969).

The *Foreign Press* is a handbook of the press.[40] After a brief discussion of the foreign press in respect to quality, circulation, control, and news agencies, the authors give an overview of the press of the continents and regions with a sketch of each country and a descriptive and statistical note on each of its major newspapers.

The first volume of the *Working Press of the Nation*[41] is a directory and guide to newspapers of all kinds—daily, weekly, foreign, and special interest. It also lists news services, feature syndicates, and photo services. The other two volumes are directories and guides to magazines, radio, and television.

The *Newspaper Press Directory* emphasizes British newspapers, but lists the newspapers of the world.[42] It has lists of newspapers and periodicals (general, specialized, trade and technical, and house organs), news and feature service agencies, press photographers, engravers, stereotypers, typesetters, commercial art studios, market research services, press cutting agencies, journalists, press clubs, and so on, for the United Kingdom and Republic of Ireland. After these lists come the press directories for the British Commonwealth, principal foreign countries, the United States, and South Africa. Quite extensive information is given for the United Kingdom and Republic of Ireland newspapers while less extensive information is given for the others.

Another current directory that is primarily British is *Willing's Press Guide*.[43] It lists newspapers and periodicals in the United Kingdom, the Republic of Ireland, the Commonwealth, and foreign countries. The newspapers in one list and the periodicals in a second list are arranged alphabetically by country. *Willing's Press*

---

[40] John C. Merrill, Carter Bryan, and Marvin Alisky (Baton Rouge, Louisiana State University Press, 1964).
[41] Tom Farrell, ed. (New York, Farrell Publishers, 1947–). Biennial: annual since 1959.
[42] *Newspaper Press Directory and Advertisers' Guide* (London, Benn Brothers, 1846–). Annual.
[43] Willing's Press Guide (London, Willing's Press Service, 1874–). Annual.

Guide and the *Newspaper Press Directory* contain much the same information for each entry.

Willing's European Press Guide is now in its second edition and claims to be the single most comprehensive guide to the European press.[44] It includes fifty thousand newspapers, periodicals, and annuals in eleven European countries. For each serial it gives its name and address, the publisher, frequency, and price. A gazetteer to the towns and cities of the eleven European countries included in this publication and an international monetary conversion table are new features. The entries are arranged under more than 180 subjects with subject headings, cross references, and indexes in four languages—English, French, German, and Italian.

Several directories list daily newspapers. United States dailies are given comprehensive coverage in the *Ayer and Son's Directory* and good coverage in *Editor and Publisher International Yearbook* and the *Working Press of the Nation*. The *National Directory of Weekly Newspapers* is a directory to weekly American hometown newspapers.[45] Entries are arranged alphabetically by state. For each state there is a map, a list of counties and county population, and a list of cities (designated by symbol as agricultural, industrial, mining, oil, resort, and county seat) and city population, the name of the paper, its circulation, publisher, day of publication, number of columns, advertising rate, policy on liquor advertising, and production information (offset, letterpress, use of color, and so on).

Bibliographies and Union Lists

The history student must know not only what newspapers contain the information he needs, but also where these newspapers are located. Clarence S. Brigham's *History and Bibliography of American Newspapers, 1690–1820*[46] is a union list for this early

[44] (New York, R. R. Bowker, 1968–).
[45] *National Directory of Weekly Newspapers Including Semi-Weekly and Tri-Weekly Newspapers* (New York, American Newspaper Representatives, 1927/28–). Annual.

period of American history. It lists 2,120 newspapers and is arranged alphabetically by state and town. For each newspaper, the author provides a historical note, with changes of title and dates, the names of publishers, printers and places of publication, and the names of libraries having files with their holdings. With *American Newspapers, 1821–1936,* it forms a comprehensive record of American newspaper files from 1690 to 1936.

The authoritative union list of American newspapers is *American Newspapers, 1821–1936: A Union List of Files Available in the United States and Canada,* edited by Winifred Gregory.[47] It presents, in a geographical arrangement of places of publication, files of newspapers from 1821 to 1936 found in the libraries of the United States and Canada and, as far as possible, those that are preserved in county courthouses, newspaper offices, and private collections. In compiling the list, Gregory used the trade dictionaries: *Rowell's American Newspapers and Periodicals 1869– 1879, Ayer and Son's Directory of Newspapers and Periodicals,* from 1880 on, and Brigham's *History and Bibliography of American Newspapers, 1690–1820. American Newspapers, 1821– 1936* is arranged alphabetically by state or province and city. Under each city the newspapers are listed alphabetically by the first important word. Bibliographic information given for each entry includes the name of the newspaper, whether it is a daily or weekly, dates, changes of titles, and names of libraries having files. Library holdings are listed by date.

There are two other important reference aids for research requiring the use of American newspapers. The *Check-List of American 18th Century Newspapers*[48] is more limited than Brig-

---

[46] 2 vols. (Worcester, Mass., American Antiquarian Society, 1947). Clarence S. Brigham, *Additions and Corrections* (1961). Reprinted from the *Proceedings* of the American Antiquarian Society (April, 1961).

[47] Under the auspices of the Bibliographical Society of America, 2d ed. (New York, H. W. Wilson, 1943).

[48] U.S., Library of Congress, Periodicals Division, *A Check-List of American 18th Century Newspapers in the Library of Congress,* new rev. and enl. ed. by Henry S. Parsons (Washington, D.C., Government Printing Office, 1936).

ham's *History and Bibliography of American Newspapers* because it is a record of only the newspapers in the Library of Congress. Arranged alphabetically by state, town, and title, this union list of 506 newspapers gives the changes of title, date of founding, the printer, publisher, editor, and the Library of Congress holdings.

S. N. D. North's *History and Present Condition of the Newspapers and Periodical Press of the United States*[49] is a useful adjunct to Brigham's *History and Bibliography of American Newspapers* and Gregory's *American Newspapers, 1821–1936.* It is a history of the press for three periods in United States history: 1639–1783, 1783–1835, and 1835–80. Statistical tables in the appendix provide the numbers of newspapers and periodicals (grouped by periods of issue, classes or characteristics, and languages) published in the United States during the census year and an analysis of circulation figures. The appendix also includes a directory of periodical publications by state and county published in 1879–80, a chronological history of the newspaper press of the United States by state and county, and a list of bound files of agricultural newspapers in the American Antiquarian Society in Worcester, Massachusetts.

There are also union lists of foreign newspapers. For example, the Library of Congress has compiled a list of its holdings of foreign newspapers, the *Check-List of Foreign Newspapers in the Library.*[50] Countries are arranged in one alphabet and cities and towns are alphabetized under the country in which they are located. This edition lists 2,689 titles covering newspapers published in seventy-nine countries in twenty-one languages. Each entry gives such bibliographical details as the date of establishment, changes in title, and frequency.

The Library of Congress has also compiled two lists of news-

[49] *History and Present Condition of the Newspaper and Periodical Press of the United States with a Catalogue of the Publications of the Census Year* (Washington, D.C., Government Printing Office, 1884).

[50] U.S., Library of Congress, Periodicals Division, *Check-List of Foreign Newspapers in the Library*, comp. by Henry S. Parsons (Washington, D.C., Government Printing Office, 1929).

papers of interest to the student of Russian history: *Russian, Ukrainian, and Belorussian Newspapers*[51] and *Newspapers of the Soviet Union*.[52] The first, a list of 859 papers issued since 1917, records the holdings of the Library of Congress and other major libraries, while the second is a record of newspapers in the Union of Soviet Socialist Republics (Slavic-language newspapers for 1954–60 and non-Slavic–language newspapers for 1917–60). Both publications list the material alphabetically by place of publication and alphabetically by title under the place of publication. Both have indexes of titles and guides to places of publication arranged by the republic. The following information is given for each entry: the latest place of publication; the title of the publication, the frequency of issue, the date of establishment, the name of the issuing body, changes in these factors, and the language if non-Russian. In *Russian, Ukrainian, and Belorussian Newspapers* the holdings in the Library of Congress and other libraries are listed for each entry. For *Newspapers of the Soviet Union* only the holdings in the Library of Congress are listed for each entry.

The Pan American Union is responsible for the *Union List of Latin American Newspapers in Libraries in the United States*,[53] an extremely important reference tool for the student of Latin-American history. It lists more than five thousand titles in fifty-six libraries. Arranged alphabetically first by country and city and then by title, this union list gives the title of the newspaper, its frequency, date of establishment, cessation if known, and an indica-

[51] U.S., Library of Congress, Slavic and Central European Division, *Russian, Ukrainian, and Belorussian Newspapers, 1917–1953: A Union List*, comp. by Paul L. Horecky (Washington, D.C., Library of Congress, 1953).

[52] U.S., Library of Congress, Slavic and Central European Division, *Newspapers of the Soviet Union in the Library of Congress* (Slavic, 1954–60; Non-Slavic, 1917–60), prepared by Paul L. Horecky with the assistance of John Balys and Robert G. Carlton (Washington, D.C., Government Printing Office, 1962).

[53] Arthur E. Gropp, comp. (Washington, D.C., Department of Cultural Affairs, Pan American Union, 1953).

tion of whether the title is still current. Notes give information on the language of the newspaper when it is not in the language of the country, changes in frequency, suspension, absorption into another paper, continuation under another title, changes in the place of publication, and holdings by date of the paper.

Historians and librarians have promoted the development of extensive programs for the preservation of newspaper files by microfilming them. Microfilm preserves the newspaper files and makes possible more extensive research in primary source material through purchase and interlibrary loan. In the United States many current daily newspapers are being microfilmed by or for their publishers. Weeklies and older files are generally the microfilm projects of libraries on a statewide basis. The University of Nevada, for example, has been working on the microfilming of all the back files of all Nevada newspapers for deposit at the University Library in Reno.[54] The Association of Research Libraries has a Foreign Newspaper Microfilm Project, which provides a national pool of current foreign newspapers, usually beginning with the 1956 issues.

Newspapers on Microfilm[55] contains approximately 21,700 entries representing 4,640 foreign newspapers and nearly 17,100 from the United States and its possessions. The foreign newspapers are from 136 countries; the American, from the fifty states, American Samoa, Guam, Okinawa, Puerto Rico, and the Virgin Islands. This union list of positive and negative microfilm is arranged geographically by country, by state and city for the United States, and by province and city for Canada. It lists the newspaper

[54] Two books on the history and bibliography of Nevada newspapers that perform the function of a union list for these papers are: Richard E. Lingenfelter's *The Newspapers of Nevada: A History and Bibliography, 1858–1859,* intro. by David F. Myrick (San Francisco, John Howell, 1964) and John Gregg Folkes, *Nevada's Newspapers: A Bibliography: A Compilation of Nevada History, 1854–1964,* Nevada Studies in History and Political Science no. 6 (Reno, University of Nevada Press, 1966).

[55] Comp. by the Library of Congress under the direction of George A. Schwegmann, Jr., 6th ed. (Washington, D.C., Library of Congress, 1967).

under its latest title. For some of the larger city dailies, notes on former titles are given. It updates the listing of Russian newspapers appearing in Horecky's *Russian, Ukrainian, and Belorussian Newspapers* to 1962, and it stars the Foreign Newspaper Microfilm Project titles. This list is a companion volume to the *National Register of Microform Masters.*

Indexes

For newspapers there is no general index which corresponds to the *Readers' Guide to Periodical Literature.* News is reported on the dates the events are news; thus an index to one newspaper will furnish a workable approach to other newspapers for subjects of general interest. It will not, however, be of any help for local news, special feature articles, editorials, or most obituaries of less than international interest. Two great newspapers publish indexes: the *New York Times* and *The Times* (London).

The *New York Times* was founded in 1851 by Henry J. Raymond, a protégé of Horace Greeley. It is a fact-filled, objective newspaper with unsurpassed financial and world coverage. The index now covers the paper from its beginning in 1851 to the present. It was the earliest newspaper index in the United States.[56] It gives the student a day-by-day history of the world in all branches of activity including politics, economics, science, agriculture, military affairs, religion, fine arts, book reviews, plays, crime, deaths, motion pictures, speeches, sports, music, and so on. The news is summarized and classified chronologically under subject headings (often inverted) and names of individuals and organizations. Information for each entry includes the date, page, and column of the issue. For example, the assassination of President Abraham Lincoln is listed under Political, "Lincoln, President, Assassinated, April 15-1-1," indicating that the student

[56] *New York Times Index* (New York, The New York Times, 1913–). Semimonthly with annual cumulations. R. R. Bowker Co., New York, is publishing the indexes from 1851 up to 1913 in book form and reprinting the volumes from 1913 to the present.

should go to the *New York Times* for April 15, 1865, to page one, column one, for the story.[57]

The Times (London) is one of the oldest, most respected, and most influential newspapers in Great Britain. John Walter I started publishing the *Daily Register* in 1785. The *Daily Register* quickly developed into a national newspaper, and its name was changed in 1788 to *The Times*. Under its proprietor, John Walter II, and editor, Thomas Barnes, *The Times* won the nickname "The Thunderer." Barnes, a friend of Charles Lamb and Leigh Hunt, has been considered the greatest journalist of the nineteenth century. He won *The Times* freedom from political interference and was responsible for many reforms. With a circulation of 256,123 in 1966, this independent-conservative newspaper appeals to the intelligentsia and government and business leaders.

The Times Index to "The Times" (London)[58] is the master key to the history of the twentieth century. It is an alphabetical index referring to the date, page, and column of the issue in which the specific reference is found. Events about a person are entered under his name. Other topics are grouped under broader headings, such as food, labor, law cases, and shipping, with cross references from individual items. There are comprehensive groupings relating to the affairs of single nations. It indexes the supplements to *The Times*, such as the *Times Literary Supplement*. Palmer's *Index to "The Times"*[59] runs from 1790 to June, 1941. While *The Times Index to "The Times"* has briefer entries and is less accurate than the *Official Index*, it is indispensable because it goes back almost to the beginning of *The Times*. It gives date, page, and column. It also has broad headings, for example, deaths are

[57] *New York Times Index*, 1863–74, 96.

[58] (London, *The Times*, 1906–). Published, 1906–13, as the *Annual Index to "The Times,"* January, 1914–February, 1957, as *The Official Index to "The Times."* Monthly with annual cumulations, 1906–June, 1914; quarterly, July, 1914–56; bimonthly, 1957– .

[59] *Palmer's Index to "The Times" Newspaper*, 1790–June, 1941 (London, S. Palmer, 1868–1943).

grouped under this heading with no cross references from the names of the people.

An index to a newspaper with specialized coverage is the *Wall Street Journal Index.*[60] The *Wall Street Journal* was established in 1889 by a Connecticut farm boy, Charles H. Dow. His Dow Jones Company had been so successful that he decided to put out a whole newspaper that would specialize in business news. The *Wall Street Journal Index* indexes accounts of current business and political trends and developments in its first section, "General News" and the items about a company, such as mergers, layoffs, earnings, incomes, and sales, under the name of the company in its second section, "Corporate News." The *Wall Street Journal* is published in four editions (New York, Dallas, Chicago, and San Francisco). The New York edition is the one indexed and issued on microfilm. According to the publishers, almost the same news material appears in each edition on the same day although a given story may not be in exactly the same spot. This is not always true; sometimes an article has appeared the day before, will appear the day after, or has been left out.

The *Current Digest of the Soviet Press*[61] is another specialized index. Besides abstracting in English articles from Soviet periodicals and newspapers, it also includes a complete weekly index to the contents of the two leading Russian newspapers—*Pravda* and *Izvestia.*

[60] (New York, Dow Jones & Co., 1959–). Monthly with annual cumulations.

[61] Trans. from the Soviet Press by John Murra, Robert M. Hankin, and Fred Holling (New York, King's Crown Press, 1951–).

7

Geographical Aids

It has always been important for the historian to identify the location of a historical event; hence, geographical bibliographies, gazetteers, and atlases are essential for historical work. Similarly, place names are important for historians. As Mario Pei has said, "A country's place names offer an almost sure index to that country's history."[1] In the United States, for example, the names of towns, rivers, and mountains are a guide to the movements of ethnic groups. Spanish explorers are recalled by Sangre de Cristo, Santa Fe, and Boca Grand; French settlers, by Eau Claire, Baton Rouge, and Des Moines; the Hudson Valley Dutch, by Schuykill and Kinderhook; the Scandinavians, by Valhalla and Gothenburg; the Germans, by Germantown and Hanover; the Poles, by Kosciuszko; and the Italians, by Paoli and Lodi.

In this chapter the geographical aids most useful to the student of history will be discussed.

BIBLIOGRAPHIES, INDEXES, AND GUIDES

There are several guides, a bibliography, and an index which the history student will find helpful in his study of geography. *Aids to Geographical Research* is old but still useful.[2] This comprehen-

[1] "Faraway Places with Strange Sounding Names," *Saturday Review* (February 10, 1968), 64.

[2] John M. Wright and Elizabeth T. Platt, *Aids to Geographical Re-*

sive guide to 1,174 research aids in many languages is divided into sections on general aids, topical aids, and regional aids and general geographical periodicals from each country. Geography and history often merge, and the history student will find bibliographies, historical atlases, and atlases for specific countries listed in this invaluable source.

There are two guides to atlases. The first, *General World Atlases in Print*,[3] evaluates general world atlases for the average American user at home, school, or office; it does not evaluate historical or other topical atlases. This publication is a reliable and up-to-date guide which will help the history student locate a good general world atlas. A second guide to atlases, *Whyte's Atlas Guide*,[4] may be more useful to the history student. It indexes twenty standard atlases and gives entries for continents, groups of countries, individual countries (when much material is devoted to them), individual city plans, island groups, oceans, unique areas, agriculture, canals, climate, deserts, highway maps, races of man, and so on. There are thirteen pages under the entry for historical maps.

The *Bibliographie géographique internationale*[5] is the most convenient, comprehensive, and, in many respects, the best of all current geographic bibliographies.[6] It lists titles of books, periodical articles, and maps that have appeared during the year, and it is divided into two parts. The first part (general) covers sections on human geography, including anthropology, political geography, economic geography, and colonization; the second part (regional), covers sections on individual countries with a subsection on human geography.

search: Bibliographies, Periodicals, Atlases, Gazetteers, and Other Reference Books, American Geographical Society Research Series no. 22, 2d rev. ed. (New York, published for the American Geographical Society by Columbia University Press, 1947).

[3] S. Padraig Walsh, *General World Atlases in Print: A Comparative Analysis* (New York, R. R. Bowker Co., 1966).

[4] Fredrica Harriman Whyte, *Whyte's Atlas Guide* (New York, Scarecrow Press, 1962).

[5] (Paris, A. Colin, 1891–). Annual.

[6] Wright and Platt, *Aids to Geographical Research*, 57.

The American Geographical Society's *Index to Maps in Books and Periodicals*[7] and *Research Catalogue of the American Geographical Society*[8] are useful tools. Its library, the largest geographical library in the Western Hemisphere, is strong in periodical articles. The entries in the *Index to Maps* are arranged by subject and geographical-political divisions in one alphabet. Within the geographical division, the entries are arranged chronologically. The *Research Catalogue of the American Geographical Society* includes books, periodical articles, pamphlets, and government documents arranged in a systematic and regional classification. It is kept up to date by *Current Geographical Publications*.[9]

GAZETTEERS

Geographical dictionaries or gazetteers are useful in locating and providing essential data about places. According to the editor of the *Columbia Lippincott Gazetteer of the World*, a gazetteer in the geographical sense "is used to describe several kinds of works which list geographical names in alphabetical order. . . . The comprehensive gazetteer . . . is an *encyclopedia of places*."[10] The major English-language world gazetteer is the *Columbia Lippincott Gazetteer of the World*. It lists in one alphabet the countries, regions, provinces, states, counties, cities, towns, islands, lakes, mountains, deserts, seas, rivers, canals, dams, peninsulas, and capes of the world and gives information about variant spellings, pronunciation, population, geographic and political location, altitude, trade, industry, agriculture, mineral and other natural re-

---

[7] 10 vols. (Boston, G. K. Hall, 1968).

[8] 15 vols. (Boston, G. K. Hall, 1962).

[9] *Current Geographical Publications: Additions to the "Research Catalogue" of the American Geographical Society* (New York, American Geographical Society, 1938–), 10 a year.

[10] Leon E. Seltzer, ed., *Columbia Lippincott Gazetteer of the World*, with the 1961 *Supplement* (New York, Columbia University Press, 1962), v. This volume is the successor of the old *Lippincott's New Gazetteer*, which was published from 1855 to 1931.

sources, irrigation works, river lengths, communications, history, cultural institutions and monuments, battles, and other facts pertinent to the place.

Designed to complement atlases by providing information not obtainable from maps and written in English for English-speaking readers, the *Columbia Lippincott* lists places under their English names and gives cross references from transliterated names, native names, names that have changed throughout history, and names in local usage. The history student will especially appreciate this feature.

A smaller volume than the *Columbia Lippincott*, which contains 130,000 place names, *Webster's Geographical Dictionary*[11] identifies about 40,000 place names. It gives full information on the spelling, syllabic division, and pronunciation of the names with concise geographical and, in many cases, historical information about the entries. If the historical information is of sufficient length or importance, it is placed in a separate paragraph introduced by the label *History*. Written in English for English-speaking readers, *Webster's Geographical Dictionary* gives special emphasis to the United States, Canada, and other parts of the English-speaking world. Like the *Columbia Lippincott*, it has many alternative names and spellings. Unlike the larger gazetteer, it has maps scattered throughout the text and twenty-four maps, twelve in color and twelve in black and white, in the back.

PLACE-NAME LITERATURE

The correct spelling of geographical names is quite a problem. Gazetteers and atlases may not be reliable and may vary. Official agencies of the United States and British governments have prepared certain approved lists for writers in English. *Decisions*, part 3 of the United States Board on Geographical Names' *Sixth Re-*

---

[11] *Webster's Geographical Dictionary: A Dictionary of Names and Places with Geographical and Historical Information and Pronunciations* (Springfield, Mass., G. & C. Merriam Co., 1962).

132

port[12] is a dictionary of thousands of place names, which the *Columbia Lippincott Gazetteer* calls invaluable. It incorporates the material of the *Fifth Report*, subsequent decisions, and the 2,500 foreign place names included in the *First Report on Foreign Geographic Names*. The information supplied for each name includes the approved form, the location, rejected forms, and, in some cases, pronunciation. It is kept up to date by *Decisions*,[13] which contains general lists of decisions and lists for special locations or specific foreign countries.

The British counterpart to the United States Board on Geographical Names is the Permanent Committee on Geographical Names for British Official Use. This organization is responsible for an unnumbered series of pamphlets which Winchell's *Guide to Reference Books* entitles *Lists of Names*.[14] These lists give the correct spelling and pronunciation of the names, rejected forms of the name, and location. A new series is being published now which updates the older lists.[15] The *Columbia Lippincott* has made use of this list too.

There is a great amount of literature on place names. In European countries the names of rivers, lakes, and mountains are often the only records of peoples who have disappeared without leaving any written records. Place names show migrations, shifting linguistic boundaries, natural resources, and cultural manifestations. European place-name research has been concerned with the etymology and evolution of geographical terms. Place-name research in the United States is recent; it has been undertaken systematically on a scholarly basis only in the present generation.

Richard B. Sealock is the authority on place-name research in the United States and Canada. His *Bibliography of Place Name*

[12] *Sixth Report, 1890–1932* (Washington, D.C., Government Printing Office, 1923).

[13] United States Board on Geographical Names (Washington, D.C., Government Printing Office, 1936–). Now issued quarterly.

[14] (London, Royal Geographical Society, 1921–38).

[15] Permanent Committee on Geographical Names for British Official Use, *Lists of Names*, new series (London, 1954–).

Literature[16] includes all the available published material on place names in books, periodicals, and manuscripts in libraries. The section on the United States is arranged alphabetically by state, and the section on Canada, alphabetically by province. An author index and a subject index with entries for specific names, broad categories (for example, mountains), foreign-language names, and types of names help the reader find what he wants.

An excellent example of a guide to place names in one country is George R. Stewart's *American Place Names: A Concise and* mology and evolution of geographical terms. Place-name research *Selective Dictionary for the Continental United States of America.*[17] This useful reference aid contains approximately 12,000 entries arranged in dictionary form. Each entry gives the meaning and derivation of the place name, the date and occasion of its naming, if possible, and the namer and his motivation.

ATLASES

An atlas is "a collection of maps bound into a volume. The figure Atlas supporting the heavens was used as a frontispiece in certain early collections of maps, e.g., in Mercator's *Atlas* (1595), and the term came to be used for the collection itself."[18]

Atlases vary considerably in content and quality. In addition to verbal (table of contents, index, and notes) and graphic (maps) information, they often present additional information, such as historic maps, guidebook information, tables of social, economic, and political data, major products, population tables, and map projections. The student needs to consider certain points in evaluating an atlas: the scope, country of origin, date, index, supple-

[16] Richard B. Sealock and Pauline A. Seely, *Bibliography of Place Name Literature: United States and Canada*, 2d ed. (Chicago, American Library Association, 1967).

[17] (New York, Oxford University Press, 1970).

[18] Wilfred G. Moore, *A Dictionary of Geography: Definitions and Explanations of Terms Used in Physical Geography* (New York, Frederick A. Praeger, 1967), 13.

mentary material, and maps.[19] The place and country of publication, for example, are often pertinent. An American atlas usually includes more maps of regions of the United States than does a European atlas, and conversely a European atlas usually emphasizes the Continent. In the past European atlases have been considered superior in workmanship to those made by American cartographers.

Geographical atlases might be classified broadly as reference atlases and atlases devoted to special topics. The universal reference atlas attempts to give, on a relatively large scale, as complete an image as possible of all the regions of the world; it is quite general. General reference and school atlases are as comprehensive as a universal atlas but on a smaller scale. National and regional atlases deal with smaller areas and treat a wide variety of subject matter in more detail.

Because several guides to atlases are available, only two outstanding reference atlases, those of most use to the history student, will be pointed out here. The outstanding universal reference atlas of the world is *"The Times" Atlas of the World*.[20] It has been called "the most significant world atlas in English that has appeared since World War II."[21] Carl White calls it "a superb up-to-date and detailed universal atlas."[22] *"The Times" Index-Gazetteer of the World* combines the indexes of the five volumes of the *"The Times" Atlas* in one volume, plus about 150,000 additional entries.[23] It is a list of towns, villages, mountains, rivers, and other geographical features in alphabetical order, with an italicized reference to where or in which country or state (for United States references) the feature belongs, followed by latitude and longitude. It is a most comprehensive reference aid.

[19] Winchell, *Guide to Reference Books*, 453–54.

[20] John Bartholomew, ed., mid-century ed., 5 vols. (London, Times Publishing Co., 1955–59).

[21] *The Booklist and Subscription Books Bulletin* (September 1, 1961), 5.

[22] *Sources of Information in the Social Sciences*, 106.

[23] (London, Times Publishing Co., 1965).

The *National Geographic Atlas of the World*[24] is a compilation of updated versions of the maps that have been folded and tucked into issues of the *National Geographic Magazine* with accompanying text. Both the maps and the text treat the world by geographic regions. Each region is first discussed as a unit, then, summaries of the political divisions making up the unit are presented. Statistical digests follow the country summaries; they give the area, population, type of government, language spoken, religious and racial background, climate, industries, and national resources. The areas to be mapped are divided into related geographical units rather than into separate political divisions. The atlas uses various projections (oblique cylindrical, two-point equidistant, Chamberlin trimetric, and so forth), and it uses various map scales for each area. Special features include a chart of temperature and rainfall in 321 places scattered around the world, a map of ocean bottoms, population tables, and inset maps of cities and metropolitan areas.

The foreign atlases are usually much more detailed for European countries. The German cartographers are especially renowned for their fine work. Two of their atlases are *Stieler's Atlas of Modern Geography*[25] and *Der grosse Bertelsmann Weltatlas*.[26] The first, a revision of *Stieler's Handatlas*, was one of the best prewar German atlases. In the international edition, the maps are in the languages of the countries mapped. The notes are in English, French, German, Italian, Portuguese, and Spanish. *Der grosse Bertelsmann Weltatlas*, a new German atlas, has excellent maps with indexes, a separate section of twenty maps on central Europe with its own index, a 2,400-word table of geographical equivalents, and an eleven-page key to languages.

[24] Meville Bell Grosvenor, ed., 2d ed. (Washington, D.C., National Geographic Society, 1966).

[25] Adolf Stieler, *Stieler's Atlas of Modern Geography: 263 Maps on 114 Sheets, Engraved in Copper*, 10th ed., international ed., published by Herman Haack with the co-operation of Berthold Carlberg and Rudolf Schleifer, 34 parts (Gotha, J. Perthes, 1934–38).

[26] Bertelsmann Cartographic Institute, ed., 10th ed. (Leitung, W. Bormaann, Guterloh, Bertelsmann, 1961).

136

The *Pergamon World Atlas* is an outstanding atlas in a loose-leaf binder.[27] It is an English edition of the *Polish Atlas Swiata*, which has been prepared and printed by the Polish Army Topographical Service. There are more than two hundred pages of geographical maps and more than four hundred thematic maps. There are maps of cities and an exceptionally large-scale and detailed map of Eastern Europe, the USSR, and the Far East based on sources not readily available to Western publishers. In addition to general updating, the *Pergamon World Atlas* contains additional maps for the United Kingdom and Canada. Scale bars in miles and altitudes in feet have been added for convenience in countries not using the metric system. Most map pages fold out, allowing presentation of large-scale maps while avoiding the problems presented by conventionally bound double-page layouts. There is an index to over 140,000 names.

There are many smaller reference atlases, but *Goode's World Atlas*[28] is the outstanding one. John Paul Goode, a distinguished cartographer, was the original editor of this atlas, which was first published more than thirty years ago as *Goode's School Atlas*. It consists of 168 pages of colored maps, including insets of metropolitan areas, plus some special maps in the text section. The maps are mainly physical-political, but there are over one hundred special maps for economics, vegetation, language, population, climate, and so on. In addition to these maps, there are tables of the principal islands, mountains, rivers, oceans, and so forth of the world; tables of the principal countries and regions of the world; and a glossary of foreign geographical terms and abbreviations. The index of more than thirty thousand entries includes pronunciations, altitudes, and latitude and longitude.

There are excellent general atlases which are limited in scope to specific regions or to special topics in specific regions. The *Atlas of Britain and Northern Ireland* is a good example.[29] An especially

[27] Stanley Knight et al., eds. (Oxford, Pergamon Press, 1968).

[28] Edward B. Espenshade, Jr., ed., 12th ed. (Chicago, Rand McNally, 1964).

beautiful atlas, its two hundred pages give a picture in maps of modern Britain's physical, economic, and industrial resources. Comparative statistics, for which the sources are given, are printed on the maps. Material for the maps was provided by 137 authorities (government departments, university departments, and so forth) and 420 scholars and experts. The gazetteer index includes over sixteen thousand names.

The *Rand McNally Commercial Atlas* is an excellent topical-regional atlas.[30] Primarily an atlas of the United States, about three-fourths of the content is devoted to the United States, though a section of maps to foreign countries is included. It was first published in 1876 as the *Rand McNally and Company Business Atlas*, and it has been published annually ever since, with complete revision of the marketing data each year. There are colored maps plus retail sales maps for each state. The maps for the states are primarily commercial-political-physical maps, and there is a separate road atlas of the United States, Canada, and Mexico. There is an individual index with each state map, and an estimated population figure is given for cities of more than two thousand. Statistical information is given about population, transportation, airports, banks, and trade (retail trade, trading areas, and principal business centers). There is a separate general index for foreign places.

Atlases devoted to special topics cover a wide variety of subject information and include economic, climatological, meteorological, agricultural, mineralogical, and demographic atlases as well as historical. The history student probably will find the economic and historic atlases the most helpful.

The *Oxford Economic Atlas of the World*[31] is in the series of Oxford regional atlases. These atlases deal in much greater detail

[29] Planned and directed by D. P. Bickmore and M. A. Shaw (Oxford, Clarendon Press, 1963).

[30] Rand McNally and Company, 99th ed. (Chicago, Rand McNally & Co., 1968).

[31] Prepared by the *Economist* Intelligence Unit and the Cartographic Department of the Clarendon Press, 3d ed. (London, Oxford University Press, 1965).

with separate areas and include such titles as *The U.S.S.R. and Eastern Europe*,[32] *The Middle East and North Africa*,[33] and *Africa*.[34] Since these regional atlases contain large-scale geographic and economic maps, the world volume does not include the large-scale maps for the areas. The *Oxford Economic Atlas of the World* is arranged in two parts: world commodity maps grouped in ten sections and a statistical index arranged by country. The maps give the world economic pattern, and the index provides the actual figures for each country, for example, world oil production can be seen from the maps while the amount of Canadian oil production can be obtained from the index. In addition to the two main parts, there are three sections providing essential information on the commodity maps. The first section contains a series of world maps dealing with physical geography; the second, demography; and the third, communications.

Norton S. Ginsburg has compiled an *Atlas of Economic Development*,[35] which has a text analyzing the statistics. This atlas shows the world pattern of distribution of certain cultural, economic, and social factors by country and region. On the page facing each map is a statistical table giving the basic data from which the map was compiled, the value and rank for individual countries, and a commentary of about one thousand words describing the limitations of the data, the characteristics of the distribution by region and country, and a comparison of the patterns displayed on the map with those found on other maps in the atlas. This is the only

[32] *Oxford Regional Economic Atlas: The U.S.S.R. and Eastern Europe*, prepared by the *Economist* Intelligence Unit and the Cartographic Department of the Clarendon Press (London, Oxford University Press, 1956).

[33] *Oxford Regional Economic Atlas of the Middle East and North Africa*, prepared by the *Economist* Intelligence Unit and the Cartographic Department of the Clarendon Press (London, Oxford University Press, 1960).

[34] *Oxford Regional Economic Atlas: Africa*, prepared by Peter H. Ady and the Cartographic Department of the Clarendon Press (London, Oxford University Press, 1965).

[35] Foreword by Bert F. Hoselitz and Pt. 8, *A Statistical Analysis*, by Brian J. L. Berry (Chicago, University of Chicago Press, 1961).

atlas that attempts to rate or to rank countries or regions according to the level of development.

Historical atlases show the state of the world and of special areas at particular periods. There are many atlases concerned specifically with United States history.

Charles O. Paullin's *Atlas of the Historical Geography of the United States*[36] concerns physical maps; reproductions of old maps; and maps concerning exploration, settlement, territories, states, boundary disputes, and social, economic, military, and political history. It covers United States history from earliest times to the late 1920's. The first part contains a descriptive text which gives the sources on which each map is based and an explanation of each map's historical significance. An index is included. The second part contains the maps, which are arranged chronologically under major topics, such as material environment, settlement, population and towns, political parties and opinions, military history, and boundaries. This comprehensive and authoritative atlas was the first major historical atlas of the United States to be published.

Clifford and Elizabeth Lord's *Historical Atlas of the United States*,[37] though not intended as a reference atlas, supplements Paullin's *Atlas of Historical Geography* and James T. Adams' *Atlas of American History*. It is organized into chronological sections: the first contains general maps; the second, maps of the colonial period; the third, maps of the 1775–1865 period (from the beginning of the American Revolution through the Civil War); and the fourth, maps of the 1865–1950 period (from the end of the Civil War through the first five years of the era after World War II). The maps in each section are arranged by topic and are concerned with political, economic, and social data.

James Truslow Adams' *Atlas of American History*,[38] a supple-

[36] John K. Wright, ed., Carnegie Institution Publication 401 (Washington, D.C., Carnegie Institution of Washington and American Geographical Society, Institution of Washington, 1932).

[37] Rev. ed. (New York, Holt, 1953).

[38] (New York, C. Scribner's Sons, 1943).

mentary and companion volume to the *Dictionary of American History*, is chiefly concerned with discovery, exploration, frontier posts, settlement, territorial organizations, the extension of communications, and the like. It locates all the places mentioned in the *Dictionary of American History* on the 147 black and white maps arranged in chronological order. The index, with its cross references from variant spellings of names, is very useful. The history student can locate a place, such as Kaskaskia, Fallen Timbers, South Pass, or Logtown, or trace a particular subject, such as the advance of the frontier, from period to period and from area to area. There is little duplication of the material in Paullin's *Atlas of Historical Geography*.

The *American History Atlas*[39] is the American history counterpart of the Breasted *European History Atlas*.[40] The maps are reductions or adaptations of large wall maps, and the text helps interpret the maps. The authors, who were history professors, have attempted to cover all aspects of world history (political, economic, and social) on the maps.

A new atlas of American history is the *American Heritage Pictorial Atlas of United States History*.[41] This large, handsome atlas, which covers United States history from the Ice Age to 1966, includes 210 new maps, illustrations, and a text by Roger Butterfield. The picture portfolios show battles of the American Revolution and Civil War, America's natural wonders, and nineteenth-century American cities. The maps, many in color, show the geographic, political, economic, social, and cultural history of the United States. A map on colonial economy, for example, shows the colonial sources of cattle, grain, tobacco, rice, indigo,

[39] Adapted from the large wall maps and ed. by Albert Bushnell Hart, David M. Matteson, and Robert E. Bolton (Chicago, Denoyer Geppert Co., 1947).

[40] *European History Atlas: Ancient, Medieval, and Modern European and World History*, adapted from the large wall maps and ed. by James H. Breasted, Carl F. Huth, and Samuel Bannester Harding, 7th rev. ed. (Chicago, Denoyer Geppert Co., 1947).

[41] (New York, McGraw-Hill Book Co., 1966).

furs, and skins, and pinpoints industries like shipbuilding. The Vinland Map, which shows the discoveries made in the western Atlantic by Vikings in the eleventh century; maps of the explorations and surveys of the American West in the nineteenth century; the twenty-two maps on World War II; the maps on the Korean War; and maps showing the international involvement of the United States in international alliances make this an up-to-date treatment of United States history.

There are historical atlases dealing with special periods in American history. For example, *The West Point Atlas of American Wars*[42] was written for the use of West Point cadets and military personnel in the study of military history. Although emphasis is on American actions, the wars are treated in their entirety. Most of the maps in the World War I section, for example, cover events before the United States entered the war, and many in the World War II section concern engagements in which the United States did not participate or in which the United States fought with the Allies. Air and naval forces are recognized in the narrative, but only the land forces are shown on the maps. The narrative pertaining to each map is tailored to fit on the blank page opposite the map; thus the map and text are side by side for joint study. There are chronological charts for the major wars. *The West Point Atlas of the Civil War*[43] is an adaptation from volume 1 of *The West Point Atlas of American Wars*.

The companion atlas to *The War of the Rebellion*,[44] the official war records of the Union and Confederate armies, is *The Official*

[42] Department of Military Art and Engineering, the United States Military Academy, comp., Colonel Vincent J. Esposito, ed., with an introduction by Dwight D. Eisenhower (New York, Praeger, 1959). Vol. 1, 1689–1900; vol. 2, 1900–55.

[43] Department of Military Art and Engineering, the United States Military Academy, comp. Colonel Vincent J. Esposito, ed. (New York, Praeger, 1962).

[44] *The War of the Rebellion: A Compilation of the Official Records of the Union and Confederate Armies*, 128 vols. (Washington, D.C., Government Printing Office, 1880–1901).

Atlas of the Civil War.[45] Very little of the territory over which the Union and Confederate armies fought for four years had been mapped. While General Ulysses S. Grant was attacking General Robert E. Lee in the Wilderness campaign, Congress authorized the Union Army to preserve the record of the war. In 1874 provision was made for publication of the official records, and six years later the first volume of what was to be a set of 128 volumes appeared. The editorship of the *Atlas* to accompany this set was entrusted to Lieutenant Calvin Duvall Cowles and the engraving and printing to Julius Bien. The serious history student who is using *The War of Rebellion* volumes will need to use this atlas.

Shepherd's Historical Atlas is a basic historical atlas that is standard in its field of world history.[46] It covers the world from ancient Egypt (about 2000 B.C.) to the United Nations and the Cold War in 1955. The special supplementary section of maps, prepared by C. S. Hammond, concerns European history from 1929 through 1955. Arranged chronologically with emphasis on political history, this concise, convenient atlas is one of the best general historical atlases available.

Another standard atlas is *Muir's Historical Atlas*.[47] Ramsay Muir's historical atlases were pioneer works. They demonstrated for the first time how a modern study of historical geography might illuminate the study of history; they represented historical data on colored maps in such a way as to facilitate comparison between successive maps over long periods of time. In the tenth edition a few old maps have been dropped, others have been reduced from double to single-page size, and ten totally new plates illustrating world history since 1926 have been added. These changes have resulted in a drastic change of the geographical and chronological balance of the *Atlas*. The emphasis has been shifted to contemporary times and away from European preoccupations.

[45] Introduction by Henry Steele Commager (New York, Thomas Yoseloff, 1958).
[46] William R. Shepard, 9th ed. (New York, Barnes & Noble, 1963).
[47] R. F. Treharne and Harold Fullard, eds. *Muir's Historical Atlas: Ancient, Medieval, and Modern* (New York, Barnes & Noble, 1963).

This comprehensive historical atlas offers political, economic, anthropological, linguistic, and cultural information.

Two other atlases of interest to the world history student are the older Breasted *European History Atlas* and the newer *Rand McNally Atlas of World History*.[48] The older atlas concentrates on Europe while the *Rand McNally Atlas* uses a world approach. The latter also depicts more than political history; it has excellent maps of economic and social history. Unlike Shepherd's *Historical Atlas*, the *Rand McNally Atlas* has an accompanying text which gives explanatory background for each map or series of maps. The text material alternates with the maps, and both are arranged chronologically. A statistical appendix projects data in historical time periods for population, immigration, size of cities, mortality, disease, commodity production, and transportation. The excellent index, which covers ethnic and state names, explorers' routes, and place names, adds to the value of this volume compiled by specialists.

There are atlases for specialized periods in European history. One of these is the *Atlas of the Classical World*,[49] originally published as the *Atlas van der antieke Wereld*.[50] Specialized maps showing the Greek colonies from 800 to 600 B.C., the empire of Alexander the Great, centers of Greek cults, and the Roman Empire are combined in this excellent atlas with text and outstanding photographs.

Another specialized atlas is Colin McEvedy's *Penguin Atlas of Medieval History*,[51] which is designed to show the unfolding of medieval history in Europe and the Near East as a continuous story from the fall of Rome to the sack of Constantinople. There is neither geographical detail nor any dissection of political units

[48] Robert R. Palmer, ed. (New York, Rand McNally and Co., 1957).

[49] A. A. M. Van der Heyden and Howard H. Scullard (London, Thomas Nelson & Sons, 1959).

[50] (Amsterdam, Elsevier's Wetenschappelijke, 1958).

[51] (London, Penguin Books, Ltd., 1961). Colin McEvedy's *The Penguin Atlas of Ancient History* was published in London in 1967 by Penguin Books.

on the maps. There is, however, great chronological detail. Each state is shown at many different points in time. The thirty-eight maps of the same area—Europe, North Africa, and the Middle East—are arranged in five sections, and the bulk of each section is made up of five or six maps showing the political state of the area at intervals that average forty years.

There is a series of atlases which deal with special topics in world affairs. Frederick A. Praeger has published *An Atlas of World Affairs*,[52] *An Atlas of African Affairs*,[53] *An Atlas of European Affairs*,[54] *An Atlas of Soviet Affairs*,[55] *An Atlas of Latin American Affairs*,[56] and *An Atlas of Middle Eastern Affairs*.[57] These are attempts to keep up with changes in the regions of the world. As Andrew Boyd says in his preface to *An Atlas of World Affairs*, "Today's map is changing fast. Every six months, on an average, during this generation, a new sovereign state has come into being, vibrant with fresh nationalism."[58]

There are other atlases which are excellent for studying current affairs but which give more background for the modern history student. There is the *Atlas of Russian and East European History*,[59] which contains one hundred black and white maps with the text and deals with the wars, expansion, and political events of Russia and East Europe from the barbarian invasions in the fourth century down to the Communist position in 1965. *The Atlas of*

[52] Andrew Boyd, maps by W. H. Bromage, 4th rev. ed. (New York, Frederick A. Praeger, Inc., 1962).

[53] Andrew Boyd and Patrick Van Rensburg, maps by W. H. Bromage, 2d ed. (New York, Frederick A. Praeger, Inc., 1965).

[54] Norman J. G. Pounds, maps by Robert C. Kingsbury (New York, Frederick A. Praeger, Inc., 1964).

[55] Robert N. Taaffe, maps by Robert C. Kingsbury (New York, Frederick A. Praeger, Inc., 1965).

[56] Ronald M. Schneider, maps by Robert C. Kingsbury (New York, Frederick A. Praeger, Inc., 1964).

[57] Norman J. G. Pounds, maps by Robert C. Kingsbury (New York, Frederick A. Praeger, Inc., 1964).

[58] P. 5.

[59] Arthur E. Adams, Ian M. Matley, and William O. McCagg (New York, Frederick A. Praeger, Inc., 1967).

South-East Asia,[60] the second of a series of regional atlases issued by the St. Martin's Press, was produced by the Netherlands atlas publisher Djambatan, with the aid of seven geographers, six of whom were from Asia. The maps include physical location maps; topical maps which show the patterns of climate, population, agriculture, vegetation, communications, minerals, and industries; special maps which include plans of many of the major cities; and historical maps. A complete index makes the volume easy to use. The *Historical Atlas of Latin America*[61] supplies what A. Curtis Wilgus calls a "window of history" through which the reader may look out upon the past or contemporary scene from the vantage point of historical perspective. Wilgus has tried to make the maps accurate in construction and simple in detail. This new edition extends the coverage from ancient times down to the 1960's. Maps and text are interleafed; there is no index.

[60] Introduction by D. G. E. Hall (New York, St. Martin's Press, Inc., 1964). The St. Martin's Press published *Atlas of African History*, by J. D. Fage, in 1958.

[61] A. Curtis Wilgus, *Historical Atlas of Latin America: Political, Geographic, Economic, Cultural,* new ed. (New York, Cooper Square Publishers, 1967).

8

Biographical Materials

Who? When? Where? Why? These are the questions the history student asks about the people he discovers in his research. He needs to find the facts to answer these questions.

Biographical dictionaries are general, national or regional, and professional or occupational. Each may be retrospective, contemporary, or both. Retrospective biographical dictionaries are usually scholarly works including sketches of persons no longer living. These dictionaries often include bibliographies of works by the person and bibliographies of works about him. The current biographical material is often contained in various types of who's who volumes, which usually follow an established pattern of giving concise personal and career information. There is an overwhelming amount of biographical material available, and this chapter will try to point out the most obvious and most useful biographical reference tools.

GUIDES AND INDEXES

A very important new guide to all kinds of biographical material about all kinds of people is *Biographical Dictionaries and Related Works*.[1] Special emphasis is on biographical dictionaries. Also in-

[1] Robert B. Slocum, ed., *Biographical Dictionaries and Related Works: An International Bibliography of Collective Biographies, Biobibliographies, Collections of Epitaphs, Selected Genealogical Works, Dictionaries of*

cluded, however, are other types of material, such as collective biographies, which treat relatively obscure areas or subjects, and directories or registers of members of specific organizations and professions, which give the basic facts of birth and death dates, educational background, and positions. Biographical dictionaries dealing with small units of government or relatively limited geographical areas are excluded. The 4,800 entries in the volume are arranged by geographic area with author, title, and subject indexes at the end of the volume. Complete bibliographical information is given for each entry, and a concise note is added if it is necessary to clarify a foreign or obscure title.

The *Biography Index* is the best current index to general sources.[2] It includes important and less important, famous and infamous figures of history and figures in the news, men and women from all countries and from every age. This index covers most major periodicals (about fifteen hundred), books in English, portions of books, obituaries in periodicals, and selected obituaries from the *New York Times*. The biographies are arranged in alphabetical order, and the following information is given for each entry: dates, profession, nationality, the location of the biography, and the information as to whether there is a portrait or illustration. The index is arranged by profession or occupation, which is subdivided by country in cases where there is a great deal of material.

The *New York Times* has published two very helpful biographical tools. The first is the *New York Times Obituaries Index*,[3] which is largely derived from the past issues of the *New York Times Index*. It brings together in one alphabet all the names entered under the heading "Deaths" in the *Index* from September, 1858, through December, 1968; the entries for 1907 through 1912 (for

Anonyms and Pseudonyms, Historical and Specialized Dictionaries, Biographical Materials in Government Manuals, Bibliographies of Biography, Biographical Indexes, and Selected Portrait Catalogs (Detroit, Gale Research Co., 1967).

[2] (New York, H. W. Wilson Co., 1947–). Issued quarterly with annual and triennial cumulations.

[3] *New York Times Obituaries Index*, 1858–1968 (New York, 1969).

148

which indexes are still in preparation); and names through 1925 that were not listed in the published indexes. Entries for each of the 353,000 names include the name of the deceased; his title if given in the original index entry; his pseudonym or nickname, if any; and the reference by year, date, section, if any, page, and column to the original news story. Entries for funerals, memorial services, and wills are often included in parentheses between the name and date reference for the obituary.

The *New York Times Biographical Edition*, a second helpful reference aid published by the *New York Times*, is a weekly publication of profiles of people in the news.[4] Articles are reprinted in full from the *New York Times*. Each week's profiles, which are consecutively numbered, are accompanied by an alphabetical index, which cumulates every four and twelve weeks. In January of the new year all issues of the preceding year are combined in one annual cumulative volume.

There are other important indexes to biographical material. Max Arnim's *Internationale Personalbibliographie* is an international index with emphasis on German names.[5] This comprehensive work indexes bibliographies in books, periodicals, biographical dictionaries, and *Festschriften*. *A Dictionary of Universal Biography of All Peoples*[6] is an index to the names appearing in twenty-four standard biographical dictionaries. *Index to Contemporary Biography and Criticism*[7] is an index to material about persons born since the mid-nineteenth century in 420 collections of biography. *Analytical Biography of Universal Collected Biography*[8] is an attempt to index every volume of collected

[4] *New York Times Biographical Edition: A Compilation of Current Biographical Information of General Interest*, vol. 1– (New York, 1970).

[5] Max Arnim, *Internationale Personalbibliographie, 1800–1943*, 2 vols. (Leipzig, Anton Hiersemann, 1944–52).

[6] Albert M. Hyamson, 2d ed. (New York, E. P. Dutton & Co., 1951).

[7] Helen Hefling and Eva Richards, rev. and enl. by Helen Hefling and Jessie W. Dyde (Boston, F. W. Faxon Co., 1934).

[8] Phyllis M. Riches, *Analytical Biography of Universal Collected Biography, Comprising Books Published in the English Tongue in Great Britain*

biography in the English language before 1933. Some 56,000 biographies are arranged alphabetically by the names of people of various periods, nationalities, and professions and occupations. For each entry there is a two- or three-word description with a brief citation to books in which the biography appears. The indexes include a chronological list by century of the biographees, a list arranged by professions or occupations, and an author and subject index of biographical dictionaries.

There are indexes to biographies by period. Cyr Ulysse Joseph Chevalier's *Répertoire des sources historiques du Moyen Age: Biobibliographie,*[9] a most comprehensive and important work including lesser known figures, is the authoritative index to biographies of the Middle Ages.

The Library of Congress has published two guides to biographical sources. The first, *Biographical Sources for Foreign Countries*[10] is a four-volume work. The first volume, compiled by Helen D. Jones, is concerned with general biographical sources; the second, compiled by W. R. Burr, with Germany and Austria; the third, compiled by Helen D. Jones, the Philippines; and the fourth, also compiled by W. R. Burr, with the Japanese Empire. The second title, *Biographical Sources for the United States,*[11] is a guide to biographical information about living Americans who have made outstanding contributions in the arts, business, and military and public affairs. Jane Kline collected the titles from publications of the 1945–60 period in the Library of Congress. The biographies in the volumes listed vary in number from less than 100 to more than 250,000; they vary in length from brief

and Ireland, America, and the British Dominions (London, Library Association, 1934).

[9] For full bibliographic information, see Chapter 3, note 32.

[10] U.S., Library of Congress, General Reference and Bibliography Division, 4 vols. (Washington, D.C., Government Printing Office, 1944–45).

[11] U.S., Library of Congress, General Reference and Bibliography Division, Jane Kline, comp. (Washington, D.C., Government Printing Office, 1961).

notices to short articles or chapters. The biographies are arranged by sections. The first section is concerned with general biography, the second, with regions and states, and the last, with special and professional groups. The editor has given a bibliographic description and annotation for each entry. An index of authors, broad subjects, and titles helps the reader find what he wants.

There are other guides to biography by country. There is Marion Dargan's *Guide to American Biography*.[12] It is divided into two volumes, covering 1607–1815 and 1815–1933, with each period then subdivided geographically. For each biographee the following information is given: original sources, separately published biographies, and references to sketches in collective biography. Only outstanding Americans are included (179 are listed in the first volume and 380 in the second). The *Biography Catalogue*[13] is a guide to biographies of persons connected with British imperial affairs. It is limited to the biographies in books and periodicals in the Library of the Royal Commonwealth Society. Part 3 of volume 1 of Raymond Foulché-Delbosc's *Manuel de l'hispanisant* contains a bibliography of Spanish biographies and bio-biographies.[14]

Autobiographies are primary source material for the history student. They get at the center of historical events; they are a prima facie version of what happened in the lifetime of the writer. The individual who writes his autobiography tells his own story, gives his own explanation of his actions, and often re-appraises or re-evaluates the past within his frame of reference.

There are two important guides to autobiographies. *British Autobiographies*,[15] arranged alphabetically, has an index of professions and occupations, places and regions, reminiscences, wars,

[12] 2 vols. (Albuquerque, University of New Mexico Press, 1949–52).
[13] Donald H. Simpson, Royal Commonwealth Society Library (London, Royal Commonwealth Society, 1961).
[14] For full bibliographic information, see Chapter 3, note 115.
[15] William Matthews, *British Autobiographies: An Annotated Bibliography of British Autobiographies Published or Written Before 1951* (Berkeley, University of California Press, 1955).

and general topics. Each entry includes the name of the author, a short title sufficient for identification, and a short note of evaluation.

American Life in Autobiography[16] tells the epic of America through the lives of men of all classes, of all shades of opinion, and of all occupations. Only books printed in 1900 or later are listed, though twentieth-century editions of older books and autobiographies that have been published as separate volumes are included. The entries are arranged alphabetically by occupation or profession, with a general index. For each entry, the author provides, if possible, the birth and death dates, information on the editions and reprintings of the autobiography, and an annotation indicating style and reader appeal.

GENERAL BIOGRAPHIES

If the student does not know anything about the person he is trying to track down, he needs to check the general, universal biographical dictionaries. He might begin with *Webster's Biographical Dictionary*.[17] It covers about forty thousand people of the past and present and includes lesser-known figures. Because the book is written for English-speaking people, American and British figures are given more coverage than foreign. The brief articles, giving pronunciation, dates, and the important facts about the person, vary in length because they list the major achievements of the biographee.

Chambers's Biographical Dictionary[18] is the British counterpart to *Webster's Biographical Dictionary*. The new edition of this reference book, which has been held in high repute for more than half a century, contains about fifteen thousand biographies, an increase of four thousand over previous editions. It is worldwide in coverage and ranges from contemporary figures, such as John F.

[16] Richard G. Lillard, *American Life in Autobiography: A Descriptive Guide* (Stanford, Calif., Stanford University Press, 1966).

[17] (Springfield, Mass., G. & C. Merriam Co., 1943).

[18] J. O. Thorne, ed. (New York, St. Martin's Press, 1962).

Kennedy and Nikita Khrushchev, to figures of the past, such as Peter Abelard, Herodotus, and Sitting Bull. It gives full name, dates, and pronunciation, and includes bibliographical references to other articles.

The *Universal Pronouncing Dictionary*[19] is an older and larger compilation of universal biography. It has brief entries for fifty thousand people of all nations and periods. *Lippincott's Biographical Dictionary*, as it is usually cited, was first published in 1901. The editor, Joseph Thomas, was an unusual man. He practiced medicine, taught Latin and Greek, and traveled to the Far East to study Eastern and Oriental languages. He hoped to produce a convenient and complete reference book for mythology and biography. He included individuals of all countries, living and dead, and of all occupations, with a greater representation of authors than of military, political, or scientific figures. Arranged in alphabetical order, the concise entries include pronunciation and brief bibliographic references.

Another large biographical compilation is the *New Century Cyclopedia of Names*,[20] which contains more than one hundred thousand proper names of persons, places, literary characters, historical events, titles of novels, plays, works of art, and so forth. It reorganized, enlarged, and brought up to date the old *Cyclopedia of Names*, published in 1894. Arranged alphabetically, the brief entries for people include the full name, its pronunciation, dates, and important achievements.

In addition to these works of universal biography in English, there are two sets in French. The first, *Biographie universelle ancienne et modern*,[21] is, according to Constance M. Winchell ,the "most important of the large dictionaries of universal biography."[22]

[19] Joseph Thomas, *Universal Pronouncing Dictionary of Biography and Mythology* (Philadelphia, J. B. Lippincott Co., 1930).

[20] Clarence L. Barnhart, ed., rev. ed., 3 vols. (New York, Appleton-Century-Crofts, Inc., 1954).

[21] New ed., published under the direction of M. Michaud, rev., corr. and greatly enl., 45 vols. (Paris, Mme C. Desplaces, 1843–65).

[22] *Guide to Reference Books*, 169.

A second valuable set is *Nouvelle biographie générale*.[23] The articles in *Biographie universelle* are more carefully edited than those in *Nouvelle biographie générale*. Similarly, they are longer and often better, and its bibliographies are better except that titles are translated into French. *Nouvelle biographie générale* has less names in the second half of the alphabet (N–Z) and contains more names, especially minor ones, in the first part (A–M). Some articles in *Nouvelle biographie générale* are better than the corresponding ones in *Biographie universelle*, and the bibliographies in *Nouvelle biographie générale* give titles in the original language. *Nouvelle biographie générale* began in 1852 under the title *Nouvelle biographie universelle*, which later became *Nouvelle biographie générale*. There are three editions of the first two volumes.[24] *Nouvelle biographie générale* was planned to be more concise than *Biographie universelle* and to include the names of some people alive at the time of publication.

Information about current personages of all countries who are prominent in the news can be found in several reference books and in the various who's who volumes.

Current Biography tries to provide "brief, objective, accurate, and well-documented biographical articles about living leaders in all fields of human accomplishment the world over."[25] An average of between 300 and 350 biographies are published annually. For each sketch the following information is usually given: full name,

[23] *Nouvelle biographie générale depuis les temps plus reculés jusqu'a nos jours, avec les renseignements bibliographiques et l'indication des sources à consulter*, published under the direction of M. le Dr. Hoefer, 46 vols. (Paris, Firmin Didot Frères, 1853–66).

[24] The first edition, entitled *Nouvelle biographie universelle ancienne et moderne*, contains 405 articles pirated from Michaud. Mme Desplaces, Michaud's publisher, won her suit against Didot, Hoefer's publisher, in 1855. Didot was forbidden to copy any more articles from Michaud. The second edition, called *Nouvelle biographie universelle depuis les temps les plus reculés*, omitted the Michaud articles. The third edition was called *Nouvelle biographie générale*.

[25] (New York, H. W. Wilson Co., 1940–). Monthly except August with annual cumulations. 1967 vol., Preface.

154

date of birth, occupation, reason for prominence, address, a biographical sketch of three to four columns, portrait, and references to other sources of information. Pronunciation is given for difficult names and date of death is given in obituaries; an index of occupations is included in each volume. *Current Biography* revises and updates its sketches and includes obituary notices. A cumulative index in each issue for all issues of the current year and a cumulated index in each volume to all preceding volumes for the decade are invaluable to the researcher.

The *International Who's Who* is a directory of prominent world figures which contains between eight thousand and thirteen thousand entries per year.[26] The concise and authoritative biographies give name, title, dates, nationality, education, profession, career, achievements, publications, and address. Like the who's who volumes, it is based on the biographee's answers to questionnaires.

World Biography[27] is another dictionary of international coverage of living artists, musicians, writers, scholars, scientists, physicians, jurists, lawyers, military leaders, politicians, diplomats, and business, industrial, and commercial leaders. Its biographical sketches cover about forty thousand persons from sixty countries. It is outdated now for current figures.

A new international dictionary of living notables is the *Dictionary of International Biography*.[28] It is designed as a biographical record of contemporary achievement. The fourth edition for 1967–68 contains more than ten thousand biographical sketches. These sketches are based on answers to questionnaires by the biographees and other notes submitted by them. Seven libraries agreed to be repositories for these original notes. The initials for the appropriate library and the numbers for any of the appropriate thirty-nine reference works of biography, in which the biographees

[26] (London, Europa Publications, 1935–). Annual. Slightly irregular in dating.
[27] (New York, Institute for Research in Biography, 1940–). Irregular. The fifth edition was 1954.
[28] (London, Dictionary of International Biography Co., 1963–). Annual.

are listed, are included in the short biographical sketch, which sets forth the birth date, occupation, honors, publications, and a very general address (city and country).

There are several guides to the nobility of Europe which are important for the history student but which are really genealogical works. Only two will be mentioned here. The *Almanach de Gotha* has been the standard source on the nobility in European and non-European countries.[29] Until 1940, it included two main sections: one giving the genealogies of the royal and princely houses; the other, descriptive and statistical information about the various countries. The first part has been continued by the *Genealogisches Handbuch des Adels*.[30] The *International Register of Nobility*[31] also is a genealogical dictionary of European nobility; it is divided into four parts: maisons souverains, maisons ex-souverains, noblesse européenne, and ordres de chevalerie.

NATIONAL AND REGIONAL BIOGRAPHIES

The great national biographical sets of the world are usually retrospective, that is, they are usually devoted to notables already dead. The two great English-language sets are the *Dictionary of National Biography* (*DNB*)[32] and the *Dictionary of American Biography* (*DAB*).[33]

[29] *Almanach de Gotha: Annuaire genelogique, diplomatique et statistique* (Gotha, Justus Perthes, 1763–1944). Annual.

[30] Prepared under the direction of the Committee for Questions of Nobility Law of the Organization of German Nobles in conjunction with the German Nobility Archives (Limburg Lahn, C. A. Starke, 1951–).

[31] (Brussels, International Office of Publicity, 1955–). Vol. 1, 1955; vol. 2, 1959–60.

[32] Leslie Stephen and Sidney Lee, eds., *Dictionary of National Biography*, 22 vols. (London, Smith, Elder, 1885–1901). Vol. 22, *First Supplement, Additional Names* (1901); *Second Supplement*, 1901–11, Sidney Lee, ed. (1912); *Third Supplement*, 1912–21, H. W. C. Davis and J. R. H. Weaver, eds. (1927); *Fourth Supplement*, 1922–30, J. R. H. Weaver, ed. (1937); *Fifth Supplement*, 1931–40, L. G. Wickham Legg, ed. (1949); *Sixth Supplement*, 1941–50, L. G. Wickham Legg and E. T. Williams, eds. (1959); *Index and Epitome*, Sidney Lee, ed., 2 vols.; *The Concise Dictionary*

156

The *Dictionary of American Biography* is modeled on the *Dictionary of National Biography*. The American Council of Learned Societies appointed a committee in 1922 to consider the feasibility of a national biographical dictionary comparable to the *DNB*. Adolph S. Ochs, the publisher of the *New York Times*, agreed to supply the half million dollars needed. The Council and Ochs appointed a committee to carry out the undertaking. Allen Johnson, Professor of American History at Yale, was the first editor. After his death, Dumas Malone, Professor of American History at Columbia University, who had been associated with Johnson since 1929, took over.

The 13,633 entries in the *Dictionary of American Biography* are for people no longer living who have lived in the United States and have made some significant contribution to American life. Each biographical sketch is signed with the author's initials. A key to the initials is in each volume. The biographies, which are based on primary sources whenever possible, encompass ancestry, parentage, education, achievements, and a bibliography. The biog-

---

of National Biography, 2 vols. (Oxford, University Press, 1903); Pt. 1, *From the Beginnings to 1900: Being an Epitome of the Main Work and Its Supplement*; Pt. 2, *1901–1950: An Epitome of the Twentieth Century D.N.B down to the End of 1950*. It includes a select subject index. The *Concise Dictionary* acts as an index to the *Dictionary of National Biography* and as a summary (1/14 the length of the entries in the *Dictionary of National Biography*). Frederic Boase's *Modern English Biography: Containing Many Thousand Concise Memoirs of Persons Who Have Died Since 1850, with an Index of the Most Interesting Matter*, 6 vols. (Truro, Netherton and Worth, 1892–1921) is useful for lesser known nineteenth-century personages not included in the *Dictionary of National Biography*. Thomas Humphry Ward's *Men of the Reign: A Biographical Dictionary of Eminent Persons of British and Colonial Birth Who Have Died During the Reign of Queen Victoria* (London, G. Routledge, 1885) includes some figures who are in neither the *Dictionary of National Biography* nor in Boase's *Modern English Biography*.

[33] Published under the auspices of the American Council of Learned Societies, 20 vols. and Index (New York, C. Scribner's Sons, 1928–37). *Supplement* 1, to December 31, 1936, H. E. Starr, ed., numbered vol. 29 (1944); *Supplement* 2, 1936–40, R. L. Schuyler, ed., numbered vol. 22 (1958).

raphies range from 500 to 16,500 words. The index volume lists the biographies under divisions, such as birthplace, occupation, and school attended. It also lists the contributors with the names of their articles.

The *National Cyclopaedia of American Biography* gives a large amount of accurate information on Americans of the past and present who have shaped the history of the United States.[34] It consists of the following parts: articles on deceased persons, which are collected in the Permanent Series and which are given a number; articles on living persons which are collected in the Current Series and which are marked with the letters of the alphabet, and the index volume. Some space is given to outstanding Americans before 1850, but more space is devoted to those after 1850 who have held or are holding high positions in government, the professions, and financial, industrial, and religious circles. The names of persons who have recently died are deleted from the Current Series and added to the latest volume in the Permanent Series. Revisions are also made in the Current Series to add significant facts to the lives of prominent living persons.

The staff has written the unsigned biographical articles from questionnaires, interviews, and information supplied by the biographees' families. The sketches, which vary in length from less than one column to more than several, are uneven but generally give the full name, field of activity, birth date, parents' names and ancestry, education, careers, honors and awards, membership in organizations, religious and political affiliations, favorite recreations, date of marriage, and children. There are portraits but no bibliographies. The indexes must be used to find a particular biography since the biographies in the Permanent and Current Series are not arranged alphabetically. The *National Cyclopaedia of American Biography*, which is less limited and less selective than the *Dictionary of American Biography*, has the most comprehensive list of living and dead American notables available in one source.

[34] For full bibliographic information, see Chapter 4, note 45.

158

There are several other excellent biographical tools for American biography. *Appleton's Cyclopaedia of American Biography*[35] includes the names of nonliving native and adopted citizens of the United States from earliest times. It has detailed but unsigned articles with portraits and facsimiles of the subject's autograph. The biographies are arranged alphabetically, but the members of each family are arranged under the family name according to seniority and not alphabetically. The *Dictionary of American Biography* has superseded this older work for names which it includes. However, *Appleton's Cyclopaedia* is still useful for names not included in the *Dictionary of American Biography* and for the illustrations and facsimiles of autographs, which also are not found in the *Dictionary of American Biography*. The supplements are not arranged alphabetically, and the reader must use the indexes.

The publisher of *Who's Who in America* has published the *Historical Volume, 1607–1896* of *Who Was Who in America* for those years.[36] The *Historical Volume* plus the other *Who Was Who in America*[37] volumes and the current *Who's Who in America*[38] provide a nearly complete listing of who's who in American history. The *Historical Volume* summarizes the lives of 13,450 leading Americans in the humanities, science, and government who lived during the period from 1607, when the English landed at Jamestown, to 1896, the eve of the Spanish-American War. It also has a "Time-Line Chart" that covers general history, the arts and thought, and science and invention from Leif Ericson's time

[35] J. G. Wilson and John Fiske, eds., 7 vols. (New York, D. Appleton and Co., 1888–1900).

[36] *Who Was Who in America: Historical Volume, 1607–1896, A Component Volume of Who's Who in American History*, rev. ed. (Chicago, Marquis-Who's Who, Inc., 1967).

[37] *Who Was Who in America: A Companion Biographical Reference Work to "Who's Who in America"* (Chicago, Marquis-Who's Who, Inc., 1942–). In progress. Vol. 1, 1897–1942 (1943); vol. 2, 1943–50 (1950); vol. 3, 1951–60 (1960).

[38] *Who's Who in America: A Biographical Dictionary of Notable Living Men and Women* (Chicago, A. N. Marquis Co., 1899–). Biennial.

(eleventh century) to the 1960's for the United States and the rest of the world.

The *Who Was Who in America* contains the sketches of those who have been removed from *Who's Who in America* due to death but not those removed for other reasons. The material for those sketches came from the biographee originally. Usually the date of death is added, but sometimes only the word "deceased" is affixed. Sometimes the entries are revised and minor points, such as the subject's business address or the clubs or fraternities to which he belonged, are omitted. The history student who may need to know these very minor points can find them by checking *Who's Who in America* for the full sketch.

Who's Who in America is the basic biographical dictionary of prominent living Americans and outstanding foreigners. It presents a "composite biographical portrait of our time"[39] with concise biographies of 66,000 living men and women who have achieved prominence in government, the arts, science, business, and, with this new volume, in sports. In addition to the sketches for those who filled out and returned the questionnaires sent them, there are sketches based on material the editors have gathered for very prominent people if they failed to answer the questionnaire.

The sectional who's who volumes serve as supplements to *Who's Who in America*.[40] They give representative coverage of a region,

[39] *Ibid.*, 1968–69, 7.

[40] *Who's Who in the East (and Eastern Canada): A Biographical Dictionary of Noteworthy Men and Women of the Middle Atlantic and Northeastern States and Eastern Canada* (Chicago, Marquis-Who's Who, Inc., 1948–), biennial (slightly irregular); *Who's Who in the Midwest (and Central Canada): A Biographical Dictionary of Noteworthy Men and Women of the Central and Mid-Western States (and Central Canada)* (Chicago, Marquis-Who's Who, Inc., 1949–), biennial (slightly irregular); *Who's Who in the South and Southwest: A Biographical Dictionary of Noteworthy Men and Women of the Southern and Southwestern States* (Chicago, Marquis-Who's Who, Inc., 1950–), biennial (slightly irregular); *Who's Who in the West (and Western Canada): A Biographical Dictionary of Noteworthy Men and Women of the Pacific Coastal and Western States (and Western Canada)* (Chicago, Marquis-Who's Who, Inc., 1949–), biennial (slightly irregular).

and they average about fourteen thousand names per volume. They do duplicate a few of the names in *Who's Who in America*; each volume includes the list of names from its contents that are also listed in *Who's Who in America* as well as a list of names about which data is available in the Marquis National Biographical Reference files.[41]

The *Dictionary of National Biography*,[42] was the first major biographical tool of the English-speaking world. At one time it was unmatched by any other in scope or completeness. Leslie Stephen was the first editor, and he was succeeded by Sidney Lee. It was designed to include all the noteworthy inhabitants of Great Britain, Ireland, and the British Colonies, exclusive of living persons, from the earliest historical times to the time of publication. British citizens who lived abroad, foreigners who became British subjects during their lifetime, and the legendary and the infamous are included. The sixteenth century appeared to have more great men in proportion to the total population than any other, but the nineteenth contributed the greatest number of names. The basic set contains 29,120 articles and has been brought up to 1950 by supplements. The last five supplements have cumulative indexes which index the work back to 1901.

The average length of a biography is a little less than one column and each biography is accompanied by a bibliography. The contributors, specialists who gathered their information from primary sources, signed their articles with their initials. A key to the initials is included in every volume. The entries in this comprehensive and scholarly work are objective and written in an informative and entertaining style.

The *Dictionary of National Biography*, one of the great literary and historical achievements of British historians, has been in need of a complete revision for a long time. While *Who's Who in History*[43] does not provide that revision, it does help to bring up to

[41] *Guide to Reference Books*, 173.

[42] For full bibliographic information, see note 32.

[43] Vol. 1 (New York, Barnes & Noble, 1960); vol. 2 (New York,

date the invaluable *Dictionary of National Biography* articles. Its volumes are something like a general outline of the history of Great Britain with each volume presenting a portrait of its age: volume 1, 55 B.C.–1485, by W. O. Hassall; volume 2, 1485–1603, by C. R. N. Routh; volume 3, 1603–1714, by C. P. Hill; and volume 4, 1714–1789, by Geoffrey Treasure. To implement this idea of each volume presenting a portrait of its age, a chronological approach is used. Alphabetical indexes at the end of the volume help the reader find the biographies he wants.

The editors of *Who's Who in History*, acting on the premise that each generation alters its historical perspective, change the selection of biographical subjects for this set. The editors kept the hard core of personalities but changed the second-rank personalities. In other words, they cut down on some *Dictionary of National Biography* classes, such as the enormous number of ecclesiastics, and they included classes of people who are now recognized as being important in their times, such as merchants and travelers. The biographies are accurate, as up to date as possible, and as full as the space allows. Because biographies to a great extent are verbal pictures which come to life more easily with a portrait, portraits are included. Each volume has several genealogical trees, a glossary of technical terms, and short bibliographical notes of the standard textbooks which may be useful for the general reader.

Who Was Who is a retrospective work based on biographical sketches contemporary with their subjects.[44] It consists mainly of the original sketches as they appeared in *Who's Who*. The sketches have been reprinted with the addition of the date of death and, in some cases, additional information.

Barnes & Noble, 1964); vol. 3 (New York, Barnes & Noble, 1966); vol. 4 (New York, Barnes & Noble, 1969).

[44] *Who Was Who: A Companion to "Who's Who": Containing the Biographies of Those Who Died During the Period* (London, A. & C. Black, 1929–). 1897–1915, 5th rev. ed. (1967); 1916–28, 4th rev. ed. (1967); 1929–40, 2d rev. ed. (1967); 1941–50 (1952); 1951–60 (1961). Future volumes to come out decennially.

162

The British *Who's Who*[45] began fifty years before the *Who's Who in America* and is the pioneer of the who's who publication now available in almost every country and every field. Until 1897, *Who's Who* was a handbook of titled and official classes and contained lists of names rather than biographical sketches. In 1897, called "First Year of New Issue," *Who's Who* became a biographical dictionary of prominent persons in many fields. Today it is principally British, although some important people of the United States and other countries are included. It covers many fields of activities, but it emphasizes government and public administration. There are five sections in a volume: abbreviations; obituaries for the previous year; the Royal Family; supplements (alterations and additions too late for inclusion and names included in the New Year's Honours List); and biographies. Each biographical entry includes full name, degrees, titles, occupation, birth date, parentage, marriages, children, offices, publications, recreation, addresses, and clubs. Each year a proof of each entry is sent to its subject for revision; therefore, the biographies are accurate, reliable, up to date, and fairly detailed.

Guides to peerage and landed gentry, such as *The Royalty, Peerage, and Aristocracy of the World*[46] and Burke's *Genealogical and Heraldic History of the Peerage, Baronage, and Knightage*,[47] will be of value to history students. These works, however, are outside the scope of this book.

The Canadians have begun to issue their *Dictionary of Canadian Biography*,[48] a monumental work comparable to the *Dictionary of National Biography* and the *Dictionary of American Biography* in content, style, and quality. Authoritative biographi-

45 *Who's Who: An Annual Biographical Dictionary, with Which is Incorporated Men and Women of the Time* (London, A. & C. Black, 1849–). Annual.

46 International ed., vol. 1– (London, Annuaire de France, Observatory House, Observatory Gardens, 1843–).

47 J. B. Burke (London, Burke's Peerage, 1826–). Irregular. 1963.

48 (Toronto, University of Toronto Press, 1966–). Vol. 1– . Planned in 20 vols. There is a French edition, *Dictionnaire biographique du Canada*.

cal essays with bibliographies for the notable Canadians are arranged in chronological periods, for example, volume 1 covers the subjects who have lived and died before 1700, volume 2, 1701–40. The chronological approach allows for the interpretation of the subject's life in relation to the developments of Canada.

The *Canadian Who's Who*[49] and *Who's Who in Canada*,[50] as well as the *Who's Who in the East* (*and Eastern Canada*), *Who's Who in the Midwest* (*and Central Canada*), and *Who's Who in the West* (*and Western Canada*),[51] supply information about living Canadians. The first two titles are neither identical nor comprehensive; they overlap. The *Canadian Who's Who* is arranged alphabetically with a classified index. *Who's Who in Canada*, which is illustrated, is nonalphabetical with an alphabetical index.

The Australians also have begun to issue their *Australian Dictionary of Biography*,[52] which is comparable to the *Dictionary of National Biography* and which will cover some six thousand entries when it is complete. Sponsored by the Australian National University, this projected twelve-volume work, like the *Dictionary of Canadian Biography*, will be divided into chronological periods: 1788–1850, 2 volumes; 1851–90, 4 volumes; 1891–1939, 6 volumes. Prior to this comprehensive and authoritative work, the only available biographical dictionary for Australians was the *Dictionary of Australian Biography* by Percival Serle.[53] It was good but short. This new set, like the *Dictionary of National Biography*, will give information about the background, career, and character of the subject and provide a critical assessment and

---

[49] (Toronto, Trans-Canada Press, 1910–). Annual with half-yearly supplements.

[50] B. M. Greene, ed., *Who's Who in Canada: An Illustrated Biographical Record of Men and Women of the Time* (Toronto, International Press, 1922–). Biennial.

[51] For full bibliographic information, see note 40. Canada has been included only in the 9th edition for 1964–65, the 9th edition for 1965–66, and the 9th edition for 1966–67.

[52] Douglas Pike, ed. (Melbourne, Australia, Melbourne University Press, 1966–). Vol. 1– .

[53] 12 vols. (Sydney, Australia, Angus & Robertson, 1949).

164

bibliography. The leading Australians of the first volume include governors, chief justices, aborigines, bushrangers, "wild white men," industrialists, artists, missionaries, a publican, and characters. In this first volume 250 authors, who have signed their sketches, have contributed 535 articles varying from two hundred to six thousand words.

The *Who's Who in Australia* is the contemporary biographical Australian dictionary.[54]

The *Dictionnaire de biographie française*[55] is a very important new dictionary of national biography. More extensive than the *Dictionary of National Biography* and the *Dictionary of American Biography*, it has shorter articles, signed with the author's full name, and bibliographies in most cases. It includes the outstanding French inhabitants of France and her dependent territories and the foreigners who played an important part in French history. It excludes the living.

There are several excellent sources of contemporary French biography. The first, *Dictionnaire biographique français contemporain*,[56] appeared first in 1950. It is a dictionary of contemporary French personalities, usually with bibliographies. *Nouveau dictionnaire national des contemporains*,[57] another valuable source, is an illustrated biographical dictionary of contemporary personalities, with fairly long sketches, portraits, an alphabetical list of names, and an index of names arranged by profession or occupation. *Nouveau dictionnaire national des contemporains* is similar in style to *Dictionnaire national des contemporains*,[58] a biographi-

[54] *Who's Who in Australia: An Australian Biographical Dictionary and Register of Titled Persons.* The 16th edition was published at Melbourne by the Herald and Weekly Times in 1959. Triennial (irregular). First published in 1906.

[55] (Paris, Latouzey er Ane, 1933–).

[56] 2d ed. (Paris, Pharos, Agence Internationale de Documentation Contemporaine, 1954). *Supplements* 1–2 (1955–56).

[57] 4th ed. (Paris, Les Editions du Nouveau Dictionnaire National des Contemporains, 1966). First published in 1962, covering 1961–62. Irregular.

[58] 3 vols. (Paris, Les Editions Lajeunesse, 1936–39).

cal dictionary of about three thousand personalities of the 1930's. *Who's Who in France*[59] contains concise biographical sketches in French in the usual who's who style.

The standard German biographical dictionary of deceased outstanding Germans from earliest times to the end of the nineteenth century is the *Allgemeine deutsche Biographie*.[60] It has long, signed articles with bibliographies. Supplementary material in the volumes makes it necessary to use the index to find material in the set. Prominent Germans who have died since 1913 might be written up in the *Biographisches Jahrbuch und deutscher Nekrolog*[61] or the *Deutsches biographisches Jahrbuch*.[62] Each volume of the *Biographisches Jahrbuch* contains a section of long, signed articles with bibliographies on prominent Germans who have died during the year, a necrology of briefer notices, and an index. The *Deutsches biographisches Jahrbuch*, which continues the *Biographisches Jahrbuch*, retains the section of long, signed articles with bibliographies and the shorter necrology notices; however, it has no cumulated index.

The *Neue deutsche Biographie*,[63] the *New Dictionary of German Biography* (*NDB*), is not intended to supersede the old *Allgemeine deutsche Biographie*. Edited by the Historical Committee at the Bavarian Academy of Sciences, it contains the biographies of outstanding Germans, including Austrian and Swiss Germans, who died before January 1, 1953. Each article, written

[59] *Who's Who in France: Dictionnaire biographique* (Paris, J. Lafitte, 1953–). First published in 1953, covering 1953–54; then biennial.

[60] *Allgemeine deutsche Biographie*, ed. through the Historical Commission at the Art Academy of Sciences, 56 vols. (Leipzig, Duncker and Humblot, 1875–1912).

[61] 1896–1913, ed. by Anton Bettelheim, 18 vols. and separate index volume to vols. 1–10 (1896–1905), (Berlin, G. Reimer, 1897–1917). Annual.

[62] Ed. by the Organization of German Academies, 1914–23, 1928–29 (Berlin, Deutsche Verlagsanstalt, 1925–32). Vols. 1–5, 10–11. Vol. 1, 1914–16; vol. 2, 1917–20; vol. 3, 1921; vol. 4, 1922; vol. 5, 1923; vol. 10, 1928; and vol. 11, 1929.

[63] Ed. by the Historical Commission at the Bavarian Academy of Sciences (Berlin, Duncker and Humblot, 1953–). Vol. 1– .

by a specialist who has signed it, is accompanied by a bibliography and by occasional references to a portrait. Each of the projected twelve volumes will have its own index which will cover the alphabetical entries in that volume and will include references to all entries in the *Allgemeine deutsche Biographie*. Two other volumes of German biography are *Biographisches Worterbuch zur deutschen Geschichte*,[64] a biographical handbook containing brief entries for two thousand Germans and a few foreigners important in German history from Roman times to 1933, and *Die grossen Deutschen*,[65] a collection of biographical studies of 234 great Germans from 672 to the 1950's. *Das Deutsche Fuhrenlexikon*[66] is a separate record of the Nazi movement.

The *Wer ist Wer?*[67] and *Who's Who in Germany*[68] are two volumes dealing with contemporary Germans in the usual who's who format. *Wer ist Wer?* for 1962 covers middle and East Germany in its second part. *Who's Who in Germany* is another in the English-language series of who's who of European countries; it includes biographical sketches and a directory of organizations.

There are various other retrospective and current biographical tools for other countries and areas. Russia, for instance, has *Russkie biograficheskie i biobibliograficheskie slovari*,[69] a list of biographical and bio-bibliographical dictionaries; the *Russkii biog-*

[64] Hellmuth Rossler and Gunther Franz (Munich, R. Oldenbourg, 1952).

[65] Hermann Heimpel, Theodore Heuss, and Benno Reifenbert, eds., *Die grossen Deutschen: Deutsche Biographie*, 5 vols. (Berlin, Im Propylaen-Verla bei Ullstein, 1957–58).

[66] (Berlin, Stollberg, 1934).

[67] Walter Habel, ed., *Wer ist Wer: Das Deutsche Who's Who*, 15th ed., Degenérs *Wer ist's?* (Berlin-Grunewald, Arani Verlags-Gmbh., 1966). Now quadrennial. Vol. 15, pt. 1, Federal Republic of Germany and West Berlin; vol. 15, pt. 2, Soviet Occupied Section, East Berlin.

[68] H. C. Kliemann and Stephen S. Taylor, eds., *Who's Who in Germany: A Biographical Dictionary Containing About 11,000 Biographies of Prominent People in and out of Germany and 2,400 Organizations*, 2d ed. (Munich, R. Oldenbourg, 1960). First edition, 1955.

[69] Isaak Mikhailovich Kaufman, new ed. (Moscow, Gos. Izd-vo Kulturno-Provet, Lit-ry, 1955). 1st ed., 1950.

raficheskii slovar,[70] the leading Russian biographical dictionary of Russians who died before 1893; and *Prominent Personalities in the USSR*,[71] which is kept up to date by the quarterly supplement *Portraits of Prominent USSR Personalities*.[72]

Africa has Ronald Segal's *Political Africa*;[73] Latin America, *Who's Who in Latin America*;[74] China, *A Chinese Biographical Dictionary*[75] and various who's who volumes;[76] and Japan, the *Japan Biographical Encyclopedia and Who's Who*[77] and *Who's Who in Japan*.[78]

[70] *Russkii biograficheskii slovar'* . . . *izdan pod nabliudeniem*, comp. under the supervision of the Russian Historical Association, A. A. Polovtsova, chief ed., 25 vols. (St. Petersburg, "Kadima," 1896–1918). Arranged alphabetically but not published alphabetically. The letters Y, Gog-Gia, E, M, Nik-Nia, Tk-Tia, and U were not covered when the work stopped.

[71] Institute for the Study of the USSR, comp., *Prominent Personalities in the USSR: A Biographic Directory Containing 6,015 Biographies of Prominent Personalities in the Soviet Union*, ed. by Edward L. Crowley, Andrew I. Lebed, and Heinrich E. Schulz (Metuchen, N.J., Scarecrow Press, 1968). The first volume was the *Biographic Directory of the USSR* (1950); the second, *Who's Who in the USSR*, 1961–62 (Montreal, Intercontinental Book and Publishing Co., Ltd., 1962); and *Who's Who in the USSR*, 1965–66 (Montreal, Intercontinental Book and Publishing Co., Ltd., 1966).

[72] Vol. 1, 1968– (Metuchen, N.J., Scarecrow Press, 1968–). Quarterly.

[73] *Political Africa: A Who's Who of Personalities and Parties* (London, Stevens & Sons, Ltd., 1961).

[74] Ronald Hilton, ed., *Who's Who in Latin America: A Biographical Dictionary of Notable Living Men and Women of Latin America*, 3d ed., 7 pts. (Stanford, Calif., Stanford University Press, 1945–51). First two editions, 1935 and 1940, were edited by P. A. Martin. The third edition is arranged by country.

[75] Herbert Allen Giles (London, B. Quaritch, 1898).

[76] *Who's Who in China: Biographies of Chinese Leaders*, 6 vols. (Shanghai, China Weekly Review, 1918–50); Max Perleberg, *Who's Who in Modern China (from the Beginning of the Chinese Republic to the End of 1953)* (Hong Kong, Ye Olde Printerie, 1954); H. H. Boorman and H. C. Howard, eds., *Biographical Dictionary of Republican China* (New York, Columbia University Press, 1967–); and *Who's Who in Communist China* (Hong Kong, Union Research Institute, 1966).

[77] (Tokyo, Japan Biographical Research Department, Rengo Press, 1958–). Triennial, 1st ed., 1958; 2d ed., 1961; 3d ed., 1964/1965.

[78] (Tokyo, Japanese Politics Economy Research Institute, 1963).

PROFESSIONAL OR OCCUPATIONAL BIOGRAPHIES

There are several directories of historians and politicians which can be of value to the history student. The *Directory of American Scholars*[79] is the standard work listing living American scholars. The first three editions appeared in one-volume editions. With the increasing growth of eligible entries, the fourth edition came out in four separate volumes, the first volume of which listed historians in the fine arts (musicologists and art and architectural historians), economics, business, sciences, and medicine (legal historians appear in volume 4). The new fifth edition, which is to be published in four volumes, will include 33,500 biographies, an increase of 10,500 from the 23,000 in the fourth edition. The first volume still covers historians (9,500 entries, a forty-nine per cent increase over the fourth edition); the second volume, English, speech, and drama (11,000 entries, a forty-seven per cent increase over the fourth edition); the third volume, foreign languages, linguistics, and philology (6,700 entries, a fifty per cent increase over the fourth edition). For each entry the following information is given: name, place and date of birth, citizenship, date of marriage, number of children, fields of specialization, education, position, military service, society membership, research, publication, and address.

One professional society which issues a biographical directory of its members is the American Political Science Association.[80] The members of this association filled out questionnaires to supply the facts for biographies of standard format. The information includes full name, place and date of birth, citizenship, marital status, education, honors, professional career, military service,

[79] 5 vols. (New York, R. R. Bowker Co., 1969). 1st ed., 1942; 2d ed., 1951; 3d ed., 1957; 4th ed., 4 vols., 1963–64.

[80] American Political Science Association, *Biographical Directory*, 4th ed. (Washington, D.C., American Political Science Association, 1961). A fifth edition with nine thousand biographies was published in 1968.

civil and professional contributions, publications, fields of interest, and address.

There are many biographical dictionaries which limit their coverage to specific groups of people. For example, there are *Who's Who of American Women (and Women of Canada)*,[81] *Who's Who in Colored America*,[82] *Who's Who in American Jewry*,[83] *Biographical Sketches of Those Who Attended Harvard College*,[84] *Historical Register of Officers of the Continental Army*,[85] and *Biographical Register of the Officers and Graduates of the U.S. Military Academy at West Point*.[86]

There are various biographical dictionaries to specific fields of history. The *Biographical and Bibliographical Dictionary of the Italian Humanists* answers many questions for the student of the Renaissance.[87] It includes all men and women of Italian birth who made a lifetime study of any phase of Greek and Roman civiliza-

[81] *Who's Who of American Women (and Women of Canada): A Biographical Dictionary of Notable Living Women of the United States of America and Other Countries*, 4th ed., 1966–67 (Chicago, Marquis-Who's Who Inc., 1965).

[82] G. J. Fleming and C. E. Burckel, eds., *Who's Who in Colored America: An Illustrated Biographical Directory of Notable Living Persons of African Descent in the United States*, 7th ed. (New York, Christian E. Burckel & Associates, 1950).

[83] *Who's Who in American Jewry: A Biographical Dictionary of Living Jews of the United States and Canada*, vol. 3, 1938–39 (New York, National News Association, 1938).

[84] John L. Sibley, *Biographical Sketches of Those Who Attended Harvard College with Bibliographical and Other Notes* (Boston, Massachusetts Historical Society, 1872–), in progress.

[85] Francis B. Heitman, *Historical Register of Officers of the Continental Army During the War of the Revolution, April, 1775 to December, 1783*, new rev. and enl. ed. (Washington, D.C., Rare Book Shop Publishing Co., 1914).

[86] George W. Cullum, *Biographical Register of the Officers and Graduates of the U.S. Military Academy at West Point, New York, Since Its Establishment in 1802*, 3d rev. and extended ed., 9 vols. (1891–1950), place and publisher vary.

[87] Mario E. Cosenza, ed., *Biographical and Bibliographical Dictionary of the Italian Humanists and of the World of Classical Scholarship in Italy, 1300–1800*, 2d rev. and enl. ed., 5 vols. (Boston, G. K. Hall & Co., 1967).

tion and those of foreign birth who went to Italy and became identified with the new learning in Italy. There are entries for kings, emperors, popes, cardinals, bishops, members of the religious orders, and collectors of books and manuscripts. There are also entries for Italian cities and the learned academies and libraries. The *Biographical and Bibliographical Dictionary of the Italian Humanists* removes much of the confusion due to the multiplicity of names by which the scholars were known and referred to in their own and later centuries. It gives full names whenever possible (in Latin, in Greek, and in the vernacular); the city of birth; the subject's teachers, pupils, and friends; references to the subject's portraits, burial place, and monuments; and other biographical data and explanations. It lists all editions of the subject's known works on the classical authors, the translations and the commentaries, the editions of all original works by the humanists themselves and works by other scholars on the lives and works of the humanists.

For the political historian there are tools for the various countries. The *Biographical Directory of the American Congress, 1774–1961*[88] presents 10,400 short biographical sketches of senators and representatives who were appointed to or elected to Congress from 1774 to 1961. The first part is a listing of officers of the executive branch of the government, for example, the cabinets from President George Washington through the first administration of President Dwight D. Eisenhower. The second part lists places and meetings of the Continental Congress, its presidents, and the delegates from each member; the census apportionment of representatives; and a chronological listing by state of senators and representatives from the First Congress (March 4, 1789–March 3, 1791) through the Eighty-sixth (January 3, 1959–January 3,

[88] *Biographical Directory of the American Congress, 1774–1961: The Continental Congress, September 5, 1774, to October 21, 1788, and the General Government* (Washington, D.C., Government Printing Office, 1859). There have been revisions in 1869, 1876, 1887, 1903, 1911, 1927, and 1949.

1961) with an alphabetical list of members of the Eighty-seventh Congress serving their first term.

The *Official Congressional Directory*[89] includes biographical sketches of members of Congress and the Supreme Court. It lists state delegations; terms of service; committees and commissions; sessions of Congress; governors of states; votes cast for senators and representatives; the cabinet; executive departments; independent agencies; courts; international organizations; foreign diplomatic representatives and consular offices in the United States; and United States diplomatic and consular offices. It also includes a press directory, which gives representatives of newspapers and periodicals, photographers, radio and television correspondents; an index of individuals; and a detailed table of contents.

The *Congressional Staff Directory* made its first appearance in 1959.[90] It contains information about Congress with emphasis on the staffs of members and staffs of the committees. There is a separate section of staff biographies arranged alphabetically. It was designed as a companion volume to the *Official Congressional Directory*.

The aim of *Who's Who in American Politics*[91] is to provide information on political figures and public servants active today in the United States. The first edition carries biographical data on 12,500 political figures from the president of the United States to those active on the local level. Twelve top political officials served

[89] U.S., Congress, *Official Congressional Directory for the Use of the United States Congress* (Washington, D.C., 1809–). Up to 1864, published irregularly by private firms; from 1865, printed at the Government Printing Office; currently issued for each session of Congress.

[90] Charles B. Brownson, comp. and ed. (Washington, D.C., The Congressional Staff Directory, 1959–).

[91] Paul A. Theis and Edmund L. Henshaw, Jr., eds., *Who's Who in American Politics: A Biographical Directory of United States Political Leaders*, 1st ed., 1967–68 (New York, R. R. Bowker Co., 1967). 2d ed., 1969–70 (New York, R. R. Bowker Co., 1969). A new feature in the second edition is the "Geographical Index" which lists biographies by the state in which they maintain their legal residence.

172

as an advisory committee, and information on the subjects of the biographies was gathered by direct questionnaires requesting information on full name, legal and mailing addresses, political party affiliation, birth place and date, education, family data, and present and previous political and business achievements.

A four-volume reference work devoted to United States Supreme Court justices is *The Justices of the Supreme Court, 1789–1969: Their Lives and Major Opinions.*[92] Scholars in law, history, and political science wrote the biographical essays appraising the ninety-seven justices. This is a valuable work for students interested in constitutional and political history.

The British have *Dod's Parliamentary Companion*[93] and the *British Imperial Calendar.*[94] The first title contains brief biographies of members of the House of Lords and the House of Commons; it lists major government offices and officials as well as the constituencies and votes cast at the most recent elections. The *British Imperial Calendar* usually gives sketches of the Royal household, high commissioners of London, the cabinet, the treasury, officers of the House of Peers and House of Commons; lists the public departments for England and Wales, Scotland, and Northern Ireland; and provides an alphabetical list of officers with official positions, degrees and honors, and salary (discontinued after the 1965 edition).

Various volumes list members of the British Parliament: *History of Parliament, 1439–1509,*[95] *The Long Parliament, 1640–1641,*[96] *The History of Parliament,*[97] *Members of Parliament, 1734–1832,*[98] and *"The Times's" House of Commons, 1966.*[99]

---

[92] Leon Friedman and Fred L. Israel, eds. (New York, R. R. Bowker Co., 1969).

[93] (London, Business Dictionaries, 1832–). Annual. Publisher varies.

[94] *British Imperial Calendar and Civil Service List* (London, H. M. Stationery Office, 1809–). Irregular. Title varies.

[95] Josiah C. Wedgwood, 2 vols. (London, H. M. Stationery Office, 1936–38).

[96] M. F. Keeler, *The Long Parliament, 1640–1641: A Biographical Study of Its Members* (Philadelphia, American Philosophical Society, 1956).

The French have two biographical dictionaries covering their parliaments. One, Adolphe Robert's *Dictionnaire des parlementaires français*,[100] covers the period from the French Revolution in 1789 to 1889. It has lengthy biographical sketches of the members of Parliament and the ministers. Ministries from 1871 are listed chronologically and alphabetically, and senators and deputies from 1871 to 1876 are listed alphabetically. The second biographical dictionary covering French parliaments is Jean Jolly's *Dictionnaire des parlementaires français*.[101] This volume covers the years 1889–1940 and contains fairly long biographical sketches.

For Germany, Wilhelm Kosch's *Biographisches Staatshandbuch* is the standard work.[102] This extensive biographical dictionary includes past and present Germans, Austrians, and Swiss of political importance. The brief biographies are unsigned. For the German Republic, 1874–1936, there is a *Handbuch für das Deutsche Reich*,[103] which gives a directory of governmental organizations and personnel. Since the end of World War II, East and

[97] Sir Lewis Namier and John Brooke, *The History of Parliament: The House of Commons, 1754–1790*, 3 vols. (London, published for the History of Parliament Trust by H. M. Stationery Office, 1964).

[98] G. B. Judd IV (New Haven, Conn., Yale University Press, 1955).

[99] *"The Times's" House of Commons, 1966: With Full Results of the Polling, Biographies of Members and Unsuccessful Candidates, Photographs of All Members, and a Complete Analysis, Statistical Tables, and a Map of the General Election, October 1966* (London, "The Times" Office, 1966).

[100] Adolphe Robert et al., *Dictionnaire des parlementaires français comprenant tous les membres des Assemblées françaises et tous les ministres français, depuis le 1er mai 1789 jusqu-au 1er mai 1889*, 5 vols. (Paris, Bourloton, 1891).

[101] *Dictionnaire les parlementaires français: Notices biographiques sur les ministres, sénateurs et députés français de 1889 à 1940* (Paris, Les Presses Universitaires de France, 1960–).

[102] *Biographisches Staatshandbuch: Lexikon der Politik, Presse, und Publiziestik*, continued by E. Kurk, 2 vols. (Berne, Francke, 1963).

[103] Germany, Reich Department of Interior, *Handbuch für das Deutsche Reich*, 1874–1936 (Berlin, Carl Heymann, 1874–1936). Annual. Irregular.

174

West Germany have separate publications for their governments. For East Germany there is *Die Volkskammer der Deutschen Demokratischen Republik*;[104] for West Germany, *Die Bundesrepublik*.[105]

PORTRAITS

A photograph, sketch, or painting of a man is an added bonus for the history student. In keeping with the visually oriented world of today are the guides to and books of portraits. The old *A.L.A. Portrait Index*[106] is an index to portraits of about forty thousand persons in printed books and periodicals. It is indispensable in locating portraits of persons of the nineteenth century or earlier; however, it is sixty years out of date and weak on American portraits.

The new *Dictionary of American Portraits*[107] is a collection of 4,045 portraits of the most important men and women in American history before 1905. It includes political leaders, scientists, inventors, musicians, artists, publishers, jurists, military men, explorers, pioneers, industrialists, financial figures, and even notorious figures, such as Billy the Kid. For the earliest periods the work of contemporary engravers and portrait painters is used; for the early Republic, the work of the great artists (Gilbert Stuart, John S. Copley, Benjamin West, Charles Wilson Peale, for example); for the moderns, photographs are used except when a portrait is better than the photograph. The portraits are arranged alphabetically and the indexes are arranged by variant name (aliases, pseudonyms, maiden names, and so forth) and by twenty-seven classifications.

[104] Germany (Dem. Rep. 1949– ; Kongress-Verlag, 1957–).

[105] Yearbook 65, 1956–57, with the *Handbook for the Federal Republic of Germany* (Berlin, Cologne, Carl Heymann, 1956–). Biennial.

[106] William C. Lane and Nina E. Browne, eds., *A.L.A. Portrait Index: Index to Portraits Contained in Printed Books and Periodicals* (Washington, D.C., Government Printing Office, 1906).

[107] Hayward Cirker and Blanche Cirker, eds., introduction by Robert Hutchinson (New York, Dover Publications, 1967).

9

Primary Sources
and Dissertations

A primary source gives the words of the witnesses or the first re-
corders of an event. Primary sources include manuscripts, archives,
letters, diaries, and speeches. Discoveries of old letters, diaries, and
papers are still being made. For example, in the 1960's the William
Clark field notes were discovered. In spite of all the known material
dealing with the Lewis and Clark Expedition, scholars had sus-
pected that there was more to be found. They had noticed the
clean appearance of the manuscript notebook journals in the collections of the American Philosophical Society in Philadelphia
that had been transcribed by Reuben Gold Thwaites in his *Original Journals of the Lewis and Clark Expedition*. A few had
wondered if Lewis and Clark had not made rough notes and then
used the notes later to post their notebook journals. In 1953,
William Clark's journal was discovered in an attic in St. Paul,
Minnesota. The journal, which is now in the Western Americana
Collection at Yale University, has been edited and annotated for
publication by Ernest Staples Osgood.[1]

Secondary sources are "descriptions of the event derived from
and based on primary sources." The line between primary and
secondary sources is often indistinct, for example, a single document may be a primary source on some matter and a secondary

[1] *The Field Notes of Captain William Clark, 1803–1805*, Yale Western
Americana Series, vol. 5 (New Haven, Conn., Yale University Press, 1964).

source on others. The historian must use the procedures of external criticism, internal criticism, and the evaluation of the data as evidence in his critical examination of the sources.[2]

External criticism seeks to establish the authenticity of the physical remains. It tries to expose counterfeits and to establish positive identification of the origin of a document. The history scholar needs to develop his skill in paleography, sphragistics, and diplomatics. Paleography is "the sum of the various kinds of knowledge required for the deciphering of ancient and medieval manuscripts. . . . Originally a part of diplomatics, it was developed in the eighteenth century as a distinct field, while more recently the discovery in Egypt of ancient documents and manuscripts on papyrus has brought into existence a specialized study, known as papyrology."[3]

Sphragistics is the science of seals. For many years a guarantee of the authenticity of legal and official documents was the seal. Forgeries may often be detected by examining this feature of the paper, which testifies to a legal transaction.[4]

Diplomatics has been defined as "the science of ancient writings, literary and public documents, letters, decrees and characters which has for its object to decipher such old writing and to ascertain their authenticity, dates, signatures, etc."[5] Students in many fields of history should realize that official papers need technical examination. There are tests which can determine the age of paper, ink, and binding. Students should also know the nature and practices of the offices in which public documents were and are preserved.[6]

Internal criticism tries to detect inconsistencies, errors, or falsehoods by examining the text of a document or the contents of nondocumentary sources. For example, in the famous case of "The Diary of a Public Man," Frank M. Anderson used internal criti-

---

[2] Handlin et al., *Harvard Guide to American History*, 22.
[3] Dutcher, *Guide to Historical Literature*, 35–38.
[4] *Ibid.*, 33.
[5] *Ibid.*, 33–35.
[6] Handlin et al., *Harvard Guide to American History*, 5–6.

cism to determine the diary's authorship and to challenge its authenticity.[7]

The evaluation of historical data which has been authenticated by the principles of external and internal criticism is the historian's major task. To use this material as evidence, the historian must consider its reliability. He must decide what the words of the testimony meant for the witness, whether the witness was in a position to know what he was talking about, whether the witness had the skill and competence to observe accurately, and whether he would represent the facts fairly. The student should make a general evaluation of the character of the witness, noting his witness's age, bias, and tendency to exaggerate, then search for independent corroboration of his interpretation of the facts.[8]

The purpose of this chapter is to direct the student to some of the main sources of primary materials.

MANUSCRIPTS AND ARCHIVES

According to the *A.L.A. Glossary of Library Terms*, a manuscript is: "1. A work written by hand. 2. The handwritten or typewritten copy of an author's work before it is printed."[9] Archives, a collective noun used properly only in the plural, are "the organized body of records made or received in connection with the transaction of its affairs by a government or a governmental agency, an institution, organization, or establishment or a family or individual, and preserved for record purposes in its custody or that of its successor."[10]

[7] "The Diary of a Public Man" was originally published in *The North American Review*, from August to November, 1879 (CXXIX, 125–40, 259–73, 375–88, 484–96). It has been reprinted with Prefatory Notes by F. Lauriston Bullard and a Foreword by Carl Sandburg (New Brunswick, N.J., Rutgers University Press, 1946). See, Frank Maloy Anderson, *The Mystery of "A Public Man"* (Minneapolis, University of Minnesota Press, 1948).

[8] Handlin et al., *Harvard Guide to American History*, 23–25.

[9] *A.L.A. Glossary of Library Terms*, 6.

[10] *Ibid.*, 85.

178

Research in Archives: The Use of Unpublished Primary Sources, written by Phillip C. Brook, the director of the Harry S. Truman Library in Independence, Missouri, deals only with American archives.[11] It is a reliable guide for the history student who intends to use archival materials.

The bibliographic control of manuscript and archival material is a problem. Richard Hale's *Guide to Photocopied Historical Materials*, a union list, is a pioneer attempt, but there is no provision to keep it current.[12] Sponsored by the American Historical Association, this volume supplies basic bibliographic information on photocopied manuscripts of interest to historians and held by 285 institutions in the United States and Canada. It is arranged geographically with topical subdivisions. Each entry supplies the following information: the name of the author, compiler, collector, or holder of the original material; the title of the collection; the dates; the amount and present location of the original materials; and the type of photocopy. This guide lists photocopies of 11,137 items which are international in scope and date from ancient to modern times. There is an index of about four thousand entries for mostly personal and institutional names, with few detailed subject entries to the very broad subject arrangement.

There are two very important and valuable guides to the archives and manuscripts in the United States. The first is *A Guide to Archives and Manuscripts in the United States*, edited by Phillip M. Hamer.[13] This guide to 1,300 depositories and 20,000 collections of personal papers and archival groups in the United States, Puerto Rico, and the Canal Zone, is arranged geographically. Depositories are listed alphabetically by state (or other governmental unit) and city. The following information is given for each depository: name and address, name and title of person to whom

[11] (Chicago, University of Chicago Press, 1969).

[12] Richard W. Hale, *Guide to Photocopied Historical Materials in the United States and Canada* (Ithaca, N.Y., published for the American Historical Association by Cornell University Press, 1961).

[13] U.S., National Historical Publications Commission (New Haven, Conn., Yale University Press, 1961).

communications regarding the holdings should be addressed, size of holdings, field of special interest, and specific mention of groups of papers of special interest. Summary descriptions of the major holdings are given, as are references to more extensive published information on individual collections. The papers of more than 7,600 individuals and the records of numerous business, political, social, and other organizations are identified. There is an index to proper names and subjects. The great advantage of the Hamer *Guide to Archives and Manuscripts* is the ease with which appropriate collections can be identified.

The second important guide to archives and manuscripts in the United States is the Library of Congress' *National Union Catalog of Manuscripts (NUCMC)*, which began publication in 1962.[14] A continuing publication, this national register of manuscript collections is designed to achieve bibliographic control over the manuscript resources of the United States. To date, 18,417 collections representing the holdings of 616 repositories have been described.

Entries in *NUCMC* are arranged by a manuscript number assigned by the printer. To find a specific collection or information within a collection, the student must use the indexes: a name index, which lists persons and corporate bodies in collections; a subject index, which lists collections; and a repository index, which lists collections under the name of the repository and its location. The following information is given for each entry: collection title, physical description, location, scope and content, and other information, such as restrictions on access and literary rights. One shortcoming of *NUCMC* is that it does not list collections containing fewer than fifty items.

Until 1934 each federal department took care of its own

[14] 1959–61 (Ann Arbor, Mich., J. W. Edwards, 1962); 1962 (Hamden, Conn., Shoe String Press, 1964); 1963–64 (Washington, D.C., Library of Congress, 1966); 1966 (Washington, D.C., Library of Congress, 1967); 1967 (Washington, D.C., Library of Congress, 1968). *Index, 1959–1962* (Hamden, Conn., Shoe String Press, 1964); *Index, 1963–1966* is included in the 1966 volume.

records. In that year the National Archives was established and given responsibility for accumulating, appraising, destroying or preserving, and storing all archives or records belonging to the United States government.[15] The Federal Records Act of 1950 established the statutory basis for the administration of these records. In 1966 these documents, dating from the time of the Continental Congresses, amounted to about 900,000 cubic feet.[16] They include the basic records of Congress, the courts, the executive departments, and independent agencies. The presidential libraries, such as the Franklin D. Roosevelt Library in Hyde Park, New York, are also part of the National Archives.

The *Guide to the Records in the National Archives* lists the records deposited in the National Archives up to June, 1947.[17] This publication is kept up to date by the *National Archives Accessions*.[18] A shorter guide, *Your Government's Records in the National Archives*,[19] a series of *Preliminary Inventories*,[20] and *Publications*[21] of the National Archives and Records Service give more complete and more detailed listings.

The *List of National Archives Microfilm Publications*[22] lists archival material available for purchase on microfilm. Since 1940 the National Archives has been microfilming selected groups of United States records that have high research value. This list de-

[15] Handlin et al., *Harvard Guide to American History*, 119.

[16] *List of National Archives Microfilm Publications*, 1966, National Archives Publication no. 66–5 (Washington, D.C., National Archives and Records Service, General Services Administration, 1966), iii.

[17] U.S., National Archives (Washington, D.C., Government Printing Office, 1948).

[18] (Washington, D.C., Government Printing Office, 1947–). Issued quarterly, July, 1947–June, 1952; annually, 1952–60 (irregular).

[19] (Washington, D.C., Government Printing Office, 1950).

[20] (Washington, D.C., Government Printing Office, 1941–).

[21] Publication no. 1– (Washington, D.C., Government Printing Office, 1936–).

[22] National Archives Publication no. 68–8 (Washington, D.C., Government Printing Office, 1968). Title varies; each new edition supersedes the previous edition.

scribes more than 1,300 microfilm projects which reproduce approximately seventy-four million pages of documentary material. These microfilm publications provide basic documentation for research in American, European, Far Eastern, and Latin-American history and local history and genealogy. The National Archives retains the negative microfilm and sells the positive prints, made from these master negatives, at a moderate price. This list, arranged by department, gives the price.

The various Federal Records centers also publish lists, which are often valuable for the history student in that region. The Federal Records Center at San Francisco, for example, has published a *Preliminary Inventory of the Records of the Northern California and Nevada Agencies, Bureau of Indian Affairs.*[23]

One of the major National Archives projects of interest to the history student is the *Federal Population Censuses, 1790–1890.*[24] The schedules of population contain a wealth of information useful in studying westward expansion, the status of free and slave labor, regional and local history, and immigration. The list is arranged chronologically by census year, then alphabetically by the name of the state or territory, then alphabetically by county.

Another project at the National Archives is the compilation of guides relating to the Civil War. *A Guide to Federal Archives Relating to the Civil War*[25] and a companion *Guide to the Archives of*

[23] U.S., National Archives and Records Service, General Services Administration, Thomas W. Wadlow and Arthur R. Abel, comps., rev. by Arthur R. Abel, Record Group 75 (San Francisco, Federal Records Center, 1966).

[24] U.S., National Archives, National Archives Publication no. 69–3 (Washington, D.C., Government Printing Office, 1969). Census material can be very helpful to the student. A guide to the censuses, the first and only such guide, is Ann Herbert Scott's *Census, U.S.A.: Fact Finding for the American People, 1790–1970*, which was published late in 1968 by the Seabury Press of New York.

[25] U.S., National Archives, National Archives Publication no. 63–1, Kenneth W. Munden and Henry Putney Beers, comps. (Washington, D.C., National Archives and Records Service, General Services Administration, 1962).

182

the Government of the Confederate States of America[26] have been compiled.

The National Archives also has guides to German records. Gerhard Weinberg compiled the *Guide to Captured German Documents.*[27] The first two parts list books and articles which include German documentary material; the third part lists, by location, files of the captured documents in the Library of Congress, the National Archives, and other repositories. The Committee for the Study of War Documents of the American Historical Association issued *A Catalog of Files and Microfilms of the German Foreign Ministry Archives, 1867–1920,*[28] which gives a complete record of the files of the Political Department of the German Foreign Ministry and details of the filming programs of these files. The Historical Office of the United States Department of State continued it through 1945.[29] The National Archives also has three other guides to the microfilms of the German Foreign Ministry.[30]

The National Archives has published a *Guide to Materials on*

[26] U.S., National Archives, National Archives Publication no. 68–15 (Washington, D.C., Government Printing Office, 1968).

[27] Prepared by Gerhard L. Weinberg under the direction of Fritz T. Epstein, U.S. Human Resources Research Institute, *Research Memorandum*, no. 2, vol. 1 (Maxwell Air Force Base, Ala., Human Resources Institute, 1952).

[28] (Oxford, University Press, 1959).

[29] George O. Kent, comp. and ed., *A Catalog of Files and Microfilms of the German Foreign Ministry Archives, 1920–1945* (Stanford, Calif., Hoover Institute, 1962).

[30] American Historical Association, Committee for the Study of War Documents, *Guides to German Records Microfilmed at Alexandria, Virginia* (Washington, D.C., National Archives, 1958–), in progress; American Historical Association, Committee for the Study of War Documents, *Index of Microfilmed Records of the German Foreign Ministry and the Reich's Chancellery Covering the Weimar Period, Deposited at the National Archives*, prepared by Ernst Schwandt (Washington, D.C., National Archives, 1958–); American Historical Association, Committee for the Study of War Documents, *List of Archival References and Data of Documents from the Archives of the German Foreign Ministry, 1867–1920, Microfilmed at Whaddon Hall for the American Committee for the Study of War Documents* (Buckinghamshire, Whaddon Hall, 1957).

Latin America in the National Archives.[31] Volume 1 covers general records of the government and the departments of State, the Treasury, and Defense and Navy. The second volume will cover the other departments, the independent agencies, the legislative and judicial branches, and an index to both volumes.

There are various guides to the different categories of manuscripts. There are local guides to manuscripts, such as Robert D. Armstrong's *A Preliminary Union Catalog of Nevada Manuscripts.*[32] There are general and topical guides, such as Ray Allan Billington's *Guides to American History Manuscript Collections in Libraries of the United States*[33] and Samuel Flagg Bemis and Grace Gardner Griffin's *Guide to the Diplomatic History of the United States.*[34] There are guides prepared by the Historical Records Survey, such as the *Guide to Depositories of Manuscript Collections in the United States*[35] and the *Inventory of Federal Archives in the States.*[36] There are guides to manuscripts in foreign countries, such as Charles McLean Andrews' two guides, *Guide to the Materials for American History, to 1783, in the Public Record Office of Great Britain* and *Guide to the Manuscript Material of the History of the United States to 1783, in the British Museum, in Minor London Archives, and in the Libraries of Oxford and Cam-*

---

[31] John P. Harrison, comp., *Guide to Materials on Latin America in the National Archives*, National Archives Publication no. 62–3 (Washington, D.C., National Archives and Records Service, General Services Administration, 1961).

[32] Foreword by David W. Heron (Reno, University of Nevada Library, Nevada Library Association, 1967).

[33] Reprinted from the *Mississippi Valley Historical Review*, Vol. 38, (December, 1951), 467–96 (New York, Peter Smith, 1952).

[34] For full bibliographic information, see Chapter 3, note 20.

[35] Historical Records Survey, Division of Women's and Professional Project, Works Progress Administration (Columbus, Ohio, Historical Records Survey, 1938).

[36] Survey of Federal Archives, Division of Women's and Professional Project, Works Progress Administration in co-operation with the National Archives (Oklahoma City, Historical Records Survey, 1937).

bridge;[37] Herbert E. Bolton's *Guide to Material for the History of the United States in the Principal Archives of Mexico*;[38] M. D. Learned's *Guide to the Manuscript Materials Relating to American History in the German State Archives*;[39] W. G. Leland and J. J. Meng's *Guide to Materials for American History in the Libraries and Archives of Paris*;[40] Julian Paz's *Catálogo de manuscrito de América existentes en la Biblioteca Nacional*;[41] and L. M. Pérez's *Guide to Materials for American History in Cuban Archives.*[42] There are also guides to foreign public records containing American historical material.[43]

Many universities, libraries, and foundations in the United States are carrying on extensive programs of manuscript copying to make various collections available to history students through microfilm. Materials being copied are very diverse; they include, for example, materials relating to the early Middle Ages, American science in the eighteenth and nineteenth centuries, the contest between European powers for colonies in North America, the Italian Renaissance, diplomatic relations between the United States and western Europe, Hebrew commentaries on medicine and religion, and activities of the United States government.[44]

The foreign copying program of the Library of Congress is probably the oldest and most continuous manuscript copying program in the United States. Begun in 1907 by Herbert Putnam, this copying program uses the descriptions of European collections in the *Carnegie Guides*[45] to determine which manuscripts to copy. In

[37] 2 vols. (Washington, D.C., Carnegie Institution of Washington, 1908–12); (Washington, D.C., Carnegie Institution of Washington, 1908).
[38] (Washington, D.C., Carnegie Institution of Washington, 1913).
[39] 2 vols. (Washington, D.C., Carnegie Institution of Washington, 1912).
[40] 2 vols. (Washington, D.C., Carnegie Institution of Washington, 1932–43).
[41] (Madrid, Tip. de Archivos, 1933).
[42] (Washington, D.C., Carnegie Institution of Washington, 1917).
[43] See Handlin et al., *Harvard Guide to American History*, 139–48.
[44] "Manuscripts on Microfilm, a Symposium," *Quarterly Journal of the Library of Congress*, Vol. 24 (July, 1967), 145–54.
[45] Carnegie Institution of Washington, 23 vols. (Washington, D.C.,

the many years in which this program has been active, the collection has grown to over two million pieces copied from several hundred libraries, archives, and private collections in seventy-three different countries, including Great Britain, France, Spain, Germany, Austria, the Netherlands, Italy, the Scandinavian countries, and some eastern European countries and Russia. The material is principally political and military and relates largely to American history before 1800. Unfortunately, there is no complete guide to this material, though James O'Neill has described a portion of it in "The European Sources for American History in the Library of Congress."[46] British materials copied before 1944 are described in Grace Gardner Griffin's *A Guide to Manuscripts Relating to American History in British Depositories*,[47] and French materials copied are described in James O'Neill's "Copies of French Manuscripts for American History in the Library of Congress."[48] The current copying program is described by Mme Ulane S. Bonnel in "La déléguée à Paris."[49]

A national Center for the Coordination of Foreign Manuscript Copying has been established in the Manuscript Division of the Library of Congress. Created through a grant from the Council on Library Resources, the Center is the result of the long-felt need to make copying ventures abroad more systematic, more efficient, and more useful to American researchers. It is hoped the Center will work toward the development of new co-operative copying projects, that it will serve as a clearinghouse for information on the contents and policies of foreign archives and libraries, that it will prepare a national list of the material which should and can

Carnegie Institution, 1906–43). Covers American, British, British-American, European, Spanish, and Spanish-American archives.

[46] "Manuscripts on Microfilm, a Symposium," *Quarterly Journal of the Library of Congress*, Vol. 24 (July, 1967), 152–57.

[47] *A Guide to Manuscripts Relating to American History in British Depositories Reproduced for the Division of Manuscripts of the Library of Congress* (Washington, D.C., Library of Congress, 1946).

[48] *Journal of American History*, Vol. 51 (March, 1956), 674–91.

[49] *Quarterly Journal of the Library of Congress*, Vol. 23 (July, 1966), 187–203.

be copied, and that it will create a permanent and easily available national record of what has been copied. The semiannual *News from the Center*, which first came out in February, 1967, is being published separately as well as in the appendix to the *Library of Congress Information Bulletin*. It contains news of what is going on at the Center.[50]

The Genealogical Society of the Church of Jesus Christ of Latter Day Saints also has an extensive microfilm project. In its storage vaults, blasted out of the Rocky Mountains in central Utah, are more than 475,000 reels of negative microfilm of parish registers, wills, records of church christenings, burial and marriage certificates, tax and military records, censuses, and land and probate records. Of the records at Salt Lake City, eighty per cent are foreign records and twenty per cent, records from the United States.[51]

While there are several bibliographies and catalogs dealing with ancient, medieval, and Renaissance manuscripts,[52] this book will mention briefly only a union list and a few of the copying projects.

The American Council of Learned Societies and the General Education Board furnished money for a union handlist of early manuscripts in American collections: *Census of Medieval and Renaissance Manuscripts in the United States*, edited by Seymour De Ricci.[53] De Ricci, the foremost authority on provenance, has previously published "A Handlist of Latin Classical Manuscripts in American Libraries";[54] hence, the *Census of Medieval and Renaissance Manuscripts* is a logical extension of this handlist. The *Census of Medieval and Renaissance Manuscripts* is arranged geographically by state, city, and library and is limited to

[50] George O. Kent, "Center for the Coordination of Foreign Manuscript Copying," in "Manuscripts on Microfilm, a Symposium," *Quarterly Journal of the Library of Congress*, Vol. 24 (July, 1967), 175–85.

[51] *Ibid.*, 177–78.

[52] For other bibliographies and catalogs to ancient, medieval, and Renaissance manuscripts, see Winchell, *Guide to Reference Books*, 14–16.

[53] With the assistance of William J. Wilson, 3 vols. (New York, H. W. Wilson Co., 1935–40).

[54] *Philological Quarterly*, Vol. 1 (April, 1922), 100–108.

Western manuscripts before 1600. The following information is given for each item: manuscript number or shelf mark; authors and titles, with *incipits* when appropriate; physical description; provenance; and references in scholarly literature. A *Supplement*[55] has been published, and an annual listing in the *Publications* of the Bibliographical Society of America has been proposed to keep the *Supplement* up to date. The *Supplement* follows the same arrangement with the same descriptive information. Both have general indexes of names, titles, and headings; indexes of scribes, illuminators, and cartographers; indexes of *incipits*; indexes of present owners; and indexes of previous owners. The *Supplement* has a concordance of *Census* numbers, which tie in with items in the *Supplement*.

St. Louis University has undertaken the copying of the Vatican manuscripts. In "Four Copying Projects at St. Louis University" Lowrie J. Daly states that about three-fourths of all the manuscripts in the Latin and Greek divisions of the Vatican Library, which totals over eleven million pages, have been filmed for St. Louis University.[56] The Vatican manuscripts include various textbooks used in the four faculties of the medieval universities (law, medicine, the arts—philosophy and science, and theology), materials for the High and early Middle Ages, and Italian Renaissance materials. St. Louis also has microfilm copies of the Vatican's Hebrew collections; the extensive indexes to the *Propaganda File* archives and the volumes that pertain to Latin America; an extensive collection of Jesuit manuscripts and archival material, including the Procurator General's files; and copies of miscellaneous documents in the archives in Mexico.

The Monastic Manuscript Microfilm Project of St. John's University is an extensive program of photographing the invaluable manuscripts still preserved in European monasteries; some of these

[55] Originated by C. U. Faye and continued by W. H. Bond, ed. (New York, Bibliographical Society of America, 1962).

[56] "Manuscripts on Microfilm, a Symposium," *Quarterly Journal of the Library of Congress*, Vol. 24 (July, 1967), 158–61.

manuscripts are over one thousand years old.[57] A negative micro-film and a positive copy of each manuscript are to be deposited in the Library of St. John's University in Collegeville, Minnesota. Father Oliver Kapsner, O.S.B., the director of the project, went to Europe in October, 1964, to arrange for the beginning of actual microfilming in the various abbeys by University Microfilms. After two years of operation, the Manuscript Project has photocopied over 6,500 codices in seventeen monasteries and produced three million frames of microfilm.[58]

The University of Notre Dame started its microfilm project when it received permission to microfilm the entire manuscript collections of the Ambrosian Library in Milan. More than thirty thousand classical, medieval, and Renaissance manuscripts are to be filmed. The project was conceived in 1960 when Cardinal Montini (Pope Paul VI) visited Notre Dame. The Ambrosian Library, founded in 1609, has among its treasures an illustrated copy of Homer's *Iliad* dating from the third or fourth century A.D., an edition of Virgil with notes by the Italian poet Petrarch, many ancient Bibles and fragments of Bibles, and a collection of auto-graphed designs by Leonardo da Vinci.[59] So far the project has produced microfilm copies of nine thousand manuscripts, and the Medieval Institute of Notre Dame has obtained xerox copies of the 25,000-subject card catalog of the manuscript material.[60]

The initiation of the Vatican Library microfilm project led groups of Protestant laymen and scholars to launch a similar project in the field of Reformation history. In 1957 the Founda-tion for Reformation Research was established in St. Louis to collect and preserve historical source material pertaining to the

[57] Monastic Manuscript Microfilm Library, St. John's University Li-brary, Collegeville, Minnesota, *Progress Reports.*

[58] "Manuscripts on Microfilm, a Symposium," *Quarterly Journal of the Library of Congress*, Vol. 24 (July, 1967), 178–81.

[59] "Notre Dame To Microfilm Abrosian Manuscripts," *Library Journal,* Vol. 87 (March 15, 1962), 1108.

[60] "Manuscripts on Microfilm, a Symposium," *Quarterly Journal of the Library of Congress*, Vol. 24 (July, 1967), 181.

Protestant Reformation and to make such material available through the library and research center. After the materials in this country were checked and European archives and libraries were surveyed, microfilming was started in 1960 in the Staatsbibliothek, the Westdeutsche Bibliothek, and the Universitats-bibliothek in Marburg, Germany, where the archives of Philip of Hess were microfilmed on 528 reels. The Foundation has also filmed the collection of the Simmlersche Handschriften at the Zentralbibliothek at Zurich, Switzerland.[61]

In addition to the guides mentioned earlier on United States archives and United States history in foreign archives, there is a guide to the western European archives. Daniel H. Thomas and L. M. Case have compiled a *Guide to the Diplomatic Archives of Western Europe.*[62] It contains a chapter on each of the major European countries, the League of Nations, the United Nations, and UNESCO. For each country there is a general history of the archives, a discussion of their location, arrangement, and rules for use.

The *Guide to the Contents of the Public Record Office* is the basic guide to British archives.[63] It is a revision of the earlier *Guide to the Manuscripts Preserved in the Public Record Office.*[64] In both titles the first volume is concerned with legal records and the second, with state papers and departmental records. The Historical Manuscripts Commission has completed guides to manuscripts from 1870 to 1911[65] and from 1911 to 1957.[66]

[61] *Ibid.,* 182–84.

[62] (Philadelphia, University of Pennsylvania, 1959).

[63] Great Britain, Public Record Office, rev. to 1960, 2 vols. (London, H. M. Stationery Office, 1963).

[64] Great Britain, Public Record Office, M. S. Giuseppi, 2 vols. (London, H. M. Stationery Office, 1923–24).

[65] Great Britain, Historical Manuscripts Commission, *A Guide to the Reports on Collections of Manuscripts of Private Families, Corporations, and Institutions in Great Britain and Ireland,* issued by the Royal Commissioners for Historical Manuscripts, 2 vols. in 3 (London, H. M. Stationery Office, 1914–38). Pt. 1, *Topographical Index*; pt. 2, *Guide to the Reports of the Royal Commission on Historical Manuscripts, 1870–1911.* Part 2 is

The fundamental guide to the archival sources for French history is Charles V. Langlois and Henri Stein's *Les archives de l'histoire de France.*[67] Italy has the *Gli archivi di stato al 1952,*[68] a condensed inventory of the Italian government archives; the *Pubblicazioni degli archivi di stato,*[69] a series of important collections in the Italian government archives (including the Medici archives); and the *Guida storica e bibliografica degli archivi e delle biblioteche d'Italia.*[70] Archival materials for territories which came under Prussian rule can be found in *Publikationen aus den Königlichen Preussischen Staatsarchiven, veranlasst und unterstützt durch die konigliche Archivverwaltung.*[71]

The Russians have *Gosudarstvennye archivy Seiuza SSR,* a general guide to government archives of the federal and regional governments.[72] The following information is given for each entry: name, address, brief historical note, a description of the kind and extent of the documentary material, dates of the material, and the

---

an alphabetical index of names, with references under each name to the report or reports in which some letter or document connected with the person is listed.

[66] Great Britain, Historical Manuscripts Commission, *A Guide to the Reports of the Royal Commission on Historic Manuscripts, 1911–1957* (London, H. M. Stationery Office, 1966–). Pt. 2, *An Index of Persons,* ed. by A. C. S. Hall, 3 vols., is a composite index of all persons mentioned in the indexes to these *Reports.* The Historical Manuscripts Commission has also published guides dealing with certain periods of English history, such as the *Guide to Sources of English History from 1603 to 1660 in Reports of the Royal Commission on Historical Manuscripts,* which was published in 1952. A second edition by Eleanor Stuart Upton was published by the Scarecrow Press in 1964.

[67] 3 pts. in 1 vol. (Paris, A. Picard, 1891–93).

[68] 2d ed. (Rome, 1954).

[69] Rome, Minister of the Interior (Rome, 1950–). *Annales institutorum, biblioteca* (Rome, 1932–), is a collection of guides to some of the important government archives at Rome, Parma, and Venice. Title varies.

[70] Luigi Schiaparelli et al., eds., 6 vols. (Rome, La Libreria dello Stato, 1932–40).

[71] 94 vols. (Leipzig, S. Hirzel, 1878–1938).

[72] G. A. Belova et al., eds., *Gosudarstvennye arkhivy Soiuza SSR: Kratkii spravochnik* (Moscow, 1956).

names of some of the people whose papers are included. The Russians also have a bibliographical index to archival publications and to material about archives: *Katalog arkhivovedcheskoi literatury i sbornikov documentov.*[73] It combines and continues chronologically the *Katalog arkhivovedcheskoi literatury*[74] and *Katalog sbornikov dokumentov, izdannykh arkhivnymi uchrexhdeniiami SSR.*[75]

The *Guiás de archivos y bibliotecas* is a series on the collections at the Biblioteca Nacional, the Real Academia de la Historia, and other big Madrid collections, as well as those in Barcelona.[76] In addition to the National Archives' *Guide to Materials on Latin America in the National Archives*[77] and the *Guiás de archivos y bibliotecas*, the first volume, *Período colonial español*, of Linon Gomez Canedo's *Los archivos de la historia de America*[78] presents historical and descriptive notes on the pertinent archives in both Spain and Spanish America, with a subject index.

ORAL HISTORY

Unfortunately, persons who have been active in or observers of the life of their times do not often leave memoirs. And today the telephone, automobile, and airplane are rendering obsolete the confidential letter. These facts make oral history an increasingly

---

[73] Union of Soviet Socialist Republics, Chief Administrative Archives, 1960–63, comp. by S. V. Nefedova et al., ed. by I. N. Firsova (Moscow, 1964).

[74] Union of Soviet Socialist Republics, Chief Administrative Archives, 1917–59, ed. by A. I. Loginovoi et al. (Moscow, 1961).

[75] Union of Soviet Socialist Republics, Chief Administrative Archives, 1917–60, ed. by A. I. Loginovoi et al. (Moscow, 1961).

[76] Two volumes in this series are *Guiá de las bibliotecas de Madrid* (Madrid, Dirección General de Archivos y Bibliotecas, 1953) and *Las bibliotecas de Barcelona y su provincia* (Madrid, Dirección General de Archivos y Biblioteca, 1952).

[77] For full bibliographic information, see note 31.

[78] Pan American Institute of Geography and History, Commission on History, Publication 87 (Mexico, Inst. Panamericano de Geografia e Historial, 1961–).

valuable resource for the historian. The best oral history memoirs are both as detailed and as intimate as private correspondence, and they are frequently far more reflective. Both the interviewer and the subject verify the finished transcript.[79]

Allan Nevins expressed the idea behind the oral history programs when he wrote that there should be "some organization which [makes] a systematic attempt to obtain from the lips and papers of living Americans who have led significant lives a fuller record of their participation in the political, economic and cultural life of the last sixty years."[80] He began the oral history program at Columbia University with an interview with George McAvery on May 18, 1948. Other universities, historical societies, corporations, museums, unions, and professional associations have taken up oral history projects.

The Oral History Collection of Columbia University is a catalog of what is available in this collection.[81] Sections of the catalog are arranged alphabetically. They include a biographical section, which is the main section; a list of special projects; a list of lectures, seminars, and forums; and an index of persons represented. For each entry in the main section the following information is given: the full name and dates, a terse description, the date of the concluding interview, and information as to whether the memoirs are "open"—available to be read, or "closed"—restricted or under seal. Columbia University adds ten to twenty thousand pages of new material to the collection annually; these additions are to be listed in the annual report.

The Oral History Project of the Center for Western North American Studies, at the University of Nevada, was established in January, 1965. Because very few scholarly works have been written on Nevada in the last twenty-five years, an oral history program

---

[79] Columbia University, Oral History Research Office, *Oral History Collection of Columbia University* (New York, Oral History Research Office, 1964), 9.

[80] *The Gateway to History* (New York, D. C. Heath and Co., 1938), iv.

[81] *Oral History Collection of Columbia University*, 10, 102–103.

was considered vital to research in the state's past. The primary emphasis has been to collect data on Nevada and its adjacent areas. Mining, ranching, religion, conservation and reclamation, medicine, politics, economics, education, construction, Indian activities, music and culture, funeral practices, photography, and amateur radio all figure in the first memoirs. Future interviews have been planned to cover Nevada business and industry, contemporary political problems, and ethnic minorities. A bibliography to this oral history project is available.[82]

DIARIES

Diaries are most helpful in studying the popular ideas, fashions, tastes, and manners of a period. All kinds of people kept diaries, and the diaries reflect what their writers thought and felt about events. Like other primary sources, diaries must be used with care. Because they may be limited by inadequate perspective or contain special bias, the student should use external and internal criticism in his evaluation of diaries as evidence.

In *American Diaries: An Annotated Bibliography of American Diaries Prior to the Year 1861*, William Matthews defines a diary as a personal record of what interested the diarist, usually kept day by day, with each day's record being self-contained and written soon after the events occurred. The writing style is usually free from organized exposition.[83] Diaries are apt to be published in varying forms and in many places. They may appear as separate books; in periodicals; in family histories; in biographies; in town, county, or state histories; and in small private collections.

There were no satisfactory guides or indexes to diaries available until William Matthews published his two guides: one to American

[82] Mary Ellen Glass, *The Oral History Project of the Center for Western North American Studies: A Bibliography* (Reno, Nev., Desert Research Institute, 1966).

[83] *American Diaries: An Annotated Bibliography of American Diaries Prior to the Year 1861* (Berkeley, Calif., University of California Press, 1945).

diaries and one to British diaries. In his *American Diaries*[84] Matthews omits manuscript diaries and restricts his listings to diaries which have been published completely or in substantial portions. He also limits the diaries to those written in or translated into English. The diaries are arranged chronologically according to the date of the first entry; those beginning in the same year are arranged alphabetically. For each diary there are descriptive notes; a note on content, such as the chief subjects, places, and persons dealt with; biographical information about the diarist, if readily available; and a note of evaluation in the terms of the general reader. If there is no evaluation, the usual implication is that the diary is dull or conventional. When diaries have been published more than once, the publications are arranged chronologically, with the last being the best and most reliable. When texts are complicated, the best text is listed first. There is an index to names, but there is no index to events.

Matthews' *British Diaries*[85] lists the diaries of a cross section of Englishmen, Scotsmen, Welshmen, and Irish from the sixteenth century until just before World War II. Matthews tried to include manuscript diaries in this volume. He excluded diaries relating to the British dominions and colonies and British diaries relating to Asia, Africa, and Latin America because he expected to include them in a book on Commonwealth diaries and autobiographies. As in the volume on American diaries, the diaries are arranged chronologically by year according to the date of the first entry and alphabetically within the year. The following information is given for each entry: dates; biographical details of the diarist, if available; a contents note indicating the chief subjects, places, and persons dealt with; and an evaluation. Locations are given for unpublished diaries. There is no subject index, but there is an index

[84] For full bibliographic information, see note 83.

[85] *British Diaries: An Annotated Bibliography of British Diaries Written Between 1442 and 1942* (Berkeley, Calif., University of California Press, 1950).

of names and an index of diaries extending over more than ten years.

QUOTATIONS AND SPEECHES

"Delenda est Carthago," "The New Frontier," "That's one small step for a man—one giant leap for mankind." Whether the student is hunting a quotation on a subject, such as Carthage or John F. Kennedy liberalism, or Neil A. Armstrong's words when he stepped on the moon, he will find books of quotations useful.

Bartlett's *Familiar Quotations* is the standard collection.[86] It lists famous sayings or writings of English and American authors with special sections for anonymous and Biblical quotations and for quotations from two thousand years before Christ. All thirteen of the editions of *Familiar Quotations* in its hundred years of existence are arranged chronologically by author. Authors are identified by their dates. There are two indexes: an alphabetical list by author in the front and an excellent index by word in the back. For each quotation the exact reference (title and page or line) is given. The centennial edition has been completely revised with the omission of many previous quotations and the addition of many new ones; so earlier editions must be checked for older authors.

There are other older standard books of quotations. Burton E. Stevenson's *Home Book of Quotations*[87] is arranged by subject with an index of authors and an index and concordance of words. It is fairly up to date and comprehensive; it includes more than fifty thousand extracts from authors of all ages and countries.

The *Oxford Dictionary of Quotations*[88] is arranged alphabeti-

[86] John Bartlett, *Familiar Quotations: A Collection of Passages, Phrases, and Proverbs Traced to Their Sources in Ancient and Modern Literature,* 13th and Centennial rev. ed. (Boston, Little, Brown and Co., 1955). A revised and enlarged 14th edition, edited by Emily Morrison Beck, was published by Little, Brown and Co. in October, 1968. The index was prepared with the aid of a computer.

[87] *Home Book of Quotations, Classical and Modern,* 9th ed. (New York, Dodd, Mead & Co. Inc., 1964).

[88] 2d ed. (London, Oxford University Press, 1953).

cally by authors writing in English. Quotations have been selected on the basis of familiarity. Separate sections include quotations from the *Book of Common Prayer*; the Bible; anonymous English literature, such as ballads and nursery rhymes; quotations from *Punch*; and foreign quotations. It excludes proverbs, which are indexed in William George Smith's *Oxford Dictionary of English Proverbs.*[89]

The noted journalist H. L. Mencken, author of *American Language,*[90] based his *New Dictionary of Quotations*[91] on a collection of quotations he started in 1918 for his own use. The book differs from the other books of quotations in that it is arranged by rubric and planned on strictly historical principles; that is, Mencken lists the first utterer of a saying or an idea and, except where the saying has undergone significant changes, disregards those who merely echoed it. He has omitted platitudes and cited only authors who had something to say; he includes proverbs and lesser-known Bible quotations. The author and title are given for each quotation. Unfortunately for the user, there is no index.

Also available are books of quotations which are devoted to specific sources or authors. For example, two books which deal exclusively with biblical quotations are Burton E. Stevenson's *The Home Book of Bible Quotations*[92] and Alexander Cruden's *Complete Concordance to the Old and New Testament.*[93] Examples of books dealing with the quotations from a single author are John Bartlett's *New and Complete Concordance to Words, Phrases, and Passages in the Dramatic Works of Shakespeare,*[94] Burton E.

---

[89] 2d rev. ed. by Sir Paul Harvey (Oxford, Clarendon Press, 1948).

[90] *The American Language: An Inquiry into the Development of English in the United States*, 4th corr., enl., and rewritten ed. (New York, A. A. Knopf, 1936). *Supplements* 1–2 (1945–48).

[91] *A New Dictionary of Quotations on Historical Principles from Ancient and Modern Sources* (New York, Alfred A. Knopf, 1943).

[92] (New York, Harper & Brothers, 1949).

[93] *Complete Concordance to the Old and New Testament . . . with . . . a Concordance to the Apocrypha*, 3 vols. (London, F. Warne and Co., 1769). Often reprinted.

[94] *New and Complete Concordance or Verbal Index to Words, Phrases,*

Stevenson's *Home Book of Shakespeare Quotations*,[95] and Lucile Kelling and Albert Suskin's *Index verborum Juvenalis*.[96]

Contemporary prose quotations are extremely difficult to find. An excellent aid is Simpson's *Contemporary Quotations*.[97] It is a collection of quotations since 1950. The author searched newspapers, magazines, speeches, and radio and television interviews for his quotations and organized them under thirty-nine broad headings, such as "The Nation," "The World," and "Man." There are subject and source indexes. *Contemporary Quotations* is an extension of Simpson's earlier publication, *Best Quotes of '54, '55, and '56*.[98]

Presidents of the United States are represented in the general quotation books, in books devoted to a particular president, and in collections devoted to presidents only. Caroline Harnsberger's *Treasury of Presidential Quotations*[99] is quite broad in scope, but its coverage is spread too thin. A table of succession of presidents, an index by author, and a subject-concept index help the student to find his way among the presidential greats.

Ralph J. Shoemaker started a series to index the presidents' words: *The Presidents' Words: An Index*.[100] He planned to publish

and Passages in the Dramatic Works of Shakespeare with a Supplementary Concordance to the Poems (London, Macmillan & Co., 1894).

[95] *Home Book of Shakespeare Quotations, Being also a Concordance and a Glossary of the Unique Words and Phrases in the Plays and Poems* (New York, C. Scribner's Sons, 1937).

[96] (Chapel Hill, N.C., University of North Carolina Press, 1951).

[97] James B. Simpson (New York, Crowell, 1964).

[98] (New York, Thomas Y. Crowell Co., 1957).

[99] (Chicago, Follett Publishing Co., 1964). Arthur Benson Tourtellot's *The Presidents on the Presidency* (Garden City, N.Y., Doubleday & Co., Inc., 1964) is a better and perhaps more significant compilation limited to presidents' views of the presidency.

[100] *The Presidents' Words: An Index* (Louisville, Ky., published by Elsie De Graff Shoemaker and Ralph J. Shoemaker, 1954–). Vol. 1, Eisenhower, June, 1952–May, 1954 (1954); vol. 2, Eisenhower, June, 1954–December, 1955 (1956); vol. 3, Eisenhower, 1956 (1957); vol. 4, Eisenhower, 1957 (1958); vol. 5, Eisenhower, 1958 (1959); vol. 6, Eisenhower, 1959 (1960); vol. 7, Eisenhower, 1960 through January 20, 1961, with an Addenda, Kennedy Campaign, 1960 (1961).

a new volume every two years. The index includes speeches, messages to Congress, press conferences, executive orders, letters, and statements. The index lists subjects and persons spoken about, phrases, quotations, expressions, and words used and gives the date and place where the words were spoken or written.

Beginning in August of 1965, the *Weekly Compilation of Presidential Documents*[101] contains addresses and remarks of the president, as well as other documents. This is an excellent source of presidential quotations.

Speeches are certainly primary sources of history. There is one index to speeches of the past and several collections of speeches of the day. Roberta Sutton has compiled *Speech Index*,[102] an index to 259 collections of world-famous speeches, including famous speeches of history. The entries for author, subject, type of speech, and cross references are all in one alphabet. An appendix contains a selected list of titles, which will be of help in locating speeches when the author is not known. The sources of a speech are indicated by symbols.

There are two sources of contemporary speeches with which the student should be familiar. One of these sources, *Representative American Speeches*,[103] is a collection of recent speeches on a variety of subjects, with biographical information on the speakers and introductions to the addresses. The second source is *Vital Speeches of the Day*, which prints in full the important speeches of the men and women of recognized authority in their fields.[104] The

[101] U.S., President, *Weekly Compilation of Presidential Documents* (Washington, D.C., National Archives and Records Service, 1965–). Weekly.

[102] Roberta Briggs Sutton, *Speech Index: An Index to 259 Collections of World Famous Orations and Speeches for Various Occasions*, 4th rev. and enl. ed. (New York, Scarecrow Press, 1966).

[103] Lester Thonssen, ed. (New York, H. W. Wilson Co., 1938–). *Representative American Speeches* is issued each year as one volume of The Reference Shelf series of H. W. Wilson Company.

[104] October 8, 1934– (New York, City News Publishing Co., 1934–). Monthly. *25 Year Index*, October 8, 1934–October 1, 1959 (Pelham, New York, City News Publishing Co., 1963).

publishers ask that men and women of acknowledged leadership forward copies of their speeches promptly to the editors for possible publication.

Just as there are special compilations of presidential quotations, there are special compilations of presidential messages, speeches, and papers of the presidents. James D. Richardson's *A Compilation of the Messages and Papers of the Presidents*[105] is a very well known set. It contains most of the presidential papers through Grover Cleveland's second administration. The index volume contains many of the papers of earlier presidents that were omitted in their regular place and the papers of William McKinley relating to the Spanish-American War. Successive editions have brought the compilation through the Coolidge administration.

Collections of the public papers of the presidents from Hoover to Johnson have been published in separate presidential series. The state papers of Herbert Hoover[106] and Franklin D. Roosevelt[107] have been published commercially. Beginning with Harry S. Truman, the *Public Papers of the Presidents of the United States* are being published by the government.[108]

A weekly service that publishes material similar to that in the

[105] James D. Richardson, *Compilation of the Messages and Papers of the Presidents, 1789–1897*, 53 Cong., 2 sess., *House Misc. Doc. 210*, pt. 1010. Laurence F. Schmeckebier and Roy B. Eastin give the various editions and publishers in *Government Publications and Their Use*, rev. ed. (Washington, D.C., Brookings Institution, 1961), 308–18.

[106] Herbert Hoover, *State Papers*, ed. by W. S. Myers, 2 vols. (Garden City, N.Y., Doubleday, Doran & Co., 1934).

[107] Franklin D. Roosevelt, *The Public Papers and Addresses of Franklin D. Roosevelt*, with a special introduction and explanatory notes by President Roosevelt, comp. by Samuel I. Rosenman, 13 vols. (New York, Random House, 1938–50). Macmillan Co. published volumes 6–9 and Harper and Brothers, volumes 10–13.

[108] U.S., President, *Public Papers of the Presidents of the United States, Containing the Public Messages, Speeches, and Statements of the Presidents* (Washington, D.C., published by the Office of the Federal Register, National Archives and Record Service, General Services Administration, 1958–). Annual. Harry S. Truman, 1945–48, 4 vols. (1961–64); Dwight D. Eisenhower, 1953–61, 8 vols. (1958–61); John F. Kennedy, 1961–63, 4 vols. (1962–64).

annual *Public Papers of the Presidents* is the *Weekly Compilation of Presidential Documents*.[109] Published every Monday, it contains addresses and remarks by the president, messages to Congress, appointments, nominations, letters, memorandums, and transcripts of news conferences. An "Index of Contents" is on the first page of each issue, and a cumulative index appears at the end for each quarter. It also includes lists of laws approved by the president, nominations submitted to the Senate, and a checklist of White House news releases not included in the compilation.

The State of the Union Messages of the Presidents is a new collection of the 178 State of the Union messages.[110] In his preface, Fred L. Israel quotes Charles A. Beard on the importance of the president's message:

The President's message is ordinarily printed in full in nearly every metropolitan daily, and is the subject of general editorial comment throughout the length and breadth of the land. It stirs the country; it often affects Congressional elections; and it may establish grand policy.[111]

This collection is the first to compile and index the full texts of the State of the Union messages in one place.

The inaugural addresses of the presidents from George Washington through Lyndon B. Johnson also have been collected in one compilation by the government.[112]

A list showing the depositories of the unpublished papers of the presidents appeared in the *Congressional Record* of July 12, 1939, during the debate on Senate Joint Resolution 118, which provided for the establishment and maintenance of the Franklin D. Roose-

[109] For full bibliographic information, see note 101.

[110] Fred L. Israel, ed., *The State of the Union Messages of the Presidents*, introduction by Arthur M. Schlesinger, Jr., 3 vols. (New York, Chelsea House, 1966).

[111] *Ibid.*, vol. 1, preface.

[112] *Inaugural Addresses of the Presidents of the United States from George Washington, 1789, to Lyndon Baines Johnson, 1965*, 89 Cong., 1 sess., *House Doc. 51* (Washington, D.C., Government Printing Office, 1965).

velt Library.[113] Since 1939, three presidential libraries have been established under the sponsorship of the federal government. The Harry S. Truman Library at Independence, Missouri and the Dwight D. Eisenhower Library at Abilene, Kansas were established under the Act of 1955, called the Presidential Libraries Act. The Hoover Foundation has announced that a library museum to house the papers, books, and documents of Herbert Hoover will be built at West Branch, Iowa. The documents now housed at the Hoover Library at Stanford will be moved there.[114] The John F. Kennedy Library, where his papers and the papers of Kennedy administration members will be deposited, is being built on the site donated by Harvard at Cambridge, Massachusetts.[115] Lyndon Baines Johnson has preserved the papers of his public career since 1937, and they are being deposited in the Lyndon Baines Johnson Presidential Library at Austin, on the University of Texas campus.[116] The Richard Nixon Foundation is going to file its articles of incorporation in California and will provide for the construction of a Richard Nixon library and museum.[117]

THESES AND DISSERTATIONS

Master's theses and doctoral dissertations are not primary sources. They represent original research on specific topics and are, for the most part, based on primary materials.

Lists of master's theses and doctoral dissertations are often quite important for historical research. The student hunting a subject for his thesis or dissertation can find out what topics have already been covered. Similarly, the student hunting information on his subject can find valuable, and often the only, information available, as

[113] U.S., Congress, *Congressional Record*, 76 Cong., 1 sess., 1939, 84, pt. 8:8987.

[114] Schmeckebier and Eastin, *Government Publications and Their Use*, 324–25.

[115] *Facts on File*, 23 (December 5–11, 1963), 434 A1.

[116] *Weekly Compilation of Presidential Documents*, August 13, 1965, 64–65.

[117] *Ibid.*, May 19, 1969, 683.

well as extensive bibliographic information in completed theses and dissertations. Once the student working on his thesis or dissertation and the research worker have found the titles of the theses and dissertations and at what institution they were written, they can arrange to borrow copies through interlibrary loan or to purchase microfilm or xerox copies if they cannot be borrowed.

With the increase in the number of graduate students, there is a growing need to identify unpublished master's theses or to find out whether any master's thesis has been written on a particular subject. Research workers also often want to look at master's theses as well as doctoral dissertations in order to find any original contributions that they might use in their research projects. There are no comprehensive lists of master's theses. There are, however, lists of master's theses in specific fields and at specific colleges or universities. Thomas R. Palfrey and Henry E. Coleman, *Guide to Bibliographies of Theses: United States and Canada* is a pioneer guide to lists of master's theses and doctor's dissertations.[118] It includes general lists of theses and dissertations in periodicals, lists in special fields, which included history, and lists by institution.

Dorothy M. Black's *Guide to Lists of Master's Theses*[119] incorporates the Palfrey and Coleman references where applicable; thus it includes all the lists of master's theses written in colleges and universities in the United States and Canada through 1964. The volume has four parts: part 1, sources of lists; part 2, general lists; part 3, lists of master's theses in special fields; and part 4, lists of master's theses at specific institutions. The student also should search under more specific topics. For example, if he wanted to find theses on Oregon history, he would find a reference under the subject heading, Oregon, to a list in the *Oregon Historical Quarterly*. He would also find a cross reference to Northwest, Pacific; under that subject heading, he would find Erick Bromberg's "A Bibliography of Theses and Dissertations Concerning the Pacific Northwest and Alaska" and its supplements in the *Pacific North-*

[118] (Chicago, American Library Association, 1940).
[119] (Chicago, American Library Association, 1965).

west Quarterly. If the student were looking to see whether a particular university issued lists of its theses, he would look in the fourth part under the name of the institution.

Master's Abstracts: Abstracts of Selected Master's Theses on Microfilm[120] began in 1962. It consisted of published abstracts of a selected list of master's theses from various universities that are available on microfilm. The number of abstracts in each issue has been limited, varying from six to sixty-four. The first number of the first volume listed master's theses available on microfilm from University Microfilms. The abstracts are listed in a classified arrangement, and there is no index.

The bibliographical control of doctoral dissertations is much better than it is for theses. There are various fairly comprehensive lists. In the United States there are lists of doctoral dissertations for the years from 1912 to the present. The first title, the *List of American Doctoral Dissertations,*[121] runs from 1912 through 1938 and includes: a list arranged alphabetically by author, a list arranged under the broad subject classes, an index of subjects, and a list arranged by institutions of doctoral dissertations that had been printed during the year. It also indicates the publication in which the thesis was first printed. The second title, *Doctoral Dissertations: Accepted by American Universities,* runs from 1933/34 through 1954/55.[122] This list is arranged first by subject and then by university; it has alphabetical author and subject indexes; and it gives author, title, and publication information. The *Index to American Doctoral Dissertations* took up the listing in 1955/56.[123] This list includes all dissertations, even those on microfilm, for

[120] (Ann Arbor, Mich., University Microfilms, 1962–). Quarterly.

[121] U.S., Library of Congress, Catalog Division, *List of American Doctoral Dissertations Printed in 1912–1938,* 26 vols. (Washington, D.C., Government Printing Office, 1913–40).

[122] Compiled for the Association of Research Libraries, 22 nos. (New York, H. W. Wilson Co., 1934–56).

[123] Compiled for the Association of Research Libraries (Ann Arbor, Mich., University Microfilms, 1957–). Annual. It is number 13, beginning with volume 16 of *Dissertation Abstracts.*

which doctoral degrees were granted in the United States and Canada during the academic year. It is arranged by subject, and it has an author index.

Dissertation Abstracts[124] is a compilation of abstracts of doctoral dissertations that have been microfilmed. It is useful for the dissertations it abstracts and for its complete list of all dissertations written in the United States. The student should know that this compilation does not abstract all dissertations written in the United States. A list of the universities that submit their dissertations for microfilming is given in the front of each issue; in 1968, about two hundred institutions were submitting dissertations. The abstracts are arranged alphabetically by subject and then by university. The listing for each abstract includes title, order number, author's name, the university, date, name of the supervisor, the abstract, the prices of a microfilm copy and a xerox copy, and the number of pages. There are author and subject indexes in each issue and a cumulated author and subject index to the year.

Dissertation Abstracts offers DATRIX ("Direct Access to Reference Information; a Xerox Service"), the new computer-based information development service to doctoral degree candidates and researchers in all fields. Since 1938, University Microfilms has been filming many, though not all, of the dissertations written by doctoral candidates in North America. To these 126,000 dissertations they are adding more than 18,000 annually from nearly two hundred institutions. DATRIX's base encompasses the majority of all dissertations published since 1938 to the current month. Plans call for the expansion of the data base to include all the American and Canadian dissertations published since 1851. The DATRIX computer's memory receives a constant input of

[124] *Dissertation Abstracts: Abstracts of Dissertations and Monographs Available in Microform* (Ann Arbor, Mich., University Microfilms, 1952–). Monthly. Published under the title, *Microfilm Abstracts*, 1935–51. Beginning with volume 27 (July, 1966), it appeared in two sections: A, Humanities and the Social Sciences; B, Science and Engineering. Number 13 lists dissertations submitted at all American universities, including some that are not abstracted in *Dissertation Abstracts*.

key words derived from the titles, the author's selected subject headings, and other descriptive data. Dissertations in the data base are classified into three broad areas: Chemistry/Life Sciences, Engineering/Physical Sciences, and Humanities/Social Sciences. Key word lists covering each major area provide the foundations from which the searcher can formulate his questions for the computer. The searcher looks at the key word list that fits the scope of his inquiry (Humanities/Social Sciences for history). Each key word in the lists is noted with an "occurrence number" to indicate how many dissertations are represented in the computer's memory by that word. By making a count of these "occurrence numbers," the searcher can estimate how many references the computer will turn up of interest to him.

The student can get the forms and key word lists from University Microfilms, Ann Arbor, Michigan, if his library does not have them; he fills out the form and returns it to University Microfilms, which are supposed to send the bibliography within a few working days. Each reference in the bibliography includes the complete title of the dissertation, the author's name, the university at which the dissertation was accepted, the date of publication, the page and volume of *Dissertation Abstracts* where the dissertation is listed, and the price of a microfilm or xerographic copy. The basic fee for DATRIX inquiry is five dollars, which includes the first ten or less references in the bibliography. Additional references are ten cents each.

The American Historical Association puts out the very useful *List of Doctoral Dissertations in History*.[125] Originally, it was a list of doctoral dissertations in progress. Since 1958, it has included dissertations completed, but does not indicate which are in progress and which are completed. The list is arranged by field of history and has author and university indexes.

[125] *List of Doctoral Dissertations in History Now in Progress or Completed at Universities in the United States*, 1909– (Washington, D.C., Carnegie Institution, 1909–39; New York, Macmillan Co., 1940–41; Washington, D.C., Government Printing Office, 1943; Washington, D.C., American Historical Association, 1947–). Annual; triennial (irregular).

Dissertations in History[126] is invaluable for the history student. Instead of having to check columns and columns in volumes and volumes, the history student can now use this compilation. It includes doctoral dissertations which have been written under formally organized departments of history and for which the degree of doctor of philosophy has been conferred. This useful compilation indicates what historians have been doing and what areas are overworked. It suggests innumerable subjects which have been neglected, and, by providing graduate students and their advisers with a useful finding aid, it should keep duplication of subjects at a minimum. The dissertations are arranged alphabetically by the author's name. The entry gives the title, the university, and the date. A subject index helps the student find the dissertations in the area in which he is interested. A numerical summary of United States and Canadian doctoral degrees in history is given by institution and by year after the preface.

There are other guides to dissertations in special fields, such as Jesse Dossick's *Doctoral Research on Russia and the Soviet Union.*[127] Carl White lists these guides and guides to current research projects being carried on.[128]

Countries other than the United States also have lists of dissertations. For Great Britain there is the *Index to Theses Accepted for Higher Degrees in the Universities of Great Britain and Ireland.*[129] For France the official list is the *Catalogue des thèses de doctorat soutenues devant les universités françaises.*[130] And for Germany there is *Jahresverzeichnis der deutschen Hochschulschriften.*[131]

[126] Warren F. Kuehl, *Dissertations in History: An Index to Dissertations Completed in History Departments of United States and Canadian Universities, 1873–1960* (Lexington, Ky., University of Kentucky Press, 1965), 239.

[127] Jesse J. Dossick (New York, New York University Press, 1960).

[128] *Sources of Information in the Social Sciences,* 59–62.

[129] 1950/51– (London, ASLIB, 1953–). Annual.

[130] 1884/85– (Paris, 1885–). Annual. Published by the Minister de l'Instruction Publique from 1884/85 to 1930/31. Title varies.

[131] 1885– (Leipzig, Buch-und Bibliothekswesen, 1887–).

10

Legal Sources

Legal records are basic sources for the historian as well as for the political scientist. Statute law includes constitutions, government regulations, executive orders, and rules of court. Case law consists primarily of judicial decisions. The source materials for diplomatic history include treaties, communiques, the enactments of international bodies that affect national policy, and judicial opinions in international courts. The major emphasis in this chapter will be on legal sources relating to the United States.

CONSTITUTIONS

There are many places where the text of the United States Constitution can be found, but for the serious student of American history more than the text is necessary. The student must understand the Constitution in terms of its growth, development, and alteration through judicial interpretation. Similarly, it is important to understand what the Constitution means today. Therefore, the student needs a current and precise compendium of the interpretations of the Constitution by the Supreme Court.

The Constitution of the United States of America—Analysis and Interpretation fills these needs.[1] Compiled for the use of Con-

---

[1] U.S., Constitution, *The Constitution of the United States of America —Analysis and Interpretation: Annotations of Cases Decided by the Supreme Court of the United States to June 22, 1964*, prepared by the

gress, it is detailed and authoritative. The 1964 edition is the sixth edition; the volume first appeared in 1913. Following a complete text of the Constitution and its amendments, a detailed discussion is given of the meaning of each article and section, with the citation of cases and legal decisions leading to the present interpretation. The subject index and table of cases are most helpful.

State constitutions may be found in the various state manuals and collections. Columbia University has compiled *Constitutions of the United States, National and State*,[2] a collection of state constitutions, and *Index Digest of State Constitutions*,[3] a digest of state constitutions. Both are useful. Both were part of a broad program of state constitutional studies jointly developed some years ago by the Brookings Institution, the National Municipal League, and the Legislative Drafting Fund. The aim of *Constitutions of the United States* is to make available in one place the complete, current texts of the constitutions of the states and of the United States. It is arranged alphabetically by state, with the United States Constitution placed first. The *Index Digest*, a companion volume, is a major aid to the use of this set because it supplies a comprehensive subject index to and comparative analysis of the state constitution texts.

Amos Peaslee's *Constitutions of Nations*[4] discusses the fundamental principles of government of various countries. The first

---

Legislative Reference Service, Library of Congress, Norman J. Small, ed., 88 Cong., 1 sess., *Sen. Doc. 39* (Washington, D.C., Government Printing Office, 1964).

[2] Columbia University, Legislative Drafting Research Fund, 3 vols. (Dobbs Ferry, New York, Oceana Publications, 1962–). Loose-leaf. Often there are special studies for states, for example, Eleanore Bushnell's *The Nevada Constitution: Origin and Growth*, Nevada Studies in History and Political Science, no. 8, rev. ed. (Reno, Nevada, University of Nevada Press, 1968).

[3] Columbia University, Legislative Drafting Research Fund, 2d ed. (New York, n.p., 1959). *Supplement*, September 1, 1958 to December 31, 1960.

[4] Amos J. Peaslee, 3d rev. ed., prepared by Dorothy Peaslee Xydis, 4 vols. (The Hague, Nijhoff, 1965–).

edition appeared in 1950. In the six years before the second edition, major changes occurred in the text or status of the constitutions of thirty-five of the eighty-nine nations covered, and five new countries became generally recognized sovereign nations. The first two editions are arranged alphabetically by country. The third edition is being published in separate volumes by continents. Three volumes have been published: volume 1, Africa; volume 2, in two parts, Asia, Australia, and Oceania; and volume 3, in two parts, Europe. For each nation there is the complete text of the latest constitutions and any amendments. Peaslee's *Constitutions of Nations* was the first collection of national constitutions to be published in English, and it is the most up-to-date compilation available.

The *Constitutions of the Communist Party States* is a collection of the constitutions and amendments of fourteen Communist states ruled by the Communist Party.[5] It does not include the constitutions of these states before they became Communist. The editor used the official English translations of all the documents when they were available and the most authoritative English translations when the official translations were not available. English translations of the 1924 Mongolian constitution and the 1952 Rumanian constitution were made for the first time for this volume.

LAWS AND COURTS

Laws and court decisions are important primary source materials for the historian. For the student unfamiliar with legal research methods and legal terminology, two volumes are particularly helpful: Price and Bitner, *Effective Legal Research*[6] and Harry Campbell Black, *Black's Law Dictionary.*[7]

[5] Jan F. Triska, ed., Hoover Institution Publications no. 70 (Stanford, Calif., Hoover Institution on War, Revolution, and Peace, 1968).

[6] Miles O. Price and Harry Bitner, *Effective Legal Research: A Practical Manual of Law Books and Their Use* (1953; student rev. ed., Boston, Little, Brown and Co., 1962).

[7] *Black's Law Dictionary: Definitions of the Terms and Phrases of*

210

United States

The published laws of the United States fall into three categories: series embracing all the laws printed in chronological order; codifications of all the permanent and general laws in force; and compilations dealing with laws on particular services or subjects. These groups contain only the laws since the adoption of the Constitution; they do not include the ordinances enacted by the Continental Congress during the Confederation period. The series containing all the federal laws enacted since the adoption of the Constitution are important for the historian since codifications give only the laws in force at the time of the codifications and do not tell about the development of the legislation, about appropriations, about repealed or temporary measures, or about acts for the particular benefit of individuals.[8]

The two stages in the publication of the laws are: (1) slip laws and (2) the *Statutes at Large*. Each law, as soon as it is enacted, is published separately in a slip-law edition. Slip laws are divided into two series: public acts and private acts, each of which is numbered separately. A marginal note gives the citation to the volume and page in the *Statutes at Large* in which the act will appear.[9] The slip laws, which are listed in the *Monthly Catalog* under Congress by their number, are superseded by the *Statutes at Large*.

The *Session Laws* were discontinued with the issue for the second session of the Seventy-fourth Congress (1936). They always had been superseded by the *Statutes at Large*. Up to 1936 the laws were assembled in unbound volumes, known as the *Session Laws* or *Pamphlet Laws*, at the end of each session of Congress. In their later years, the *Session Laws* were published in two parts: part 1 contained the public acts and resolutions; part 2, the

---

American and English Jurisprudence, Ancient and Modern, by the publishers' editorial staff, 4th ed. (St. Paul, Minn., West Publishing Co., 1951).

[8] Laurence F. Schmeckebier and Roy B. Eastin, *Government Publications and Their Use*, rev. ed. (Washington, D.C., Brookings Institution, 1961), 190–92.

[9] *Ibid.*, 192–94.

private acts and resolutions, concurrent resolutions, treaties, proclamations, and since 1930, executive agreements.[10]

The laws are published in their final form in the *Statutes at Large.*[11] Beginning with volume 52 (1938), each volume contains the laws enacted during a calendar year. After volume 64 (1950), treaties and international agreements other than treaties were dropped from the *Statutes at Large* and continued in a new series called *United States Treaties and Other International Agreements,* published by the State Department. The contents of the *Statutes at Large* vary, but beginning with volume 65 (1961), each volume contains public laws, private laws, concurrent resolutions, and proclamations. The arrangement under each division is chronological by the date of the passage of the act. A subject index and a personal-name index is in each volume.[12]

There are indexes to the *Statutes at Large.* The *Index* volume for 1789–1874, compiled by Middleton G. Beaman and A. K. McNamara, indexes volumes 1–17 of the *Statutes at Large,* that is, the legislation prior to the enactment of the *Revised Statutes.* The volume for 1874–1931, prepared by Walter H. McClenon and Wilfred C. Gilbert, indexes the *Revised Statutes* of 1874 and the *Statutes at Large,* volumes 18–46. The *Index* for 1874–1931 is a revision of the George W. Scott and Middleton G. Beaman *Index Analysis of the Federal Statutes, 1874–1907* and indexes all fed-

---

[10] *Ibid.,* 194–95.

[11] U.S., Laws, Statutes, *United States Statutes at Large Containing the Laws and Concurrent Resolutions Enacted . . . and Reorganization Plans and Proclamations,* 1789–1873; 1873– (Boston, Little, Brown and Co., 1845–73; Washington, D.C., Government Printing Office, 1875–). Title varies slightly. The present series of *Statutes at Large* starts with volume 18 (1873–75). It was preceded by the *Laws of the United States*: Folwell edition for the first thirteen congresses, 1789–1813; Bioren and Duane edition for the first twenty-eight congresses, 1789–1845; the Little, Brown edition, called *Statutes at Large,* covering the first forty-two congresses, 1789–1873 and ending with volume 17. The federal government took over the series with volume 18.

[12] Schmeckebier and Eastin, *Government Publications and Their Use,* 195–200.

eral legislation of a public, general, and permanent nature through 1931.[13]

The first and only real codification of the laws of the United States is contained in the *Revised Statutes*.[14] The second edition contains the corrections of texts that have been misquoted. The second edition is the one that should be used, unless the student needs the provisions regarding post roads or the District of Columbia, which were left as part 2 of volume 18 of the *Statutes at Large* for the Forty-third Congress. Two *Supplements* were published in 1891 and 1901, but they have been largely superseded by the *United States Code*.

The *United States Code* (cited as *U.S.C.*) made its first appearance in 1926.[15] It is a consolidation and codification of all general and permanent laws in force on the date of its publication, arranged under fifty titles. It is prima-facie evidence and is presumed to be the law, but the presumption is rebuttable if the *Code* is at variance with the law as given in the *Statutes at Large*.[16]

The *United States Code Annotated* (cited as *U.S.C.A.*) comprises all laws of a general and permanent nature. It is arranged like the *United States Code*. The annotations are from federal and state court reports and opinions of the United States attorneys general.[17] The *Federal Code Annotated* (*F.C.A.*)[18] differs from

[13] U.S., Laws, Statutes, *Index to the Federal Statutes General and Permanent Law* . . . , 1789–1873, 1874–1931, 2 vols. (Washington, D.C., Government Printing Office, 1911–33).

[14] U.S., Laws, Statutes, *Revised Statutes of the United States, Passed at the First Session of the Forty-Third Congress, 1873–1874: Embracing the Statutes of the United States, General and Permanent in Their Nature, in Force December 1, 1873*, 2d ed. (Washington, D.C., Government Printing Office, 1878).

[15] U.S., Laws, Statutes, 1964 ed. (Washington, D.C., Government Printing Office, 1965). Earlier editions were published in 1926, 1934, 1940, 1946, 1952, and 1958. Cumulative supplements are issued annually.

[16] Schmeckebier and Eastin, *Government Publications and Their Use*, 202–203.

[17] U.S., Laws, Statutes, (St. Paul, Minn., West Publishing Co., 1927–). Kept up to date by cumulative annual pocket parts containing amendments and additions. Replacement volumes are issued from time to time.

the official edition (*U.S.*) in that it is annotated by cases and certain author opinions.

Shepard's *A Table of Federal Acts by Popular Names*[19] is a serviceable tool for the history student. It is probably the best known of such lists. Through it the student can find information on acts such as the G.I. Bill of Rights or the Tydings-McDuffie Act. It gives references to the United States *Statutes at Large* and the *United States Code.*

Laws are made in the executive branch of the government as well as in the legislative. There has been an increasingly large number of orders, regulations, and administrative decisions having the force of law issued by administrators of government bodies. In 1937, Congress authorized the preparation of a *Code of Federal Regulations* (*C.F.R.*),[20] which bears somewhat the same relation to the *Federal Register* as the *United States Code* does to the *Statutes at Large,* in that the rules actually in force at the end of a calendar year are incorporated in the *United States Code.* Like the *United States Code,* the *C.F.R.* is divided into fifty titles. *A Codification Guide,* a checklist by title and section number of all *C.F.R.* sections which have been affected by later action, is the most im-

[18] U.S., Laws, Statutes, *Federal Code Annotated: All Federal Laws of a General and Permanent Nature . . . Fully Annotated to the Decisions of Federal and State Tribunals, Together with Annotations of Uncodified Laws and Treaties, Executive Orders, Proclamations, and Law Review Articles* (Indianapolis, Bobbs-Merrill Co., 1937–). Yearly. Volumes replaced at intervals by perpetual revision plans. *Ten-Year Cumulative Supplement* for vols. 1–13, titles 1–50, 1947– . In progress. *Index,* 2 vols. (1962).

[19] Shepard's Citations, Inc., *A Table of Federal Acts by Popular Names or Short Titles to January 1, 1964* (Colorado Springs, Colo., Shepard's Citations, 1964). In 1968, *Shepard's Acts and Cases by Popular Names, Federal and State* began. It is kept up to date by cumulative supplements.

[20] *Code of Federal Regulations, Containing a Codification of Documents of General Applicability and Future Effect as of December 31, 1948, with Ancillaries and Index,* 2d ed. (Washington, D.C., published by the Division of the Federal Register, National Archives, Government Printing Office, 1949–). In progress. Kept up to date by pocket supplements. Cumulating annually and recodified every five years. First edition was in 1938.

214

portant tool for tracing the present text of a *C.F.R.* title and section and for finding changes made since the publication of the text in the bound volume. It appears daily on the second page of each issue of the *Federal Register*; it is cumulated monthly, quarterly, and annually.

The *Federal Register* contains all presidential proclamations and executive orders, rules, regulations, and orders of bureaus and departments.[21] Beginning with the issue for June 4, 1938, the rules, regulations, and orders are arranged under fifty titles, which are sometimes parallel to those of the *United States Code*. The *Federal Register* is a daily supplement to the *Code of Federal Regulations*.

The states have their own legislatures which pass laws. The state laws are published but not usually codified regularly. Nevada, however, publishes its laws in force under the title *Nevada Revised Statutes*. This, including the supplementary and replacement pages, constitutes all of the statute law of Nevada of a general nature enacted by the legislature. In other words, it is the law of Nevada.

Marbury v. *Madison*, 1 Cranch 37 (1803); *Brown* v. *Board of Education of Topeka*, 347 U.S. 483 (1954, 1955); and *Baker* v. *Carr*, 369 U.S. 186 (1962) are three examples of historic Supreme Court decisions. Because the history student often has to work with court cases, he should learn where to locate the decisions.

The Constitution provides that the judicial power of the United States be vested in a Supreme Court, and it gives to Congress the authority to establish such lower courts as are necessary. In 1789, Congress passed the Judiciary Act, which, with its amendments, is the basis of the following courts: courts of appeal, district courts, and (since 1953) the court of claims. Congress also has estab-

---

[21] U.S., *Federal Register*, March 14, 1936– (Washington, D.C., Government Printing Office, 1936–). Daily, except Sunday, Monday, and the day following a legal holiday. Monthly, quarterly, and annual indexes of all existing regulations and rules promulgated on or before December 31, 1948, and effective after January 1, 1949.

lished other courts for special purposes: the customs court, the court of customs and patent appeals, the territorial courts, the courts of the District of Columbia, and the court of military appeals. All these courts issue decisions usually called *Reports*. Not all federal court reports are issued as governmental publications. For the most part, commercial law firms have published them. The student may find these reports in a large university library or law library.

The United States Supreme Court interprets and expounds the acts of Congress and examines federal and state laws and executive actions to determine their constitutionality by judicial review; thus it has been able to mold the shape of law. Its decisions as handed down are published as decisions of the Supreme Court. These are published on Mondays, decision days, during term time. A slip decision is a separate report published as a separate pamphlet. It lacks headnotes and the text may be corrected later. It does contain the docket number, the title, how the case came to the court, the date of the decision, the text of the opinions, and the decision.[22]

The opinions of the Supreme Court are published as the *United States Reports*.[23] Before 1922 (volume 257), the reports were the prerequisite of the official reporter of the court who had them printed by a private firm and then furnished a certain number of copies to the government for official use. Until 1875, the reports bore the names of the various reporters who collected them; and these reports are cited in law and other books by abbreviations of these reporters' names. The following is a table of the abbreviations, dates, and volumes for the set:

Dal.	Dallas	1–4	1790–1800
Cr.	Cranch	5–13	1801–1815
Wh.	Wheaton	14–25	1816–1827
Pet.	Peters	26–41	1828–1842

[22] Price and Bitner, *Effective Legal Research*, 126. Facsimile editions are published unofficially in the [Commerce Clearing House] *CCH United States Supreme Court* and the *United States Law Week*.

216

How.	Howard	42–65	1843–1860
Black	Black	66–67	1861–1862
Wal.	Wallace	68–90	1863–1874
U.S.	————	91–date	1875–date[24]

Shepard has the *Table of Cases Cited By Popular Names*,[25] a tool similar to its *Table of Federal Acts by Popular Names*, for identifying cases by the popular name. *Table of Cases Cited by Popular Name* will identify such cases as the Hot-Oil Case, the Gravel-Pit Case, or the Goat Case. It gives parallel citations to all standard report series.

Price and Bitner's *Effective Legal Research* and Ervin H. Pollack's *Fundamentals of Legal Research*[26] are two excellent guides to legal documents. The older edition of *Effective Legal Research* has an appendix listing American law reports and digests, which will provide the names of compilations the constitutional history student might need to use.

The states have their own courts. The constitution in each state provides for the judicial branch and usually leaves the detailed organization of the court system to the legislature. In Nevada, for example, Article VI, sections 1 and 2 of the state constitution established the Nevada Supreme Court. Through the years the state legislature has created and changed judicial districts and the number of judges assigned to them. The state courts publish their own decisions.

[23] U.S., Supreme Court, *United States Reports, Cases Adjudged in the Supreme Court at October Term*, vol. 1– (Washington, D.C., Government Printing Office, 1790–).

[24] Ann Morris Boyd and Rae Elizabeth Rips, *United States Government Publications*, 3d ed. rev. by Rae Elizabeth Rips (New York, H. W. Wilson Co., 1949), 92.

[25] Shepard's Citations, Inc., *Table of Cases Cited by Popular Names, Federal and State* (Colorado Springs, Colo., Shepard's Citations, 1957). *Supplement*, January 1, 1957 to January 1, 1962. In 1968, *Shepard's Acts and Cases by Popular Names, Federal and State* began. It is kept up to date by cumulative supplements.

[26] 3d ed. (Brooklyn, The Foundation Press, 1967).

Great Britain

The English common law, as modified by English statutes up to the time of the American colonial settlement and as interpreted by English decisions up to the separation of the colonies from England, is looked upon as the basis of American jurisprudence. The student of United States history, as well as the student of English history, may need to use the English statutes and decisions.

English slip laws have been available in one form or another since 1484, the year before the Tudors took over the monarchy. As is the case in the United States, each slip law is issued as a separate pamphlet by Her Majesty's Stationery Office when it is approved. The English slip laws are cumulated and bound annually into session laws. Sessional or annual volumes of the statutes have been issued continuously from the time of Richard III (1483) to the present, except during the Commonwealth when the acts and ordinances were issued separately soon after they were passed. The session laws are cited by the years of the reigns of the kings and queens. The *Public General Acts and Church Assembly Measures*[27] are the annual statutes which are comparable to the session laws of the United States. Indexes in each volume include an alphabetical list of public general acts, a chronological list, and the effects of legislation of the current year upon existing legislation, such as repeals and amendments.

There is no official English compilation by subject matter corresponding to the *United States Revised Statutes* or the *United States Code*. There is, however, *Halsbury's Laws of England*,[28] a complete encyclopedia of English law. It consists of separate

[27] Great Britain (London, H. M. Stationery Office, 1931–). Annual; formerly sessional. They have been issued in various editions and formats. Sessional or annual volumes date from 1483; church assembly measures have been included in the bound volumes since 1926.

[28] Earl of Halsbury, et al., *Halsbury's Laws of England: Being a Complete Statement of the Whole Law of England*, ed. by Viscount Simonds, 3d ed., 43 vols. (London, Butterworth & Co., Ltd., 1952–64). Current service. First published in 1907–17 with annual supplements; 2d ed., 1931–42.

218

treatises on individual subjects arranged alphabetically. On many topics it is the only convenient up-to-date source of information. A general index is in volumes 41 and 42, and a consolidated table of statutes is in volume 43.

There have been numerous chronological collections of statutes in force. One of these is the *Statutes Revised*.[29] This official publication covers the statutes from 1235 through 1948. It prints all acts in force, exclusive of those of a local, personal, or private nature. The acts are arranged in chronological order with the omission of all acts relating exclusively to North Ireland. Each volume has its own subject and chronological index, but there is no cumulative index; therefore, the student must use the annual *Index to the Statutes in Force*[30] and the *Chronological Table of the Statutes*.[31]

The *Acts and Ordinances of the Interregnum*[32] covers the period of Cromwell's Commonwealth. The acts in this publication are in none of the various compilations of the *Statutes*. The third volume of *Acts and Ordinances of the Interregnum* contains a chronological list of acts and ordinances printed, a subject index, and an index of names, places, and matters for which legislation was enacted.

Halsbury's Statutes of England[33] is a nonofficial encyclopedic

[29] Great Britain, *The Statutes Revised, 1235–1948*, Sir Robert Drayton, ed., 73d ed., 33 vols. (London, H. M. Stationery Office, 1950). Earlier editions: *Statutes of the Realm* (London, Record Commission, 1810–28); *Statutes, 1235–1920*, 2d ed., 24 vols. (London, H. M. Stationery Office, 1929). *Annotations to Acts*, 1949 (London, H. M. Stationery Office, 1951–). Annually gives directions for noting the amendments to the third edition of the *Statutes Revised*.

[30] Great Britain, (London, H. M. Stationery Office, 1870–). Annual since 1870.

[31] Great Britain, *Chronological Tables of the Statutes Covering the Legislation from 1235 to —* (London, H. M. Stationery Office, 1870–). Annual. From 1870 to 1949, it was issued as the *Chronological Table and Index of the Statutes*.

[32] Great Britain, Laws, Statutes, *Acts and Ordinances of the Interregnum, 1642–1660*, C. H. Firth and R. S. Rait, eds., 3 vols. (London, H. M. Stationery Office, 1911).

treatment of the statutes of England and Northern Ireland. Statutes in force of general public interest are classified under 174 alphabetically arranged titles. Each volume and supplement has a table of the statutes which are printed in it, a table of abbreviations, and its own subject index. The final table volume of the set cumulates the chronological tables of the statutes, adds an alphabetical list of statutes, cumulates and expands the subject index, but omits the table of cases. There are three supplements to *Halsbury's Statutes*.[34]

The English counterpart of the *United States Code of Federal Regulations* is the *Statutory Instruments*.[35] This publication consists of rules, regulations, and orders implementing formal legislation, including treaties. The headings of law correspond to those in the *Index to the Statutes in Force*. The statutory authorization and effective date are given for each instrument, and there are indexes and tables for each volume. *Statutory Rules and Orders* is an official compilation collecting all the statutes of a general and permanent character in effect in 1948, and in some cases to 1951.[36] The annual volume of the *Statutory Instruments* keeps this set up to date.

Halsbury's Statutory Instruments[37] is a nonofficial classified encyclopedic treatment of all statutory rules and orders and statutory instruments in force; it is arranged by subject on the same plan as *Halsbury's Statutes*. It prints and annotates a selection of the statutory instruments. Quarterly supplements and an annual cumulative volume keep the basic set up to date.

[33] 2d ed., Roland Burrows, ed., 26 vols. (London, Butterworth & Co., Ltd., 1948–51).

[34] *Annotated Current Statutes*, the five-times-a-year loose-leaf annotated slip law service; the *Continuation Volume*, which cumulates the preceding year's slip laws and classifies and indexes them as in the main set; and the *Cumulative Supplement*, an annual citator volume into the main set.

[35] (London, H. M. Stationery Office, 1904–). Through 1947 they were known as *Statutory Rules and Orders*.

[36] *The Statutory Rules and Orders and Statutory Instruments*, rev. to December, 1948, 25 vols. (London, H. M. Stationery Office, 1948–52).

[37] 24 vols. (London, Butterworth & Co., Ltd., 1951–52).

English courts in effect combine the courts which would be federal and state in the United States. Price and Bitner's *Effective Legal Research* has an excellent section on English law reports, search books, and indexes.[38] Sweet & Maxwell's *Guide to Law Reports and Statutes*[39] has an alphabetical list of English, Irish, and Scottish law reports with the period covered by each, a chronological list of English law reports, and a table showing the date of the volume and the concurrent series of reports from 1810 to 1962. The student needing this specialized material can check these titles for suggestions on how to find British case law. There is nothing in the British Court system that corresponds to the United States Supreme Court and its doctrine of judicial review.

International

"International law is the standard of conduct, at a given time, for states and other entities subject thereto." It is, for the most part, in a continual state of change and development, and it is embodied in international agreements, in international customs or practice, in the general norm of civilization, and in decisions of international judicial tribunals and international arbitral bodies.[40]

There are three significant digests of international law: Moore, Hackworth, and Whiteman. John Bassett Moore's *Digest of International Law*[41] is the standard work on international law up to 1906. It digests and indexes diplomatic discussions, treaties and other international agreements, international awards, the decisions of municipal courts, the writings of jurists, and the documents issued by presidents and secretaries of state of the United States, the opinions of attorneys general, and the decisions of the federal and

[38] Student rev. ed., 314–31.

[39] 4th ed. (London, Sweet & Maxwell, Ltd., 1962).

[40] Marjorie Millace Whiteman, *Digest of International Law*, Dept. of State Publication 7403 (Washington, D.C., Government Printing Office, 1963), vol. 1, p. 1.

[41] John Bassett Moore, *Digest of International Law*, 56 Cong., 2 sess., *House Doc. 551*, 8 vols. (Washington, D.C., Government Printing Office, 1906).

state courts. The index, table of cases, and list of documents are in the eighth volume.

Green H. Hackworth's *Digest of International Law*[42] carries on from where Moore's *Digest of International Law* left off to 1940. It includes the documents and files accumulated in the Department of State since 1906. Volume 8 is a general index and table of cases.

The successor to Hackworth's *Digest of International Law* is Marjorie Millace Whiteman's *Digest of International Law*.[43] The last volume is to be a comprehensive index.

Treaties are often a source for international law. Multilateral treaties may contain provisions regulating certain phases of international conduct, and bilateral treaties sometimes contain provisions declaring existing law.

The new definitive compilation of United States treaties now in progress is *Treaties and Other International Agreements of the United States of America, 1776–1949*.[44] Charles I. Bevans is the compiler of this collection of official United States government translations of treaties and other international agreements to which the United States was a party from 1776 to 1949. It will be considerably larger than earlier compilations of this kind because of the great increase in the number of treaties and other international agreements entered into by the United States from 1937 to 1950 and the inclusion of postal arrangements and agreements printed in the Executive Agreement Series.

This new series begins with several volumes of multilateral treaties and agreements, arranged chronologically according to the date of the signature. These will be followed by approximately

[42] U.S., Dept. of State, *Digest of International Law*, comp. by Green H. Hackworth, Dept. of State Publications 1506, 1521, 1708, 1756, 1927, 1961, 1998, 2100, 8 vols. (Washington, D.C., Government Printing Office, 1940–44).

[43] U.S., Dept. of State, *Digest of International Law*, comp. by Marjorie Millace Whiteman, Dept. of State Publications 7403, 7553, 7737, 7825 (Washington, D.C., Government Printing Office, 1963–).

[44] Vol. 1, Multilateral, 1776–1917, U.S. Dept. of State Publication no. 8407 (Washington, D.C., Government Printing Office, 1968).

eleven volumes of bilateral treaties and agreements grouped under the names of the countries with which they were concluded. Each volume will have a relatively brief index; there will be cumulative analytical indexes for the series. Until this series is completed, the student will need to use the older compilations: Hunter Miller's *Treaties and Other International Acts of the United States of America*[45] and W. M. Malloy's *Treaties, Conventions, International Acts, Protocols, and Agreements Between the United States of America and Other Powers, 1776–1937*.[46] The Malloy set is a fairly complete compilation except that it lacks postal conventions and Indian treaties. William M. Malloy compiled only the first two volumes, which cover 1776–1909, but the whole set is usually referred to as Malloy's *Treaties*. The third volume covers 1910–23, and the fourth, 1923–37. The fourth also includes a chronological list of the treaties in all four volumes, a list by country of treaties in volumes 3 and 4, a list of treaties submitted to the Senate, 1789–1937, with a note of the action taken, and reference to the "Treaty Series," and a numerical list of the treaty series up to December 31, 1937, with references to the *Statutes at Large*. The postal conventions and Indian treaties are in *Indian Affairs, Laws and Treaties*, a compilation by Charles J. Kappler.[47]

Hunter Miller's *Treaties and Other International Acts of the United States* is arranged chronologically with the treaty text in English and the foreign language in which it was concluded. Notes of information on background and citations to relevant judicial

[45] U.S., Treaties, Dept. of State Publications 175, 237, 453, 645, 1017, 1719, 1791, 3141, 8 vols. (Washington, D.C., Government Printing Office, 1931–48).

[46] U.S., Treaties, 4 vols. (Washington, D.C., Government Printing Office, 1910–38). Vols. 1 and 2, 1778–1909, 61 Cong., 2 sess., *Sen. Doc. 357*; vol. 3, 1910–23, C. F. Redmond, comp., 67 Cong., 4 sess., *Sen. Doc. 348*; vol. 4, 1923–37, E. J. Trenwith, comp., 75 Cong., 2 sess., *Sen. Doc. 134*.

[47] *Indian Affairs, Laws and Treaties*, vols. 1–2, 57 Cong., 1 sess., *Sen. Doc. 452*; vol. 3, 62 Cong., 2 sess., *Sen Doc. 719*; vol. 4, 70 Cong., 1 sess., *Sen. Doc. 53*; vol. 5 is the *Laws*, 76 Cong., 3 sess., *Sen. Doc. 194*.

decisions are found at the end of the text of the treaties. The Miller compilation was designed to replace the William M. Malloy collection, but only eight volumes covering treaties to the end of 1863 have appeared. No more will be published.

There are several compilations of treaties submitted to the United States Senate dating from 1789 through 1944.[48] These compilations are arranged in chronological order by date of signature. For each treaty information on the action taken on it in the Senate and its present status is given. *Treaties in Force*[49] tells the current status of a treaty. Part 1 includes bilateral treaties and other agreements listed by country, with subject headings under each country. Part 2 includes multilateral treaties and other agreements, arranged by subject headings, with a list of states that are parties to each agreement. An appendix gives a consolidated tabulation of documents affecting international copyright relations. Information on the current status of treaties and other international agreements is published regularly in the Department of State *Bulletin*.[50]

From 1950, when the texts of treaties were dropped from the *Statutes at Large*, the *United States Treaties and Other International Agreements* (cited as *U.S.T.*)[51] has been the official series in which treaties and international agreements are published. They are arranged in numerical order as they were originally published in pamphlet form in the *Treaties and Other International Acts*

---

[48] U.S., Dept. of State, *List of Treaties Submitted to the Senate, 1789–1934*, Dept. of State Publication no. 765 (Washington, D.C., Government Printing Office, 1935); *Treaties Submitted to the Senate, 1935–1944*, Dept. of State Publication no. 2311 (1945); *List of Treaties Submitted to the Senate, 1789–1931, Which Have Not Gone into Force*, U.S., Dept. of State Publication no. 382 (1932).

[49] U.S., Treaties, *Treaties in Force: A List of Treaties and Other International Agreements of the United States in Force* (Washington, D.C., Government Printing Office, c. 1929?–). Irregular; annual since 1958. Each volume has a U.S. Dept. of State publication number.

[50] (Washington, D.C., Government Printing Office, 1939–). Weekly.

[51] U.S., Treaties, 1950– (Washington, D.C., Government Printing Office, 1952–). Annual.

224

(cited as *T.I.A.S.*) series.[52] There is a subject and country index. There are several collections of the major treaties in history. Rönnefarth's *Konferenzen und Verträge* covers the major historically significant conferences and agreements from 1492 to the present.[53] The following information is given for each treaty: background, parties involved, and a summary of the provisions.

Georg F. von Martens, once a professor of international law at the University of Göttingen, Germany, is the author of *Recueil des traités*, an enormous collection of treaties signed after 1761. This was continued as a standard work by other men. Martens' Collection of Treaties is the name often given to the collection of Martens' three series, Murhard's volumes, Samwer's series, Triepel's collections, and Hopf's volumes.[54] This collection is the most com-

---

[52] U.S., Treaties, *Treaties and Other International Acts, as of December 27, 1945*, Dept. of State Publication no. 1501– (Washington, D.C., Government Printing Office, 1946–). This series, issued separately in pamphlets, continues the *Treaty Series* (18??–1946) and the *Executive Agreement Series* (1929–45). It contains texts of treaties, declarations, constitutions, and charters of international organizations.

[53] Helmuth K. G. Rönnefarth, *Konferenzen und Verträge: Vertrags Ploetz, ein Handbuch geschichtlich bedeutsamer Zusammenkünfte und Vereinbarungen*, 2d rev. and enl. ed. (Würzburg, A. G. Pletz, 1958–59), 4 vols. when complete; in progress. First ed., 1952. Vol. 1 is to cover *Altertum*; vol. 2, to cover *Mittelalter*, vol. 3, *Neure Zeit*, 1492–1914 (1953); vol. 4, *Neueste Zeit*, 1914–59 (1959).

[54] Georg F. von Martens, *Recueil des principaux traités d'alliance, de paix, de trêve de neutralité, de commerce, de limites, d'échange, etc., conclus par les puissances de l'Europe tant entre elles, qu'avec les puissances et états dans d'autres parties du monde depuis 1761 jusqu'à présent*, 7 vols. (Göttingen, F. Dieterich, 1791–1801). 2d enl. ed. by K. von Martens, 8 vols. (Göttingen, F. Dieterich, 1817–35); Georg F. von Martens, *Supplément au recueil etc. précédé de traités du XVIIIme siècle antérieurs à cette époque et qui ne se trouvent pas dans le corps universel diplomatique de Mrs. Dumont et Rousset et autres recueils généraux de traités*, 4 vols. (Göttingen, F. Dieterich, 1802–1808); Georg F. von Martens et al., *Nouveau recueil de traités d'alliance etc. depuis 1808 jusqu'à present*, 16 vols. (Göttingen, F. Dieterich, 1817–42); Friedrich W. A. Murhard, *Nouveau recueil général de traités, conventions et autres transactions remarquables, servant à la connaissance des relations étrangères des puissances et états dans leurs rapports mutuels*, 20 vols. in 22 (Göttingen, F. Dieterich, 1839–42); Karl F. L. Samwer et al., *Nouveau recueil général de*

plete and extensive collection of international agreements and negotiations in existence. The general index to Martens' first series is in two parts: part 1, which is arranged chronologically, and part 2, which is arranged alphabetically. The index to his second series is in the last volume of the set. The third series has a chronological index, an index by country, and an index by subject at the end of each volume. The general index of the third series has the chronological indexes and the indexes by country, but it does not have subject indexes.

Dumont's *Corps universel diplomatique du droit des gens*, a collection of treaties and negotiations which contains early treaties, supplements Martens' *Recueil des traites*. Dumont's *Corps* and *Supplement* cover treaties from 315 A.D. to 1738.[55] There are two other collections of treaties. Tétot's *Repertoire des traités*,[56] lists treaties from the Treaty of Westphalia in 1648 up to 1867. Gabriel

traités etc. Deuxième série, 35 vols. (Göttingen, F. Dieterich, 1876–1908), general table and index volume for the entire series (1910); Heinrich von Triepel, *Nouveau recueil général de traités etc. Troisième série*, 19 vols. (Leipzig, F. Dieterich, 1908–29); Julius Hopf, *Table générale du recueil des traités de G. F. Martens et de ses continuaterus*, 2 vols. (Göttingen, F. Dieterich, 1875–76).

[55] Jean Dumont, *Corps universel diplomatique du droit des gens: Contenant un recueil de traitez d'alliance, de paix, de treve, de neutralite, de commerce, d'échange . . . & autres contrats, qui ont été faits en Europe depuis le règne de l'empereur Charlemagne jusques à présent*, 8 vols. (Amsterdam, Chez P. Brunel, R. & G. Wetstein, les Janssons Waesberge, & L'Honore & Chatelain, 1726–31). Jean Dumont, *Supplement au Corps universel diplomatique du droit des gens, contenant l'Histoire des anciens traitez, ou Recueil historique & chronologique des traitez répandus dans les auteurs grecs & latins, & autres monumens de l'antiquité, depuis les temps les plus reculez jusques à l'empire du Charlemagne . . .*, 5 vols. (Amsterdam, Chez les Janssons à Waeberge, Wetstein & Smith, & A. Chatelain, 1739).

[56] *Repertoire des traités de paix, de commerce, d'alliance, etc., conventions et autres actes conclus entre toutes les puissances du globe, principalement depuis la paix de Westphalia jusqu'à nos jours: Table générale des recueils de Dumont, Wenek, Martens . . . etc.*, 2 vols. (Paris, Amyot, 1866–73).

de Ribiers *Repertoire des traités* continues Tétot's collection from 1867 to 1897.[57]

The *Catalog of Treaties*[58] is a list of treaties from 1814 to 1918 in chronological order, with an index by country and an index of agreements of a general international character. It is not complete and emphasizes the period after 1900. The entry for a treaty tells where and when the treaty was signed and ratified and gives references to the printed text of the treaty with a note about the languages of the text. The appendix contains a few of the most important treaties before 1814 and a few of the early treaties referred to in the main list.

Major Peace Treaties of Modern History, 1648–1947, the first comprehensive collection of peace treaties to appear in English, was published in 1968.[59] These treaties are concerned with a variety of issues that have directly affected the lives and well-being of a large percentage of the population of the world.

In diplomatic negotiations today, each country is entitled to its own national language; however, until the middle of the seventeenth century, Latin was the language used in official diplomatic negotiations. By the time of the Conference of Nimwegen (1676), French had become the general diplomatic language, but the Treaty of Nimwegen (1678), like the Treaty of Ryswick (1697) and the Treaty of Utrecht (1713), was drawn up in Latin. This continued as the common practice until the late eighteenth century when French completely replaced Latin, due to the widespread

[57] *Repertoire des traités de paix, de commerce, d'alliance, etc., conventions et autres actes conclus entre toutes les puissances du globe, depuis 1867 jusqu'à nos jours (faisant suite du Repertoire de M Tétot): Table générale des principaux recueils français et étrangérs, ouvrage* pub. sous les auspices du Ministere des affaires étrangéres, 2 vols. (Paris, A. Pedone, 1895–99).

[58] U.S., Dept. of State, *Catalogue of Treaties, 1814–1918* (Washington, D.C., Government Printing Office, 1919; reprint ed., Oceana Publications, 1964). This was originally prepared for the Paris Peace Conference and was a classified document.

[59] Fred L. Israel, ed., introductory essay by Arnold Toynbee, 4 vols. (New York, Chelsea House, 1968).

cultural influence of France beginning with Louis XIV. Since the end of the nineteenth century, English has been added as a major language in diplomatic transactions. In *Major Peace Treaties of Modern Europe*, official English translations, usually those of the British Foreign Office, have been used.

The League of Nations published *Treaty Series* from 1920 through 1946.[60] It has been superseded by the *Treaty Series* of the United Nations.[61] Included are the treaties and international agreements registered or filed and recorded with the secretariat of the United Nations since December 14, 1946. The texts are given in their original languages, with English and French translations. A chronological index is issued at the end of every one hundred treaties.

There are treaty sets for other countries. Great Britain has sets covering the nineteenth and twentieth centuries. *Hertslet's Commercial Treaties*[62] ran from 1827 to 1925 and was finally incorporated into the *British and Foreign State Papers*.[63] This set includes treaties, correspondence about foreign affairs, texts of constitutions of foreign countries, and other organic laws. The volume and cumulative volume indexes by subject and country

[60] League of Nations, *Treaty Series: Publication of Treaties and International Engagements Registered with the Secretariat of the League*, vols. 1–205 (Treaty Nos. 1–4834), September 1920–1944/1946 (London, Harrison & Sons, Ltd., 1920–46).

[61] United Nations, *Treaty Series: Treaties and International Agreements Registered or Filed and Recorded with the Secretariat of the United Nations*, 1946/1947– (New York, 1947–).

[62] *Hertslet's Commercial Treaties: A Collection of Treaties and Conventions Between Great Britain and Foreign Powers, and of the Laws, Decrees, Orders in Council, etc., Concerning the Same, So Far as They Relate to Commerce and Navigation, Slavery, Extradition, Nationality, Copyright, Postal Matters, etc.*, 31 vols. (London, H. M. Stationery Office, 1827–1925).

[63] Great Britain, Foreign Office, *British and Foreign State Papers, 1812– , with Which Is Incorporated Hertslet's Commercial Treaties* (London, H. M. Stationery Office, 1841–). Annual. Vol. 64 indexes vols. 1–63; vol. 93 indexes vols. 65–92; vol. 115 indexes vols. 94–114; vol. 138 indexes vols. 116–137.

228

are good. The Foreign Office also has published a *Treaty Series*[64] since the 1890's.

The Pan American Union has issued several publications on Pan American treaties. *Bilateral Treaties, Conventions, and Agreements* covers treaties between the United States and other American republics.[65] The other, *Inter-American Treaties and Conventions,*[66] lists treaties and conventions signed at the various conferences of the American states, gives the names of the signatory powers, and provides information on ratification. This is kept up to date by the *Status of the Pan American Treaties and Conventions,*[67] which gives current information in the form of tables.

INTERNATIONAL ORGANIZATIONS

The League of Nations was incorporated into the Treaty of Versailles; thus it automatically came into existence on January 10, 1920, when the treaty went into effect. Unable to prevent the aggressions of the Fascist and Nazi powers, which culminated in the outbreak of World War II in 1939, the League practically ceased to function during the war. On April 18, 1946, President of the Assembly Carl J. Hambro announced the League's dissolution to the delegates at the Twenty-first Session at Geneva.

While the publications of the League during its twenty-six years of existence were exceeded in sheer volume within three years by

[64] Great Britain, Foreign Office, *Treaty Series*, 1892– (London, H. M. Stationery Office, 1892–). Issued as Command Papers, which are numbered and indexed and can be bound as a separate set. General indexes are issued every few years.

[65] Pan American Union, Dept. of International Law and Organization, Division of Legal Affairs, *Bilateral Treaties, Conventions, and Agreements in Force Between the United States of America and Other American Republics, as of March 1, 1948* (Washington, D.C., Pan American Union, 1948).

[66] Pan American Union, Division of Law and Treaties, *Inter-American Treaties and Conventions* (Washington, D.C., Pan American Union, 1954).

[67] Pan American Union (Washington, D.C., Pan American Union, 1936–). Annual.

those of the United Nations, in their time they were the most significant and advanced publications of any international institution. They consisted chiefly of the following types of material: the official journal, which contained documentary materials; minutes of the council sessions after 1922; assembly records, resolutions, and recommendations; documents and records of special conferences; the treaty series; a monthly summary; documents issued by sections of the secretariat, committees, and offices; and masses of reports, statistical compilations, and monographs. Anyone working in international relations in the period of the 1920's and 1930's will definitely need to investigate this material.

Arthur Carl von Breycha-Vauthier has compiled *Sources of Information*, a most useful guide which analyzes League publications up to December 1, 1938.[68] A guide that extends the period surveyed up to 1947 is Hans Aufricht's *Guide to League of Nations Publications*.[69] It covers the whole period of the League from 1920 till the end in 1947, includes all types of documents, and is arranged by subject. As Arthur Sweetser says in the preface: "Dr. Aufricht's *Guide* is, in fact, far more than a bibliography, it is a concise historical outline of the League and its principal agencies. Its systematic layout, explanatory notes, and cumulative lists and tables give a picture of the League as a whole and show perhaps more vividly than could continuous text the sweep of its interests."[70]

The charter establishing the United Nations was signed in June of 1945, in San Francisco. The United Nations Agencies are a

[68] *Sources of Information: A Handbook on the Publications of the League of Nations*, preface by James T. Shotwell (London, George Allen & Unwin, 1939).

[69] *Guide to League of Nations Publications: A Bibliographical Survey of the Work of the League, 1920–1947* (New York, Columbia University Press, 1951). On April 18, 1946, at the final session of the Assembly of the League, the League's physical assets were turned over to the United Nations and its social and economic functions were fused with those of the Economic and Social Council. A Board of Liquidation was charged with the liquidation to be carried out between April 23, 1946, and July 31, 1947.

[70] *Guide to League of Nations Publications*, viii.

loosely united clan; they are independent in action and equal in authority. The United Nations took over the assets of the League and its publication program. In addition to dealing with top priority political problems, especially the maintenance of peace and security, the United Nations is concerned with economic, social, and technical development. In 1966, the clan numbered fifteen agencies, of which the United Nations was the largest. All were intergovernmental organizations dedicated to the improvement of the conditions of life on earth, and all were organized in a roughly similar pattern. Each agency had its own constitution, rules of procedure, budget, administrative head, membership, and special concerns.

The United Nations issues documents and publications, which range from a one-line note transmitting a report to the *Proceedings of the Second Conference on the Peaceful Uses of Atomic Energy* in 133 volumes. Broadly speaking, UN publications are intended for public consumption. They comprise publications designed for wide external distribution, such as *Everyman's United Nations, The United Nations Yearbook*, and the periodical, *The UN Monthly Chronicle*. They also include works which were prepared for internal use and are issued only incidentally as publications, such as *Official Records* of the General Assembly and a mass of reports, studies, bulletins, and so on. Both types of publications are listed in UN sales catalogs and the *Publishers' Trade List Annual*.

The documents of the UN are not intended for public use. They include draft resolutions, verbatim records of meetings, working papers, preliminary reports, administrative announcements, press releases, and so forth. If they are thought to have any lasting value or usefulness to the public, they are reprinted in final corrected form and issued as publications. The verbatim records of meetings, after they have been corrected, edited, and summarized, are released as part of the *Official Records* of the appropriate body (the General Assembly, the Security Council, and so forth). The final texts of resolutions, as documents, have gone through numerous redraftings before their appearance as publications. Other documents, such as preliminary studies and reports, are changed and corrected before they are released as publications in the form of monographs or series. The full record of the organization's work is made publicly available by the deposit of sets of its publications and documents, including even the ephemeral mimeographed material intended only for internal use and not for inclusion in the *Official Records* or other published sources, in selected libraries.[71]

The single monthly publication which lists and indexes all of the documents published by all of the agencies in the preceding calendar month is the *United Nations Documents Index* (*UNDI*).[72] It is a checklist with a subject index.

In 1963, specialized agencies' material was eliminated from the *UNDI*. Several of the agencies, such as GATT (General Agreement on Tariffs and Trade), ILO (International Labour Organization), and UNESCO, issue frequent comprehensive lists of their documents, and virtually all of them publish sales catalogs. Much of the most useful material issued by the agencies is picked up by subject indexes, such as *Public Affairs Information Bulletin* and *Index Medicus*. There has been a demand for a single index, which the *UNDI* had started out to be. A proposal has been made to the Association of International Libraries that a counterpart to *UNDI* be established to cover the specialized agencies and other international organizations, such as the Council of Europe and the OECD (Organization for Economic Cooperation and Development).[73]

Tracking down publications of international organizations is a complex operation. Even verifying the existence of an inter-

[71] Joseph Groesbeck, "United Nations Documents and Their Accessibility," *Library Resources & Technical Services*, Vol. 10 (Summer, 1966), 313–15.

[72] United Nations, Dag Hammarskjöld Library, Documents Index Unit. *United Nations Documents Index*, January 1950– (New York, 1950–). Monthly. Beginning with vol. 14 (1963), the monthly issues were replaced and superseded by two separate annual cumulations: a *Cumulative Checklist* and a *Cumulative* (Subject) *Index*.

[73] Groesbeck, "United Nations Documents and Their Accessibility," *Library Resources & Technical Services*, Vol. 10 (Summer, 1966), 318.

national organization can often be a difficult process. There are three publications which help identify international and intergovernmental agencies. One is "Current Bibliographical Control of International and Intergovernmental Documents," which is limited to intergovernmental agencies having some relation to science.[74] For the history student there is Amos J. Peaslee's *International Governmental Organizations*,[75] which lists alphabetically (by the English form of the name) international organizations created by governments and of a governmental nature and multilateral bodies (with three or more members). Unofficial private organizations are not included. For each organization the following information is given: a brief summary of the history and constitutional development, membership, functions, organs, headquarters, and a selective bibliography. Also valuable to the historian is *Annuaire des organisations internationales*,[76] which separates the entries into the United Nations family, the European community, and other intergovernmental organizations. Information for each organization includes address, history, purposes, types of membership, structure, officers, finance, activities, and publications. Unlike Peaslee's *International Governmental Organizations*, it includes governmental and nongovernmental organizations. For a listing of the international organizations to which the United States belongs, the *12th Report on the Extent and Disposition of U.S. Contributions to International Organizations for the Fiscal Year 1963* is helpful.[77]

[74] James B. Childs, "Current Bibliographical Control of International Intergovernmental Documents," *Library Resources & Technical Services*, Vol. 10 (Summer, 1966), 319.

[75] U.S., Library of Congress, International Organization Section, *International Governmental Organizations: A Guide to Their Library, Documentation, and Information Services*, prepared under the direction of Katherine O. Murra (Washington, D.C., Government Printing Office, 1962).

[76] *Annuaire des organisations internationales*, 1946– (Brussels, Union of International Associations, 1948–). Annual, 1948–50. Biennial, beginning with 1951–52.

Some of the Western European agencies, like the specialized agencies of the United Nations, issue their own catalogs. The Council of Europe and the European Economic Community have done this. The Eastern European agencies, such as the Council for Mutual Economic Aid (COMECON) and the Warsaw Treaty Organization, have not issued documents for public use. The Arab states intergovernmental agencies and the African intergovernmental agencies, such as the Organization of African Unity, have no systematic plan yet for issuing and publishing their documents.[78] For all international organizations at Geneva, the Association des Intérêts de Gèneve has published occasional directories.[79]

The Pan American Union at Washington, D.C., the secretariat for the Organization of American States, adopted in 1960 an organizational classification scheme for the official documents of the OAS (Organización de los Estados Americanos). Since Spanish is the principal working language of the Organization of American States, the combined guide, scheme, and tables, issued in April, 1961, is in Spanish.[80] The final annual list and index of the official documents of the OAS is a classified list with entries for 3,900 documents with an index.[81] Each listing gives the classification, the language (Spanish, English, French, or Portuguese), and information as to whether the item is for limited distribution or for sale. The classification is by organization, and the volume

[77] 88 Cong., 2 sess., *House Doc. 313.* The State Department also publishes *United States Participation in the United Nations.*

[78] Childs, "Current Bibliographic Control of International Intergovernmental Documents," *Library Resources & Technical Services,* Vol. 10 (Summer, 1966), 326–29.

[79] The Permanent Center of International Information, ed., *Annuaire international de Genève: Geneva International Yearbook* (Geneva, Associations des Interets du Genève, 1926–).

[80] *Serie de los documentos oficiales de la Organización de los Estados Americanos: Gúia, esquama y cuadros explicativos de categorias.*

[81] *Documentos oficiales de la Organización de los Estados Americanos: Indice y lista general,* Vol. 1 (Enero-December, 1960).

234

includes, in addition to the acts and documents of the Organization of American States, documents of the Inter-American Conference, its council, the Inter-American Economic and Social Council, the meetings of the Ministers of Foreign Relations, specialized inter-American conferences, and other central councils, commissions, and agencies. The Pan American Union's informational and technical publications are not listed in this publication; however, they are listed in separate lists issued regularly.

11

Government Publications

Much important reference material can be found in the reports, bulletins, and other publications issued by the various municipal, state, and national governments. Government publications are among the oldest written records; they are sources of the political, economic, and social history for the peoples of all times. Each nation today issues the records of its work as a government, but the government of the United States issues more publications than any other government.

United States

There are several comprehensive guides to the use of United States government publications. These have been designed primarily for the student in library science, but the history student can learn about the indexes and catalogs from them. Boyd's *United States Government Publications* is a standard work that is still excellent on publications up to the post-World War II period.[1] It lists publications according to the government division, department, or agency and annotates the most important titles.

Schmeckebier and Eastin's *Government Publications and Their Use* is another useful and more up-to-date guide.[2] The authors have

[1] Anne Morris Boyd, 3d rev. ed. by Rae Elizabeth Rips (New York, H. W. Wilson Co., 1949). 1st ed., 1931; 2d ed., 1940.

[2] Laurence Frederick Schmeckebier and Roy B. Eastin, 2d rev. ed. (Washington, D.C., Brookings Institute, 1969).

tried to describe the basic guides to government publications, to indicate the uses and limitations of available indexes, catalogs, and bibliographies, to explain the systems of numbering and methods of titling, and to list government periodicals and microfacsimile copies of government publications.

Ellen Jackson's *Subject Guide to Major United States Government Publications*[3] is a guide only to the publications issued by the Government Printing Office. Its entries give the title, author, date, pages, agency of issue, and document number. If the title of the publication does not adequately indicate its nature, an annotation and explanatory note does. For certain types of material, such as treaties, this guide gives a brief history when the form of publication has changed many times. The history student will probably get more help from Boyd's *United States Government Publications* or Schmeckebier and Eastin's *Government Publications and Their Use*.

The collected edition of United States government publications is known as the congressional edition or the Serial Set. In general, the Serial Set includes the material resulting from the work of the legislative branch and such material from the executive branch as Congress has definitely ordered to be printed in it. Today, little more than congressional material is included in the Serial Set, but during the last of the nineteenth and first of the twentieth century much material coming from the executive branch was included. This material was also printed in what was called the departmental or plain-title edition.

The material included in the congressional edition is grouped into four series for each Congress, according to its origins and character: Senate reports, House reports, Senate documents, and House documents. The *Report* volumes contain the reports of the various House and Senate committees. The *Document* volumes contain reports of special investigations made for Congress and other material Congress has ordered to be printed therein. The House and Senate *Journals* also are a part of the congressional

[3] (Chicago, American Library Association, 1968).

edition. Each publication within a series and each series is numbered consecutively through an entire Congress. All the volumes in the congressional set, beginning with the volumes for the Fifteenth Congress, have been numbered consecutively. This is the reason that the congressional edition is often called the Serial Set.

The publications for the first fourteen congresses were not issued regularly as *Journals, Reports,* or *Documents.* Complete collections of these publications did not even exist; thus it was impossible to include them in the numerical scheme that John G. Ames, an early superintendent of documents, worked out. The documents of the first fourteen congresses are called the *American State Papers* and are numbered from 01 to 0038.[4]

There have been three checklists of United States government publications. The latest general compilation of government publications is the third edition of the *Checklist of United States Public Documents.*[5] It actually is a shelflist of all the publications in the Superintendent of Documents Library, the most complete collection in existence. The *Checklist* is arranged in the following order: (1) the congressional edition by serial number through the Sixtieth Congress; (2) the departmental edition arranged by superintendent of documents number to the end of 1909; and (3) miscellaneous publications of Congress also arranged by the superintendent of documents number. At the back of the volume is a list of departments and bureaus. The publications of the first fourteen congresses listed include the following: *American State Papers,* 38 vols. (Gales and Seaton); *American State Papers,* 5 vols. (Duff Green); *State Papers,* 1st ed., 8 vols., 2d ed., 10 vols., 3d ed., 12 vols. (T. B. Wait); the *Congressional Register* (Thomas

[4] U.S., Congress, *American State Papers: Documents, Legislative and Executive,* 38 vols. (Washington, D.C., Gales and Seaton, 1832–61).

[5] U.S., Superintendent of Documents, *Checklist of United States Public Documents, 1789–1909, Congressional: To the Close of the Sixtieth Congress: Departmental: To the End of the Calendar Year 1909,* 3d rev. and enl. ed. (Washington, D.C., Government Printing Office, 1911). Volume 1 lists congressional and departmental publications. Volume 2 was to have been an index, but it was never issued.

Lloyd); *Journals of the Senate*, 5 vols. (Gales and Seaton, reprint). Papers before 1789 listed include the following: *American Archives*,[6] 6 vols. of the 4th series and 3 vols. of the 5th series (Peter Force); Elliot's *Debates on the Adoption of the Constitution*;[7] *Diplomatic Correspondence of the American Revolution* (Jared Sparks);[8] and *Diplomatic Correspondence of the United States, 1783–1789* (Francis P. Blair and Blair and Rives);[9] *Revolutionary Diplomatic Correspondence* (Francis Wharton);[10] *Journals of the Continental Congress*;[11] *Secret Journals of the [Continental] Congresses* (Thomas B. Wait);[12] and *Miscellaneous Papers of the*

[6] U.S., Continental Congress, *American Archives . . . a Documentary History of . . . the North American Colonies*, ed. by Peter Force, 4th series, 6 vols. (Washington, D.C., published by St. Clair Clarke and Peter Force, December, 1837–46); 5th series, 3 vols. (Washington, D.C., published by St. Clair Clarke and Peter Force, April, 1848–January, 1853). The *American Archives* were not published in the congressional edition, but fifteen hundred copies were supplied to Congress for distribution.

[7] Jonathan Elliot, *The Debates of the Several State Conventions on the Adoption of the Federal Constitution, . . . Together with the Journal of the Federal Convention [and Other Papers]*, 2d ed., collected and revised from contemporary publications, published under the sanction of Congress, 5 vols. (Philadelphia, J. R. Lippincott & Co., 1861).

[8] U.S., Dept. of State, *The Diplomatic Correspondence of the American Revolution . . .*, from the original manuscripts in the Department of State, conformably to a Resolution of Congress, of March 27, 1818, ed. by Jared Sparks, 12 vols. (Boston, N. Hale and Gray & Cowen; New York, G. & C. & H. Carvill, 1829–30).

[9] U.S., Dept. of State, *The Diplomatic Correspondence of the United States of America, from the Signing of the Definitive Treaty of Peace 10th September, 1783, to the Adoption of the Constitution March 4, 1789*, published under the direction of the Secretary of State, from the original manuscripts in the Department of State, conformably to an act of Congress, approved May 5, 1832, 7 vols. (Washington, D.C., printed by Francis P. Blair, 1833–34).

[10] Francis Wharton, *Revolutionary Diplomatic Correspondence of United States . . . with Preliminary Index, and Notes Historical and Legal*, 50 Cong., 1 sess., *House Misc. Doc. 603, Pts. 1–6*, serial no. 2584–89.

[11] U.S., Continental Congress, *Journals of the Continental Congress, 1774–1789*, edited from the *Original Records in the Library of Congress*, by W. C. Ford et al., 34 vols. (Washington, D.C., Government Printing Office, 1904–37).

[12] U.S., Continental Congress, *Secret Journals of Acts and Proceedings*

Continental Congress. The student will need to use the *Checklist of United States Public Documents* to find the serial number for congressional documents. The student will also find the lists of publications of departments and bureaus useful.

There are catalogs and indexes which give a complete chronological index key to United States government publications from the Continental Congress to the present. Poore's *Descriptive Catalogue*[13] was the first and only attempt to make a complete list of all government publications. This is a chronological listing of congressional and departmental publications. Poore's *Descriptive Catalogue* gives the full title, author, and date of each publication, a brief abstract of its contents, and where it can be found. Executive and judicial publications, being less frequently issued, are entered first at the beginning of the year; Congressional publications are entered by the date on which they were ordered to be printed. The index at the end is a subject and name index, but it gives only the page number without any identifying word or phrase. It is estimated that the *Descriptive Catalogue* contains 63,063 titles and has omitted 10,000 others. In spite of inconsistencies, inaccuracies, and omissions, it is still the indispensable guide for the period from 1774 to 1881.

The next index chronologically is John Griffith Ames's *Comprehensive Index*.[14] It contains both congressional and departmental publications. Whereas Poore's *Descriptive Catalogue* is weak in executive documents, Ames's *Comprehensive Index* is weak in departmental documents. Arranged alphabetically by sub-

of Congress, from the First Meeting Thereof to Dissolution of Confederation by Adoption of Constitution of United States Published Conformably to Resolution of March 27, 1818, and April 21, 1820, 4 vols. (Boston, Thomas B. Wait, 1821).

[13] Benjamin Perley Poore, *A Descriptive Catalogue of the Government Publications of the United States, September 5, 1774–March 4, 1881,* comp. by the order of Congress, 48 Cong., 2 sess., *Sen. Misc. Doc. 67* (Washington, D.C., Government Printing Office, 1885).

[14] *Comprehensive Index to the Publications of the United States Government, 1881–1893,* 2d ed., 58 Cong., 2 sess., *House Doc. 754,* 2 vols. (Washington, D.C., Government Printing Office, 1905).

ject, the *Comprehensive Index* has a personal-name index at the end of the second volume. The following information is given for each entry: the author's name or government body responsible for the publication; the subject by which the alphabetization is made; and the reference to the Congress, session, volume, and number of the series in which the document is found. The *Comprehensive Index* enumerates the different editions in which a publication was issued and gives the serial numbers in tables under the subject "Congressional documents" in the first volume. It is a monumental work, although it does not include all the publications of the period.

The *Comprehensive Index* was succeeded by the biennial *Catalog of the Public Documents*, which was discontinued with the 1940 volume.[15] This comprehensive dictionary catalog of congressional and departmental publications lists all the documents under author (governmental or personal), subject, and, occasionally, title. It gives full catalog information for each book or pamphlet. There are many helpful, explanatory notes about publications and agencies. Serial numbers for congressional publications are given with the main entry. A numerical list with reference to the main entry and a schedule of volumes with serial numbers can be found under the heading, "Congressional documents lists." Three *Supplements* to the *Monthly Catalog*[16] were published to fill in the period for the Seventy-seventh to the Seventy-ninth congresses (1941–April, 1947) when publications, which would have been listed in the next *Catalog of the Public Documents*, were omitted from the *Monthly Catalog*.

No more supplements were published because all documents beginning in April, 1947, were to be listed in the *Monthly Cata-*

[15] U.S., Superintendent of Documents, *Catalog of the Public Documents of Congress and of All Departments of the Government of the United States for the Period, March 4, 1893 to December 31, 1940*, 45 vols. (Washington, D.C., Government Printing Office, 1896–1945).

[16] U.S., Superintendent of Documents, *Monthly Catalog of United States Government Publications: Supplements*, 1941–42, 1943–44, 1945–46, 3 vols. (Washington, D.C., Government Printing Office, 1947–48).

log[17] as they were received, regardless of publication date. The *Monthly Catalog* is the current listing of publications issued by all branches of the government; it includes both the congressional and the department and bureau publications. The publications are arranged by department and bureau, with an annual index.

The *Numerical Lists and Schedule*[18] have been issued as a separate publication for each session of Congress since the discontinuance of the *Catalog of the Public Documents,* which included this information in a section.

Catalogs or indexes covering special classes of publications have been issued. Some have constituted a continuing series, and some have been isolated issues. All of the publications set forth in the special lists are listed in the comprehensive catalogs, but the special lists are easier to use if references in a limited field are needed. The State Department, for example, publishes *Publications of the Department of State,* a semiannual list arranged by series.[19]

There are some nongovernmental bibliographies in governmental publications of research. One is Adelaide R. Hasse's *Index*

[17] U.S., Superintendent of Documents, *Monthly Catalog of United States Government Publications,* 1895– (Washington, D.C., Government Printing Office, 1895–). Monthly. Title varies: *Catalogue of the United States Public Documents,* 1895–June, 1907; *Monthly Catalogue, United States Public Documents,* July, 1907–39; *United States Government Publications, Monthly Catalog,* 1940–50. There is a *Decennial Cumulative Index,* 1941–50 (Washington, D.C., Government Printing Office, 1934).

[18] U.S., Superintendent of Documents, *Numerical Lists and Schedule of Volumes of the Reports and Documents of the 73rd Congress,* 1933/34– (Washington, D.C., Government Printing Office, 1934). Prior to 1951, the set, which is a separate volume for each session of Congress, was superseded by the "Congressional Documents" tables in the *Catalog of the Public Documents.* From the 77 Congress, 1 session, January 3, 1941 on, it has to be used to obtain serial numbers for the congressional reports and documents which are now listed only in the *Monthly Catalog* and without serial number.

[19] U.S., Department of State, October 1, 1929–January 1, 1953 (Washington, D.C., Government Printing Office, 1954); January 1, 1953–December 31, 1957 (1958); January 1, 1958–December 31, 1960 (1961). Appears semiannually in January and July.

242

to United States Documents Relating to Foreign Affairs, 1826– 61.[20] This valuable volume indexes the reports of Congress, the *Senate Executive Journal* for diplomatic and consular appointments and treaty ratifications, the opinions of the attorney general for decisions of questions of international controversy, the *Statutes at Large,* and the *Congressional Globe.* Two others are Jerome Wilcox's *Guide to the Official Publications of the New Deal Administrations*[21] and his *Official War Publications.*[22]

In 1970, the *CIS/Index* (the Congressional Information Service's *Index to Publications of the United States Congress*) made its first appearance. The first part of this index consists of abstracts of United States congressional documents issued in the previous month. The second part is the main index covering subjects; names of hearing witnesses, authors, and subcommittees; affiliations of witnesses or authors; and popular names of the laws, reports, or bills. Additional indexes give bill numbers, public law numbers, report numbers, document numbers, and the superintendent of documents number. The user can find the abstract from the CIS accession number in the index; he may also send to the Congressional Information Service for a microfiche copy of a complete document if his library does not have it. Issued monthly, the *CIS/Index* has quarterly index cumulations, and the whole data bank will be cumulated annually into a hardbound volume.

The documents belonging to the beginning and early periods of United States history are found mainly in report editions or in compilations and collections which Congress had ordered prepared or purchased from private parties.

[20] Carnegie Institution Publication no. 185, 2 vols. (Washington, D.C., Carnegie Institution, 1914–21).

[21] Jerome Kear Wilcox (Chicago, American Library Association, 1934). *Supplements,* April 15, 1934–January 1, 1937, 2 vols. (1936–37).

[22] Jerome Kear Wilcox, *Official War Publications: Guide to State, Federal, and Canadian Publications,* June, 1940–January 1, 1945, 9 vols. (Berkeley, Bureau of Public Administration, University of California, 1941–45).

The *American Archives*[23] originally were planned to comprise six series, consisting of a collection of records, state papers, debates and letters; the whole was to form a documentary history of the North American colonies from their beginning through the ratification of the Constitution. Only six volumes in the fourth series and three volumes in the fifth were published.

The most important publication of the Continental Congress was its *Journals*, which contained the public proceedings and other important material. The *Journals* have been printed in various editions, but the most complete is the one edited by Worthington Chauncey Ford, Gaillard Hunt, and others.[24] Certain portions of the *Journals*, known as the *Secret Journals*, were withheld from publication with the *Journals*. They were published by Wait in 1821.[25]

Collections of diplomatic correspondence relating to the revolutionary period are especially important. There are several collections of this correspondence. There is *Diplomatic Correspondence of the American Revolution*, edited by Jared Sparks,[26] and *Diplomatic Correspondence of the United States*, edited by Francis Blair.[27] The most complete and authentic set is *Revolutionary Diplomatic Correspondence*, by Francis Wharton.[28]

The proceedings and debates of the Constitutional Convention are most important for the period. Elliot's *Debates*[29] is the most complete and valuable of the several editions.

The *American State Papers* is the collection of documents of the first fourteen congresses.[30] It is made up of executive and legislative documents from the archives and manuscript records of the

[23] For full bibliographic information, see note 6.
[24] For full bibliographic information, see note 11.
[25] For full bibliographic information, see note 12.
[26] For full bibliographic information, see note 8.
[27] For full bibliographic information, see note 9.
[28] For full bibliographic information, see note 10.
[29] For full bibliographic information, see note 7.
[30] For full bibliographic information, see note 4.

244

Senate and House. It is not complete; there is no complete set anywhere.

A. W. Greely has compiled the important bibliography *Public Documents of the First Fourteen Congresses.*[31] It is an attempt to give a complete list of publications of the period. The publications are arranged chronologically by Congress, then by classification of journals, documents, and reports.

Other documents for the early congresses are the proceedings and debates in the early congresses, namely, the *Annals of Congress,* the *Register of Debates,* and the *Congressional Globe.* These will be discussed later.

Because all congressmen and one-third of the senators are elected every two years, there is a new Congress every two years. From the beginning of the government in 1789, each Congress has been numbered consecutively and is always referred to by number and by session, such as the Sixty-ninth Congress, first session. The important publications of Congress grow out of its activities connected with the making of laws and out of the investigations which it conducts or authorizes to be conducted as an aid in the legislative program. The two bodies of Congress, the Senate and the House of Representatives, have similar administrative and functional organizations. Both are organized and perform their duties under a complicated body of rules, which may be found in the Senate and House *Manuals,* in the Senate and House *Journals,* and in the Senate and House *Precedents.*

Congress conducts its work through committees, boards, and commissions. There are several kinds of committees: standing, conference, joint, special, and select. The standing committees of the Senate and House are composed of elected members, who study the bills and resolutions referred to them and make recommendations as to what should be done. Conference committees are

[31] A. W. Greely, *Public Documents of the First Fourteen Congresses, 1789–1817: Papers Relating to Early Congressional Documents,* 56 Cong., 1 sess., *Sen. Doc. 427,* serial 3879 (1900). *Supplement,* reprinted from the *Annual Report* of the American Historical Association, 1 (1903); 343–406.

temporary; they consist of members selected from both houses to adjust their differences over a specific bill or resolution which is being considered in Congress. Joint committees consist of members selected from both houses: their duties are similar to those of standing committees, plus certain administrative duties when Congress is not in session. Congress creates special and select committees to make special investigations not necessarily related to legislation. They vary from one session of Congress to another. Commissions and boards are created by Congress to make special investigations. They are usually composed of members selected wholly or in part from outside Congress.

To enact a law, a bill or resolution is drafted and introduced into the Senate or House where it is referred to a standing committee. The committee studies the bill and holds hearings, if desired. The committee then reports the bill with the committee's recommendations to the house where the bill originated and where it is debated. If the bill is passed, it is sent to the other house where it goes through the same procedure. If the second house amends the bill, it returns to the first house where it is debated again. If the bill passes, it goes to the president for his approval and signature. If the president does not approve, the bill goes back to the original house with his objections. A bill may be passed by both houses over a presidential veto. If the two houses cannot agree, the bill goes to a conference committee. This committee reports to both houses, and the houses may debate the bill again. The bill may or may not be passed.

Congress conducts investigations through its special committees and commissions. They conduct their investigations in a manner suggesting judicial procedure, that is, they hold hearings, require witnesses to attend, and books, papers, and documents to be produced. Their hearings, special reports, and studies are valuable sources of data for the student.

Bills are private or public and are used for general legislation. Private bills include all bills for the relief of private parties. All other bills are public. A bill is called a bill as long as it remains in the house in which it originates; it becomes an act when it has passed one house and goes to the other house. It does not become an act or statute in the legal sense until it has passed both houses and received the signature of the president or the two-thirds vote of both houses over the president's veto.

Resolutions are simple, joint, or concurrent. Simple resolutions concern the business of one house only and are not preserved as laws. Joint resolutions are used for incidental or inferior legislation, such as extending national thanks to individuals. They are passed by Congress in the same way that bills, except those proposing amendments to the Constitution, are, and they have the full force of law. Concurrent resolutions have developed as a means of expressing facts, principles, opinions, and the purposes of both houses. Both houses have to agree in order to make the resolutions binding.[32]

Bills and resolutions are not printed in the congressional edition. They are printed when referred to committee, when favorably reported back, and after passage by either house. They are numbered when they are introduced; they retain the same number until they become a law, at which time they are printed in leaflet form, called a slip law, and given a new number in a consecutive series. The slip laws are sent to the State Department which edits them and has them printed in the United States *Statutes at Large*.[33]

Bills and resolutions are neither listed nor indexed directly in any of the regular government catalogs or indexes except when a special edition is printed for general distribution. Older bills and resolutions are listed indirectly in the *Catalog of the Public Documents* under the entries for committee reports, which refer to them. Current bills and resolutions are listed by number and title with the stage of their progress in the indexes to the *Congressional Record* and in the *Appendix* to the Senate and the House *Journals*. They also are listed in the Library of Congress Legislative Refer-

[32] Boyd and Rips, *United States Government Publications*, 50–53.
[33] For full bibliographic information, see Chapter 10, note 11.

ence Service's *Digest of Public General Bills* and in the *House Legislative Calendar.*

Congressional hearings are the printed or processed transcript of the stenographic record of testimony given before committees. Technically speaking the hearings are not publications of Congress because they are not ordered by either house. Occasionally they are printed as documents or parts of reports. They are most important for the historian. The *Monthly Catalog* index gives references to the hearings under committees and subject matter. There are other indexes to hearings. *Public Affairs Information Service Bulletin* lists important current hearings on political, economic, and social matters. Hearings prior to the Sixty-first Congress are listed in the *Checklist of United States Public Documents*, and the Library of Congress has issued a *Checklist of Hearings Through the 67th Congress* by Harold O. Thomen, in nine parts.[34]

[34] *Checklist of Hearings Before Congressional Committees Through the Sixty-seventh Congress* (Washington, D.C., Library of Congress, Legislative Reference Service, 1941, 1942–58).

The 1924 edition of the *Senate Catalogue* is a guide to most hearings issued up to March 3, 1923. The list of hearings has been published several times, both before and after 1924; one publication is the *Index of Congressional Committee Hearings (Not Confidential in Character) Prior to January 3, 1935, in the United States Senate Library* (Washington, D.C., Government Printing Office, 1935), *Supplement, January 3, 1935–January 3, 1941* (1941). The Microform Division of the Greenwood Publishing Corporation, Westport, Connecticut, is publishing a microfiche collection with hardbound index of congressional hearings entitled *Congressional Hearings: Testimony Before Committees of the United States Congress*, 41 Congress through 73 Congress, 1869–1934. It is based on the *Index of Congressional Committee Hearings (Not Confidential in Character) Prior to January 3, 1935 in the United States Senate Library* (1935). The latest edition is the *Cumulative Index of Congressional Committee Hearings (Not Confidential in Character)* from the 74 Congress (January 3, 1935) through the 85 Congress (January 3, 1959) in the United States Senate Library, indexed and compiled under the direction of Felton M. Johnston, Secretary of the Senate, by Richard D. Hupman, Librarian [et al.] (Washington, D.C., Government Printing Office, 1959). *Quadrennial Supplement to Cumulative Index of Congressional Committee Hearings (Not Confidential in Character)*, from 86 Congress (January 7, 1959) through

248

When a committee has completed studying a bill or resolution, it prepares a report to its respective house, setting forth recommendations and the reasons for its decisions. This report ordinarily does not include the text of the bill or the hearings, though the report refers to the bill and hearings by number and title. Committee reports on bills and resolutions are printed as individual numbered publications when reported to either house. Congress orders them printed and bound in the congressional edition, arranged numerically in the series called *Senate Reports* and *House Reports*. Before the first session of the Sixteenth Congress (1819–20), House committee reports were included in the *Documents* series and in the *State Papers*, and Senate committee reports were not issued in separate volumes until the Thirtieth Congress (1847–48). Since the Forty-seventh Congress, reports of committees have been numbered consecutively for a Congress and for each house. Volumes of reports on private bills and simple and concurrent resolutions, beginning with the third session of the Fifty-eighth Congress (1904), have been designated alphabetically instead of numerically for each session.

Current committee reports are listed in the *Monthly Catalog* and indexed under subject in its index. The *Congressional Record* index lists current committee reports under the name of the committee, under the name of the congressman making the report, and under the bill number. The *Journals* refer to them in the section "History of Bills and Resolutions." Older reports are indexed in the *Catalog of the Public Documents* under subjects, with a cross

87 Congress (January 3, 1963) together with selected committee prints in the United States Senate Library, comp. and indexed by Mary F. Sterrett (Washington, D.C., Government Printing Office, 1963). The hearings in the House of Representatives are listed in the *Index to Congressional Committee Hearings in the Library of the United States House of Representatives Prior to January 1, 1951*, comp. by Russell Savill (Washington, D.C., Government Printing Office, 1954) and *Supplemental Index to Congressional Committee Hearings*, January 3, 1949, to January 3, 1955, 81, 82, and 83 congresses, in the Library of the United States House of Representatives, comp. by John A. Cooper under the direction of Ralph R. Roberts (Washington, D.C., Government Printing Office, 1956).

reference from the name of the committee, in Ames's *Comprehensive Index*, and in Poore's *Descriptive Catalogue*. Very early reports are listed individually in Poore's *Descriptive Catalogue*, Greely's *Public Documents of the First Fourteen Congresses*, and the *Checklist of United States Public Documents*.

To locate a committee report in the congressional edition, it is necessary to have the number of the report and the number and session of the Congress. Using this information it is possible to find the serial number of the volume from the *Checklist of United States Public Documents*, the schedules in the *Catalog of the Public Documents*, or in the *Numerical Lists and Schedule of Volumes*.

Thomas Hudson McKee's *Compilation of Committee Reports* is a list of committee reports of the Fourteenth to Forty-ninth congresses (1815–87).[35] These reports for each committee of each house are grouped together and arranged chronologically: 178 volumes of Senate committee reports and 335 volumes of House committee reports with ninety-five indexes (thirty-six for the Senate and fifty-nine for the House). The indexes were published separately for sale.

Staff of legal and research experts often make studies on aspects of the subject a committee is investigating. These studies are issued as "Committee prints," which contain much valuable data.

There is a guide to government reports associated with identification of a person by name. *Popular Names of U.S. Government Reports*[36] contains 479 significant reports of executive, legislative, and judicial bodies published within the last seventy-five years. The reports are arranged alphabetically by popular name. The entries are reproductions of Library of Congress printed catalog cards. The index is by subject. It does for government reports what Shepard's *Federal Acts by Popular Names or Short Titles* does for laws.

[35] (Washington, D.C., Government Printing Office, 1887).
[36] U.S., Library of Congress, Serial Division, Reference Department, *Popular Names of U.S. Government Reports Catalog*, comp. by Donald F. Wisdom and William P. Kilroy (Washington, D.C., Government Printing Office, 1966).

Each house of Congress is required to keep a journal of its proceedings; therefore, the *Journal of the Senate* and the *Journal of the House of Representatives* have been issued since the first session of Congress in the congressional edition. They contain a list of bills and resolutions introduced each day by number and title (not the text or debate), titles of memorials or petitions to Congress, the annual message of the president, presidential veto messages, and other communications to both houses. The *Journal* of the Senate also includes inaugural addresses and proceedings of impeachment trials in the Senate. In the appendix of each Senate and House *Journal*, a section called "History of Bills and Resolutions" contains a complete numerical list of all Senate and House bills and resolutions arranged as: House bills, Senate bills, House resolutions, Senate resolutions, House joint and concurrent resolutions, and Senate joint and concurrent resolutions. Each entry includes the following information: the title of the bill or resolution; the name of the committee to which the bill or resolution was referred, with the name of its chairman; the number of the committee's report (if any); the action taken by the two houses on the bill or resolution; the page number of the *Journal* where the bill or resolution is mentioned; and the law number if the bill or resolution is passed and signed by the president. There also are subject indexes to the section of bills and resolutions and to the *Journal*. There are indexes to the early *Journal*s. Albert Ordway compiled two, the *General Index of the Journals of Congress*[37] and the *General Personal Index of the Journals of Congress*.[38] They are in the congressional edition. Ordway's *General Personal Index* is incomplete.

[37] *General Index of the Journals of Congress, from the First to the Tenth Congress, Inclusive* [1789–1809], 1880, 46 Cong., 2 sess., *House Rept. 1776; General Index of the Journals of Congress* [1809–21], 1883, 47 Cong., 1 sess., *House Rept. 1559.*

[38] *General Personal Index of the Journals of Congress, from the 1st to the 8th Congress, Inclusive* [1789–1805], 1885, 48 Cong., 2 sess., *House Rept. 2692; General Personal Index of the Journals of Congress, Inclusive* [1805–21], 1887, 49 Cong., 1 sess., *House Rept. 3474.*

The *Executive Proceedings of the Senate* is a separate series of journals printed for the secret or executive sessions of the Senate.[39] The president's nominations to office and the treaties which he has negotiated with foreign countries are considered in these sessions. They are printed separately some years after the events, by special order of the Senate. Only seven printings of the *Executive Proceedings of the Senate* have been authorized.

Senate Executive Documents also come out of the secret or executive sessions of the Senate. They contain the actual documents (treaties, agreements, and the like) which were considered by the Senate in executive session and to which the *Executive Proceedings of the Senate* refer. When they are printed, after the injunction of secrecy is removed, they are issued in lettered series. They are not included in the congressional edition unless they are so ordered by the Senate, at which time they are printed in the Senate Document series. Committee reports that accompany *Senate Executive Documents* are issued as *Senate Executive Reports*.

Printed reports, mainly from stenographic records, of debates and proceedings in both houses of Congress exist from the beginning of the government on March 4, 1789. These reports have appeared in four series: *Annals of Congress, Register of Debates, Congressional Globe*, and *Congressional Record*. Though they are not included in the congressional edition, they are among the most important historical documents of the government.

[39] *Journal of the Executive Proceedings of the Senate of the United States*, 1789– . Order of April 4, 1828, *Journals* of the 1 to the 19 Congress, 1789–1829, vols. 1–3, printed by Duff Green; Order of June 28, 1886, *Journals* of the 20 to 40 Congress, 1829–69, vols. 4–16; Order of January 21, 1901, *Journals* of the 41 to the 51 Congress, 1869–91, vols. 17–27; Order relating to the 52 to the 58 Congress, 1891–1905, vols. 28–34; Order of February 28, 1931, *Journals* from the 59 Congress to the end of the 71 Congress, 1905–31, vols. 35–39; Order of July 6, 1929, provided for five hundred copies of all journals beginning with the 72 Congress, 1 session, and continuing for each session thereafter; Order of February 9, 1950, provided for disposing of volumes from December 1, 1901, through December 31, 1948, also cut federal printings to 50 copies of each volume. Schmeckebier and Eastin, *Government Publications and Their Use*, 130–31.

The *Annals of Congress*[40] was the first attempt to record the daily proceedings in both houses, and the *Register of Debates in Congress*[41] was the second. Both have indexes for each session in the printed volume. The *Congressional Globe*[42] includes messages of the president and reports of the cabinet officers in its appendices until the end of the Thirty-ninth Congress. There is an index for each session in the volume and an index to each *Appendix*.

The *Congressional Record*[43] is issued daily while Congress is in session. It is revised and issued in permanent form at the end of each session. It contains presidential messages, congressional speeches and debates in full, and a record of voting. The texts of bills are excluded beginning with the Eightieth Congress (March 17, 1947). A section called the "Daily Digest" has been added to the daily issues, which is a great help in tracing the legislative his-

[40] U.S., Congress, *The Debates and Proceedings in the Congress of the United States with an Appendix Containing Important State Papers and Public Documents and All the Laws of a Public Nature, with Copious Index* (1 to 18 Congress, 1 sess. . . . March 3, 1789–May 27, 1824), comp. from authentic sources, 42 vols. (Washington, D.C., Gales and Seaton, 1834–56). (Commonly known as the *Annals of Congress*.)

[41] U.S., Congress, *Register of Debates in Congress, Comprising the Leading Debates and Incidents of the Second Session of the 18th Congress Together with an Appendix Containing Most Important State Papers and Public Documents to Which the Session Has Given Birth, to Which Are Added the Laws Enacted During the Session, with a Copious Index to the Whole*, December 6, 1824, to the 25 Cong., 1 sess., October 6, 1837, 14 vols. in 25 (Washington, D.C., Gales and Seaton, 1825–37).

[42] U.S., Congress, *Congressional Globe: Containing the Debates and Proceedings . . . 23d Congress to the 42d Congress, December 2, 1833 to March 3, 1873*, 46 vols. (Washington, D.C., printed at the Globe Office for the editors, 1834–73). The United States Historical Documents Institute, Washington, D.C., has published the *Proceedings of the U.S. Congress, 1789–1964* (i.e., the *Annals*, the *Register of Debates*, the *Congressional Globe*, and the *Congressional Record*, 1873–1964) on 479 reels of microfilm, with reprint volumes of the indexes to all the regular and special sessions, the indexes to the appendices, and the histories of bills and resolutions.

[43] U.S., Congress, *Congressional Record: Containing the Proceedings and Debates*, March 4, 1873– (Washington, D.C., Government Printing Office, 1874–).

tory of important current bills. It lists for each house the action taken on bills and bills signed by the president; it also notes committee meetings and reports. There are biweekly indexes in addition to the final index in the permanent edition. The index is divided into two parts: (1) alphabetical index of names and subject; (2) history of bills and resolutions arranged by bill number. This second section is the best source for tracing the history of a bill.

There are several tools for finding current information on legislation prepared by the federal government. The *Digest of Public General Bills*[44] contains a digest of the provisions of every bill, which is public and general in character. It does not contain a complete history of the bill, but it does give the introduction, the committee reference, and the last action. The arrangement is by bill number, with a subject index.

The *Calendar of the United States House of Representatives and the History of Bills and Resolutions Introduced into the United States Senate During . . . Congress* is for the official use of Congress and is not readily available to the student. The *Commerce Clearing House Congressional Index*,[45] however, is an excellent nongovernmental tool for following current legislation.

The publications of the executive branch of the government are also quite important for the history student. The president is the chief executive and exercises his executive powers through departments created by act of Congress and presided over by major officials, called secretaries, appointed by the president with the consent of the Senate. These secretaries compose the president's cabinet. Although the cabinet as a whole does not issue any publications, the departments are organized for administrative and functional purposes into many bureaus, and they issue publications. Many small boards, commissions, and committees, such as

[44] U.S., Library of Congress, 74 Cong., 2 sess., 1936– (Washington, D.C., Government Printing Office, 1936–). At first, weekly; later irregular; and now, four or five cumulative issues per session.

[45] (New York, Commerce Clearing House, 1937–38–). Loose leaf, biennial.

the Central Intelligence Agency and the Council of Economic Advisors, have been created during the twentieth century with independent status because either Congress or the president did not want to subordinate them to any of the executive departments. These independent institutions, however, do belong to the executive branch of the government, and they do issue publications.

Executive publications constitute by far the greatest number of government publications. This chapter will mention only a few of the presidential documents and a few of the State Department documents which could be useful to the history student. All publications originating in the executive branch are issued in the so-called departmental edition. Up to 1908, practically all publications in the departments and independent agencies were issued in both the departmental and congressional editions. In 1908, annual reports and serial publications of the executive agencies were removed from the Serial Set and distributed to depository libraries. It also was provided that the departmental edition should be printed concurrently with the congressional edition and that publications not large enough to bind should be distributed unbound.[46] The departmental publications are, in general, well indexed. Since 1895 they have been included in the *Catalog of the Public Documents*, and the current ones are listed in the *Monthly Catalog*. Many of the early department publications are listed in Poore's *Descriptive Catalogue* and Ames's *Comprehensive Index*. Many of the bureaus publish their own indexes and the general periodical indexes, such as the *Public Affairs Information Service Bulletin*, which indexes many of the more important executive publications.

The publications of the president include his messages, addresses, and speeches. In addition to the compilations mentioned earlier, there are several government sources for presidential records. *Annual Messages* are printed in the *Senate* and *House*

[46] Boyd and Rips, *United States Government Publications*, 100–101. A depository library is "a library legally designated to receive without charge copies of all of selected United States government publications," *A.L.A. Glossary*, 45.

Journals, in the *Congressional Record* since 1873, and in *Papers Relating to Foreign Relations* since 1861. They also are printed immediately on receipt in pamphlet form. The early ones can be located in the *American State Papers: Foreign Relations, 1789–1828*; the *Annals of Congress, 1790–1823*; the *Register of Debates*, 1824–36; and the *Congressional Globe*, 1833–72.

Veto messages are always printed in the *Journal* of the house in which the vetoed bill originated and in the *Congressional Record*. They are also printed in the congressional edition of the documents series. Poore lists the early ones in his *Veto Messages of the Presidents*.[47] Richard D. Hupman has directed the Senate Library in the compilation of *Presidential Vetoes*, a list of the bills vetoed and a notation of the action taken on them by the Senate and House, 1789–1961.[48]

Special Messages and other communications except routine letters and notes are printed in the *Congressional Record* and as separate documents in the congressional edition. A transmittal letter is printed with the reports or documents if they are printed in the congressional edition. In addition to the compilation *The State of the Union Messages of the Presidents*, by Fred L. Israel,[49] the presidents' inaugural addresses are printed in the *Journals* of the Senate, in the *Congressional Record*, and separately. The presidential speeches are sometimes printed in the *Congressional Record*, sometimes issued separately, and sometimes not printed. If the messages and addresses are printed by the government, the *Monthly Catalog* and the *Catalog of the Public Documents* list them under the heading, "President of the United States." The *Checklist* lists the older ones and presidential papers under the same heading, with a chronological arrangement by the name of the president; Poore's *Descriptive Catalogue* and Ames's *Compre-*

[47] Benjamin Perley Poore, *Veto Messages of Presidents of the United States, with Action of Congress Thereon . . . 1792–1886*, 49 Cong., 2 sess., *Sen. Misc. Doc. 53*.

[48] U.S., Congress, Senate, Library (Washington, D.C., Government Printing Office, 1961).

[49] For full bibliographic information, see Chapter 9, note 110.

hensive Index list the older ones under the name of the president. Presidents issue executive orders, which virtually have the force of law. They also issue proclamations, which do not always have the force of law; sometimes they are merely notifications or appeals to the public. Most executive orders relate to the conduct of government business or to organization of the executive departments, but some have a wider significance, for example, Executive Order no. 2796 prescribes rules and regulations under the Trading with the Enemy Act. Most of the emergency agencies created in 1933 were established by the executive orders of President Franklin D. Roosevelt. The executive orders and proclamations which were published in the *Federal Register* are not issued separately. Those that are not published in the *Federal Register* are issued separately. The proclamations are collected and printed in the *Statutes at Large*. The *Monthly Catalog* listed both the executive orders and proclamations under "President of the United States prior to September 1947." The *Catalog of the Public Documents* lists them by number and date, with reference to subject under the main entry, "President of the United States," with subentries, "Executive orders" and "Proclamations." If compilations have been made on particular subjects, they are indexed under the subject or the name of the issuing body. Executive Order no. 10006 of October 9, 1948, required current publication of all executive orders and proclamations in the *Federal Register*. Beginning with Proclamation no. 2287 of June 6, 1938, and Executive Order no. 7906 of the same date, proclamations and executive orders have been published by the Office of the Federal Register in supplements to Title 3 of the *Code of Federal Regulations*.[50] The proclamations are collected now in one section of the *Statutes at Large*.

List and Index of Presidential Executive Orders, Unnumbered

[50] Boyd and Rips, *United States Government Publications*, 103–105; Schmeckebier and Eastin, *Government Publications and Their Use*, 318–21. As of January 1, 1960, the entire series was made up of the following volumes: 1. Title 3, Book 1, *Cumulative Supplement*; 2. Title 3, 1943–48, *Compilation*; 3. Title 3, 1949–53, *Compilation*; 4. the 1954–58 *Supplements* to Title 3.

Series and *Numbered 1–8030* are two lists of executive orders which were prepared under government sponsorship but published privately.[51] Margaret Fennell has prepared a *Table of Executive Orders Appearing in the "Federal Register" and the "Code of Federal Regulations" for 1936–1954.*[52] It supplements the two series of presidential executive orders mentioned above. Executive orders relating to Indian affairs in effect up to June 29, 1938, are contained in Kappler's *Indian Affairs, Laws and Treaties.*[53]

There is no index to all the proclamations; however, citations are given for the *Statutes at Large*, which contain proclamations prior to March 4, 1931, on certain subjects, in the *Index to the Federal Statutes, 1789–1931.*[54]

Presidential committees and commissions are similar to the boards and commissions set up by Congress to make special investigations, but they are appointed by the president instead of by legislative action. The reports of these commissions often are of great significance.

The Executive Office of the President issues several publications that are significant and valuable for the student of American history and life. There is the *Economic Report*,[55] an annual report to Congress prepared by the president and the Council of Economic Advisors. The council studies national economic developments and trends and recommends to the president certain national economic policies. The council provides the president with studies and reports on federal economic policy and legislation as re-

---

[51] Historical Records Survey, New Jersey, *List and Index of Presidential Executive Orders, Unnumbered Series, 1789–1941* (Newark, N.J., 1943); Historical Records Survey, New York City, *Presidential Executive Orders, Numbered 1–8030, 1862–1938*, 2 vols. (New York, Archives Publishing Co., a division of Hastings House, 1944).

[52] U.S., Library of Congress, Legislative Reference Service (Washington, D.C., Reference Department, Library of Congress, 1955).

[53] For full bibliographic information, see Chapter 10, note 47.

[54] For full bibliographic information, see Chapter 10, note 13.

[55] U.S., President of the United States, *Economic Report of the President to Congress*, January, 1947– (Washington, D.C., Superintendent of Documents, 1947–).

quested, and the president, in turn, submits his annual *Economic Report.*

The Bureau of the Budget was created in 1921 as an aid to the president in preparing his annual *Budget of the United States Government.*[56] Supplements, such as the *War Supplements* of 1944–47 and the *Corporation Supplement,* are issued when needed. The budget for each fiscal year is now contained in two volumes and divided into four parts: part 1 contains summary tables; part 2, the details of the budget for federal funds, including various types of tables and schedules, explanatory statements of the work to be performed and the money needed; part 3, a summary table on trust and deposit funds and detailed schedules and explanatory statements on the various trust funds; and part 4, special analyses of budget data and federal programs. The *Appendix* consists of schedules showing details of the personal services which are reflected in the budget.

The *United States Government Organization Manual,*[57] another publication of the executive branch, contains information on the organization, functions, and action of the federal government bodies and refers to the laws or other authority creating them. Charts show the organization of the major bodies. Appendix A lists executive agencies and functions of the federal government that have been abolished, transferred, or terminated subsequent to March 4, 1953. Appendix B lists representative publications from all agencies publishing. If the student learns about the structure of the government, he will learn the sources of its documents.

Taylor's Encyclopedia of Government Officials, by John Clem-

[56] U.S., Bureau of the Budget, *Budget of United States Government, Fiscal Year . . . 1922–* (Washington, D.C., Government Printing Office, 1921–).

[57] U.S., National Archives, Federal Register Division, 1935– . It superseded the *Daily Revised Manual of Emergency Recovery Agencies and Facilities Provided by the United States Government,* which had been issued in 1934 by the National Emergency Council. It was entitled *United States Manual* and was published by the Government Reports Office in 1935–48.

ents, is a privately published directory of government agencies and departments of the United States and of the states.[58] Updated supplements are published quarterly, and a completely revised edition is published every two years.

The first executive department of the United States government to be established was the Department of Foreign Affairs, which soon changed its name to the Department of State. The Department of State's functions pertaining to foreign relations are most important in United States history.

Beginning October 1, 1929, all State Department publications, except laws and translations, have been numbered consecutively in the order in which they are sent to the press. They have been divided into numbered series according to their general character and subject. Current publications are listed quarterly in the *Department of State Bulletin* for the preceding three months, and a cumulated list is issued regularly.[59] It is arranged by series.

The diplomatic correspondence between the United States and foreign countries is most significant. The *Foreign Relations of the United States* has been published since 1861.[60] It is a collection of official papers relating to the foreign relations of the United States, with the annual message of the president to Congress. The long delay (currently about fifteen years) in the publication of these papers is primarily due to the reluctance of the foreign powers to consent to the publication of their documents.

Prior to 1861 there was no annual publication of the general diplomatic correspondence carried on through the State Depart-

[58] *Taylor's Encyclopedia of Government Officials: Federal and State*, 2d ed. (Dallas, Texas, Political Research Inc., 1969–70).

[59] U.S., Dept. of State, *Publications of the Department of State*, October 1, 1929–January 1, 1953, Department of State Publication 5059 (Washington, D.C., Government Printing Office, 1954). *January 1, 1953–December 31, 1957* (1958); *January 1, 1958–December 31, 1960* (1961).

[60] U.S., Dept. of State, *Foreign Relations of the United States*, 1861– (Washington, D.C., Government Printing Office, 1862–). Title varies: *Papers Relating to the Foreign Relations of the United States*, 1861–1931. *General Index, 1861–1899, 1900–1918*, 2 vols. (Washington, D.C., Government Printing Office, 1902–41).

ment. It was the custom of Congress to call from time to time for the correspondence on which it desired information; the material supplied in response to such calls was published in the congressional document series at irregular intervals. The most important correspondence relating to foreign affairs between 1789 and 1838 was reprinted in the *American State Papers*. Wharton's *Revolutionary Diplomatic Correspondence* contains the documents on foreign relations for that period.[61] In 1861, Secretary of State William Seward submitted a volume made of the general diplomatic correspondence of the year. Every year since, with the exception of 1869, a similar volume has been sent to Congress. In 1870 the title was changed from *Papers Relating to Foreign Affairs* to *Papers Relating to the Foreign Relations of the United States*.[62] Several volumes are now issued for each year, with subtitles designating the country or area of the world to which they relate. The volumes of *Foreign Relations* for 1861–99 are indexed in the *General Index to the Published Volumes of the Diplomatic Correspondence and Foreign Relations of the United States of America, 1861–1899*.[63] Later volumes are indexed in *Papers Relating to the Foreign Relations of the United States: General Index, 1900–1918*.[64]

Hasse's *Index to United States Documents Relating to Foreign Affairs, 1828–1861*,[65] is a useful guide to early publications containing foreign relations, and Samuel Flagg Bemis and Grace

[61] For full bibliographic information, see note 10.

[62] Supplements have been issued containing the *Lansing Papers, 1914–1920*, 2 vols.; the *Diplomatic Correspondence Relating to the World War, 1916–1918*, 7 vols.; *Relations with Russia, 1918–1919*, 4 vols.; and *Relations with Japan, 1931–1941*, 2 vols. A series of thirteen supplementary volumes has been issued on the Paris Peace Conference, 1919; volume 13, an annotated text of the Treaty of Versailles, was also published as Conference Series no. 92.

[63] U.S., Dept. of State, vols. 1–56 (Washington, D.C., Government Printing Office, 1902).

[64] U.S., Dept. of State, vols. 57–96 (Washington, D.C., Government Printing Office, 1942).

[65] Adelaide R. Hasse, Carnegie Institution Publication no. 185, 2 vols. (Washington, D.C., Carnegie Institution, 1914–21).

Gardner Griffin's *Guide to the Diplomatic History of the United States*[66] is the basic important guide to all the materials on foreign relations. John Basset Moore's *Digest of International Law*,[67] Hackworth's *Digest*,[68] and Whiteman's *Digest*[69] can also be used as indexes to diplomatic discussions and correspondence of the United States.

The government has published many papers relating to specific events or issues of foreign affairs. For example, *The Conferences at Malta and Yalta*, a volume containing the records of these conferences, with preconference background material, was issued in 1955 in a special series of *Foreign Relations* volumes and as a House document.[70] The Carnegie Foundation for International Peace, which is not a government agency, also is responsible for two collections of official papers: *Diplomatic Correspondence of the United States Concerning the Independence of the Latin American Nations*,[71] selected and arranged by William R. Manning of the State Department, and *Diplomatic Correspondence of the United States: Inter-American Affairs, 1831–1860*.[72]

In 1929 the State Department started a special series relating to conferences. Each number in the *Conference Series* relates to a particular conference or to some development resulting from a conference. Beginning in 1948, this material was included in a new series, the *International Organization and Conference Series*, which was divided into groups of publications concerning general, regional, United Nations, and specialized agencies. In the spring of 1959, these groups were discontinued, and the publications on international organizations and conferences were numbered in one sequence.

[66] For full bibliographic information, see Chapter 3, note 20.
[67] For full bibliographic information, see Chapter 10, note 41.
[68] For full bibliographic information, see Chapter 10, note 42.
[69] For full bibliographic information, see Chapter 10, note 43.
[70] *The Conferences at Malta and Yalta*, 1945, 84 Cong., 1 sess., *House Doc. 154* (Washington, D.C., Government Printing Office, 1955).
[71] 3 vols. (New York, Oxford University Press, 1925).
[72] 12 vols. (Washington, D.C., Carnegie Endowment for International Peace, 1932–39).

262

Since 1932 the record of United States participation in international conferences has been available in two series of Department of State publications: *American Delegations to International Conferences, Congresses, and Expositions*[73] and *Participation of the United States Government in International Conferences.*[74]

The weekly *Department of State Bulletin*[75] contains information on current developments in the field of foreign relations and the work of the Department of State and the Foreign Service, including press releases, official statements of policy, texts of important documents, the United States position in the United Nations, and articles by department officials. It replaced the series entitled *Press Releases*, which had been issued weekly from 1929 to 1939, with an index every six months and a cumulative index for October 5, 1929–December 29, 1934, and the *Treaty Information Bulletin*, which was discontinued in June of 1939.

Documents and State Papers[76] complement the weekly *Bulletin* by providing documentary information on international relations in the form of reports, statements of policy, background studies, texts of treaties and agreements, and similar long-range materials. It includes a calendar of international meetings and current references on the United Nations.

The basic documents on American foreign policy covering 1941–49 were published under the title, *A Decade of American*

[73] U.S., Dept. of State, *American Delegations to International Conferences, Congresses, and Expositions and American Representation on International Institutions and Commissions with Relevant Data*, July 1, 1932–June 30, 1941– (Washington, D.C., Government Printing Office, 1932–).

[74] U.S., Dept. of State, Division of International Conferences, *Participation of the United States Government in International Conferences Including the Composition of United States Delegations and Summaries of the Proceedings*, July 1, 1941– (Washington, D.C., Government Printing Office, 1932–).

[75] U.S., Dept. of State, July 1, 1939 (Washington, D.C., Government Printing Office, 1939–). Weekly.

[76] U.S., Dept. of State, April, 1948– (Washington, D.C., Government Printing Office, 1939–).

Foreign Policy: Basic Documents, 1941–1949;[77] and those for 1950–55, as *American Foreign Policy, 1950–1955: Basic Documents.*[78] The first of the annual volumes, *American Foreign Policy: Current Documents, 1956* was issued as Department of State publication 6811.[79]

The *Biographic Register* contains a biographical sketch of each employee of the State Department, the United States Mission to the United Nations, the International Cooperation Administration, the United States Information Agency, and the Development Loan Fund in grades GS-12 and above and ES-12 and above.[80] In the Foreign Service groups there are biographies for ambassadors, ministers, Foreign Service officers, Foreign Service reserve officers, and Foreign Service staff officers of classes one to nine inclusive. Chiefs of overseas missions and employees of comparable grades of the International Cooperation Administration, the United States Information Agency, and the Foreign Agricultural Service of the Department of Agriculture are included.

Three valuable series for checking diplomatic personnel and their assignments are the *Diplomatic List*,[81] a list of the foreign diplomatic representatives in Washington, arranged by country; the *Foreign Service List*,[82] a list of American diplomatic and con-

---

[77] U.S., Dept. of State (Washington, D.C., Government Printing Office, 1950). Also available as 81 Cong., 1 sess., *Sen. Doc. 123.*

[78] U.S., Dept. of State, Department of State Publication no. 6446, 2 vols. (Washington, D.C., Government Printing Office, 1957).

[79] The volumes for 1957 as Department of State Publication 7101; for 1958, as Publication 7322; for 1959, as Publication 7492; for 1960, as Publication 7624; for 1961, as Publication 7808; for 1962, as Publication 8007 (Washington, D.C., Government Printing Office, 1958–).

[80] U.S., Dept. of State, *Biographic Register* (Washington, D.C., Government Printing Office, 1870–). Annual. Not published in some years (1881, 1885, 1889–91, 1943). Title varies: *Register of the Department of State,* 1869–1942.

[81] U.S., Dept. of State, March, 1893– (Washington, D.C., Government Printing Office, 1894–). Monthly.

[82] U.S., Dept. of State, comp. by the Publishing and Reproduction Services Division, Office of Operations (Washington, D.C., Government Printing Office, 1929–). Quarterly.

sular officers with their classification and assignment, arranged alphabetically by the country where they are stationed; and the *Foreign Consular Offices in the United States*,[83] a list of foreign consular offices in the United States with their jurisdictions and personnel, arranged alphabetically by country.

Great Britain

The invaluable but bibliographically confusing British Parliamentary Papers are of immense importance to historians. The nineteenth-century Parliamentary Papers, which total close to seven thousand folio volumes have been described as "the richest important nineteenth century collection of printed government records in existence in any country." Similarly, James T. Shotwell, a social historian, has stated, "If any one type of source must be regarded as the most important for English social and economic history in modern times the Blue Books of Parliamentary Papers must be chosen." The Blue Books cover enclosures, game laws, trade conditions, river pollution, railroads, wages, conditions of employment, migration, emigration, sewage, smoke prevention, charities, and so on. They are one of the few sources where evidence of what all classes of people thought about a question can be found. The illiterate and day laborers are reported in the same detail as the wealthy landlords.[84]

The editors of the Irish University Press in Shannon, Ireland, have identified, isolated, and grouped into sets of volumes all the basic source material on many significant subjects, such as the industrial revolution, the slave trade, and workhouses, from the nineteenth-century Parliamentary Papers. The pattern of publication for each subject is as follows: reports of select committees; reports of commissioners; correspondence; and returns. Each section is to be arranged in chronological order. The Irish University

[83] U.S., Dept. of State, 1932– (Washington, D.C., Government Printing Office, 1932–). Annual.

[84] T. P. O'Neill, *British Parliamentary Papers: A Monograph on Blue Books* (Shannon, Ireland, Irish University Press, 1968), 15–18.

Microforms, a Division of the Irish University Press, will prepare the microforms of the IUP series of Parliamentary Papers and the IUP Bibliographical Division will provide subject indexes to every subject set of them.

Percy Ford and Grace Ford have written *A Guide to Parliamentary Papers: What They Are; How To Find Them; How To Use Them.*[85] Albert Walford's *Guide to Reference Material* points out that the guide is more useful for the serious researcher than for the ordinary user; however, it is the only work of its kind and it is a valuable introduction to this complex resource. A projected manual of British government documents, which will be a companion volume to Boyd and Rip's *United States Government Publications*, is being compiled by Frank Rodgers and Rose B. Phelps. Three chapters on Parliamentary Papers have appeared in *A Guide to British Parliamentary Papers*, a condensed version.[86]

The term "Parliamentary Papers" is used in two different senses. The more comprehensive includes all material emanating from both the House of Commons and the House of Lords. This material can be divided into three broad categories: 1. journals, votes, and proceedings; 2. bills, reports, and papers; and 3. acts of Parliament, which include public and general acts, local and private acts, and measures passed by the National Assembly of the Church of England. The documents listed in the second group are often known as Parliamentary Papers. They may also be known as Sessional Papers. Groups of Parliamentary Papers are bound together to form separate series of volumes. These series differ from one another in size and arrangement according to the nature of their contents and according to the historical processes through which they were preserved.

The papers relating to the agenda, proceedings, and debates of the House include Procedure Papers, the Journals, the Debates, and the Standing Committee Debates. The Procedure Papers cover

[85] (Oxford, B. Blackwell, 1955).
[86] University of Illinois Graduate School of Library Science, Occasional Paper no. 82 (April, 1967), 31.

votes and proceedings, notices of questions, motions, and amendments; the agenda; the proceedings of recent sittings of standing committees; and collected lists of amendments to be proposed. The papers on the procedure of the House are issued separately. In the British Museum these papers are bound up as follows: votes and proceedings, divisions, notices of motion, questions and orders of the day, and private business.

The Journals of both houses have existed since the sixteenth century, although they were not referred to by that title until the seventeenth century. The extant Journals of the House of Lords began in 1509, the first year of the reign of Henry VIII; those of the House of Commons, in 1547, the year in which Edward VI became king. The Journals of the House of Commons show the long struggle of the lower house for power and its emergence as a dominant force. The Journals are printed at the end of each session with a Sessional Index. Since 1880 this index has also been consolidated into separately issued decennial ones. Before the regular decennial indexes, there were indexes compiled by individuals.[87]

The Debates[88] have been the official records of parliamentary debates since 1909, when the House of Commons set up a reporting staff of its own. These debates are substantially verbatim and in the first person. From 1803 to 1909 some speeches were given in full; the rest were abbreviated accounts in a mixture of first and third person. Originally the Debates were published privately by

[87] Percy Ford and Grace Ford, *A Guide to Parliamentary Papers*, 21–23, 3–4. Cunningham's Index, 1547–1659, vols. 1–7; Flexman's Index, 1660–97, vols. 8–11; Forster's Index, 1697–1714, vols. 12–17; Moore's Index, 1714–74, vols. 18–23; Dunn's Index, 1774–1800, vols. 35–55.

[88] Great Britain, Parliament, *Parliamentary Debates*, vols. 1–41 (1803–20); 2d ser., vols. 1–25 (1820–30); 3d ser., vols. 1–356 (1830–1890/91); 4th ser., vols. 1–199 (1892–1908); 5th ser., Commons, vol. 1– (1909–), Lords, vol. 1– (1909–). Generally cited as *Hansard* or *Debates (Hansard)*. Publisher varies. In 1909, H. M. Stationery Office took over publication. The first, second, third, and fourth series are unofficial; thus they do not contain complete or verbatim reports of debates. The fifth series is official. It contains complete and verbatim accounts of debates.

William Cobbett. They were designed to form a continuation of *The Parliamentary History of England from the Earliest Period to the Year 1803*,[89] of which the first twelve volumes were Cobbett's *Parliamentary History of England, from the Norman Conquest in 1066 to the Year 1803* and the remaining twenty-four were Hansard's series.

Standing Committee Debates are the minutes of the proceedings of standing committees, which are appointed each session to deal with bills after the second reading. It is usual to publish an official report of the debates on a government bill, but a report in the case of an unofficial member's bill is published only when the chairman of the committee considers that it is required in the public interest.

Papers giving Parliament information and other material bearing on questions of policy, administration, and other matters include: House Papers, papers arising outside the House, and Command Papers and Non-Parliamentary Papers. House Papers are those papers which arise out of the deliberations or are needed for the work of the House and are "Ordered by the House of Commons to be Printed." They include bills, reports of committees of the House, returns, and Act Papers.

Bills are divided into two classes: public bills, which relate to matters of public policy and are introduced directly by members of the House, and private bills, which are for the particular interest of individuals, public bodies, or local authorities, and are solicited by the interested parties. Bills are printed on their introduction into either House, and they are usually reprinted with the amendments made during their passage through Parliament. Bills from the House of Commons are arranged and numbered as a separate series. The Queen's Printer prints public and general bills. Private bills are not officially printed until they have received royal assent as acts.

The Committee of the Whole House, that is, the whole House sitting as a committee, arose in the seventeenth century during the period of the struggle between the Crown and the House of Com-

[89] 36 vols. (London, Hansard, 1806–20).

mons. It was a device to allow informal discussion on a particular issue and for enquiry. Today, this form of committee is used only for deliberation.

Select committees consist of members of the House of Commons or the House of Lords chosen to represent the parties and the opinions of their House. A joint select committee consists of members of both Houses. Each session a number of select committees, known as sessional committees, are appointed to deal with matters of a particular class arising during the course of a session. The rest are appointed to deal with particular subjects. Before and during the early nineteenth century the select committee was the chief means by which Parliament conducted its investigations as is evidenced by the *Index to Reports from Select Committees, 1801–1845*.[90] The select committee is still an important parliamentary investigating instrument, but the royal commissions and departmental committees have undertaken more of the work of investigation. The reports of the select committees contain the report on the subject referred to them; a record of the proceedings of the committee, which normally includes the text of the draft report submitted by the chairman, and amendments proposed; a record of the voting; and the minutes of evidence taken by the committee.[91]

Returns are the papers Parliament requires from the departments while carrying out its work. Parliament can order them printed as House Papers. Act Papers are papers which an act of Parliament has required should be laid before the House and which the House has ordered to be printed. Many of them are financial reports and accounts.

Papers arising outside the House include the reports of the royal commissions and departmental papers. Royal commissions and departmental committees or other investigating bodies report to their appointing authority (the Crown or a minister). Their reports and papers can be brought to the notice of the House by being presented to it "By Command." Instead of being "Ordered by the

[90] See note 97.
[91] Percy Ford and Grace Ford, *A Guide to Parliamentary Papers*, 4–7.

House of Commons to be printed," Command Papers are technically "Presented by Command of the Crown." Since 1921 the principle has been that only those departmental papers are presented which are likely to be the subject of early legislation or which are essential to members of Parliament.

A royal commission of inquiry consists of a body of persons appointed by the Crown to inquire into the subjects named in a royal warrant. A royal commission may be composed of people whom the minister considers experts and who are usually not members of Parliament. When time is needed to finish an investigation, a commission's inquiry may last over a period of years. The commission need not stop its work when Parliament is not sitting, and it can send members abroad to take evidence. It is a more powerful and more flexible instrument of investigation than a select committee. This form of investigation suited the needs of the government in the nineteenth century; however, today only the more complicated investigations are conducted by royal commissions. Arthur Harrison Cole identified royal commission reports of the nineteenth century in *A Finding List of British Royal Commission Reports*.[92] Entries in this list are arranged chronologically under broad subject headings. It is continued by one of the Stationery Office series of *Sectional Lists*.[93] The listing is alphabetical by the name of the commission.

As Parliament extended its supervision over the economic and social life of the country, the work and number of departments grew, and the departments developed new investigating committees. These included departmental committees, advisory and consultatory committees, and working parties. These committees may or may not include members of Parliament as members, they may extend their inquiries over a considerable time and outlast any

[92] *A Finding List of British Royal Commission Reports: 1860–1935*, with a preface by Arthur Harrison Cole (Cambridge, Mass., Harvard University Press, 1935).

[93] Great Britain, Government Publications, *Royal Commissions 1936–1961*, sectional list no. 59, rev. to April 30, 1964 (London, H. M. Stationery Office, 1964).

given Parliament. They report to a minister; their reports may or may not include evidence taken, but they do not include a record of proceedings. The researcher will learn little from their reports, which appear first as House Papers and then as Command Papers. The departmental committee has replaced the royal commission in all but major investigations.[94]

Before the nineteenth century there was no systematic way of preserving the Sessional or Command Papers; therefore, those papers that have come down are not complete. The three official sources for those preserved are the Journals, the First Series, and the Abbot Collection. References to papers printed in the body of the Journals are found in the indexes under the headings "Printing" and "Reports of Committees." The First Series, 1715–1801, is a reprint of a selection of the reports which have been printed in the Journals or had been printed separately. There are fifteen volumes with an index, which contains a list of reports of committees which were inserted in the Journals but not in the reprints. The Abbot Collection, 1731–1800,[95] is made up of 111 volumes of separately printed papers which were in storage at the time the First Series was printed. Charles Abbot ordered that they should be gathered together and bound. They were arranged in three groups: bills, reports, and accounts and papers. Each group was arranged in chronological order, with a serial numbering of each paper. There is an index to this collection.

From 1801, at the end of each session, the papers which had been before Parliament were bound into volumes called the Bound Sets of Sessional Papers. Each set of papers was arranged in four groups: bills, reports of committees, reports of commissioners, and accounts and papers. Within each group the papers are bound in alphabetical order. These papers bear one of three series of numbers. A new series of numbers is started each session. From the

---

[94] Percy Ford and Grace Ford, *A Guide to Parliamentary Papers*, 8–12.

[95] *Catalogue of Papers Printed by Order of the House of Commons, 1731–1800*, reprint, H. M. Stationery Office, 1954. This is the Abbot Catalogue to the Abbot Collection of bound volumes of papers.

beginning of the bound set in 1801, a printer's number was placed in the bottom corner of all House Papers. When the first alphabetical index was printed for the session 1814–15, this number was inserted in round brackets and was used as the sessional index reference number to the paper in the bound set.

Papers presented "By Command" bear a legend to that effect and a serial command number. They are listed in the Sessional Index as Command Papers. Unlike the House Papers, which start a fresh series of numbers each session, command numbers may stretch over many sessions. Up to 1869, however, it is not possible to identify a Command Paper from the command number in the index due to a mix-up in which Command Papers were given a command number, but the number was not printed on the paper. There are four series of Command Papers.[96]

There are indexes to the Bound Sets of Sessional Papers.[97] The Sessional Index is the last volume of the Sessional Bound Set. It contains a list of bound volumes, a numerical list of bills, a numeri-

[96] 1833–68/69, no. 1 to no. 4222, not printed on the papers; 1870–99, C. 1 to C. 9550, number printed on the paper; 1900–18, Cd. 1 to Cd. 9239; 1919–55/56, Cmd. 1 to Cmd. 9899; 1956/57– , Cmd. 1– .

[97] Great Britain, Parliament, House of Commons, *General Alphabetical Index to the Bills, Reports, Estimates, Accounts, and Papers Printed by Order of the House of Commons and to the Papers Presented by Command*, 1801–48/49, 4 vols. (London, H. M. Stationery Office, 1853–1960), in progress. Consists of unnumbered volumes: general index to the accounts and papers, reports of commissioners, estimates, and so on, 1801–52; indexes to bills and reports, 1801–52, in two sections (general index to the bills and general index to the reports of select committees); general index, 1852–99; and general index, 1900–48/49. Great Britain, Parliament, House of Commons, *General Alphabetical Index to the Bills, Reports, Estimates, Accounts and Papers Printed by Order of the House of Commons and to the Papers Presented by Command*, 1950–58/59– (London, H. M. Stationery Office, 1963–). Decennial cumulation of the annual indexes. A continuation of the decennial indexes, 1870–1949, now superseded by the fifty-year indexes. Great Britain, Parliament, *List of the Bills, Reports, Estimates, and Accounts and Papers Presented by Command . . . with a General Alphabetical Index Thereto* (London, H. M. Stationery Office, 1801–). Annual. The index section is superseded through 1958/59 by the fifty-year and ten-year indexes listed above, but the numerical lists are still the only ones available.

cal list of papers, a numerical list of Command Papers, and an alphabetical index. Except for the interruption in the war years, 1914–18 and 1939–45, there have been decennial indexes since 1870. Before that date they were published at irregular intervals; however, the decennial indexes have been consolidated into three volumes covering 1801–52 and one volume covering the years from 1852–53 to 1868–69.

The annual Consolidated List is the sales list of Her Majesty's Stationery Office. The first part deals with Parliamentary Papers; the second, with non-parliamentary lists. Issued daily and monthly, the lists are consolidated into the annual list at the end of the year. The Parliamentary Papers are arranged in it as in the Sessional Index; therefore, the annual Consolidated List provides access to the Parliamentary Papers until they are found and the sessional list is in print.[98]

An advisory committee is made up of experts to whom the minister can refer problems in a particular field of his department's work or who provide expert assistance to him in the administration of acts of Parliament. A working party is a small group or committee charged with the investigation of some problem or the preparation of some plan. After World War II, the departments began to use this form of inquiry—forty-nine working party reports were published between 1946 and 1952, only two of

[98] Great Britain, Stationery Office, *Catalogue of Government Publications*, 1922– (London, H. M. Stationery Office, 1923–). Annual. Title varies: *Consolidated List of Parliamentary and Stationery Office Publications*, 1922; *Consolidated List of Government Publications*, 1923–50; *Government Publications: Catalogue*, 1954–55; *Catalogue of Government Publications*, 1956– . Continues the *Quarterly List . . . of Official Publications* (London, H. M. Stationery Office, 1897–1922). Great Britain, Stationery Office, *Consolidated Index to Government Publications*, 1936/40– (London, H. M. Stationery Office, 1952–). Quinquennial. Four of these five-year indexes have now appeared and consolidated the indexing of the annual lists. Great Britain, *Government Publications Monthly List* (London, H. M. Stationery Office, monthly). This last title is primarily a sales catalog and is superseded by the *Catalogue of Government Publications*.

which were presented as "Commands." Evidence is not published, but the reports often contain important memoranda.

The annual reports of various departments and bodies created by Parliament are the chief sources of information on the particular fields they cover; they are indispensable. Some are required by statute to be laid before Parliament; others are presented to Parliament "By Command"; and others are published by departmental authority. Some of these series have been in existence for many years. A list of the more important of these series and their appropriate page numbers is given in appendix 4 in Percy and Grace Ford's *Select List of British Parliamentary Papers, 1833–1899.*[99] The annual reports may contain supplementary reports or accounts of special investigations of importance in public policy.

Other official papers include: the published awards of the Industrial Court and the National Arbitration Tribunal and the larger reports of the Court of Inquiry into major industrial disputes; selected decisions on income tax cases; large numbers of statutory instruments (or statutory rules and orders as they were formerly called); and other information papers.

Before 1921, Parliamentary Papers included nearly all documents of importance. The official description of Non-Parliamentary Papers was simply "Official Publications." The House and Command Papers, known together as the Sessional Papers or "Blue Books" because for most of the nineteenth century the printer used a blue paper cover on many of them,[100] were distributed free to members of Parliament and a number of other bodies and organizations. In the government economy programs after World War I, the Treasury issued Circular no. 38/21 instructing departments to modify their practice of issuing departmental papers as Parliamentary Papers and directing that papers were not to be presented by command unless the matter seemed likely to be the subject of early legislation or the papers were otherwise essential to members of Parliament as a whole. The

[99] (Oxford, B. Blackwell, 1953).
[100] O'Neill, *British Parliamentary Papers*, 5.

result has been a reduction in the proportion of departmental papers presented and an increase in the number and proportion not presented. The Non-Parliamentary Papers now consist of more than official papers and include reports on public policy, which would have been parliamentary but for the economy rule. The old term "Official" was replaced by the term "Non-Parliamentary" to describe them.

Departments' interpretations of the rule was neither consistent nor uniform; hence, there has been confusion in the arrangement of Parliamentary Papers. A smaller and smaller proportion are presented to Parliament as commands and more and more have become Non-Parliamentary. The Sessional Bound Sets, Parliament's own papers, once regarded as containing all the necessary papers on public policy, have declined in relative importance. Parliamentary Papers also have declined in importance because they do not present evidence. Departmental committees or the departments themselves have exercised their freedom not to publish their evidence, with the result that a printed public version may not be obtainable.

The *Annual Consolidated List* is the only index for the Non-Parliamentary Papers.[101] The departments are arranged in alphabetical order and the Non-Parliamentary Papers are arranged under the department of origin. A separate section lists royal commissions. Sales lists go back to 1836, when Parliamentary Papers were put on sale.

There are some nonofficial breviates and catalogues of British Parliamentary Papers besides the official ones mentioned earlier. These breviates and catalogues can help the student with his research. They include the *Catalogue of Parliamentary Reports and a Breviate of Their Contents*;[102] Percy and Grace Ford's select lists,

---

[101] For full bibliographic information, see note 98.

[102] Great Britain, House of Commons, *Catalogue of Parliamentary Reports and a Breviate of Their Contents, Arranged Under Heads According to the Subjects, 1696–1834* (London, 1834; reprint ed., with an introduction by Percy Ford and Grace Ford, Oxford, Blackwell, 1953).

which run from 1833 through 1954;[103] *A Guide to the Principal Parliamentary Papers Relating to the Dominions, 1812–1911*;[104] *A Century of Diplomatic Blue Books*;[105] Robert Vogel's *A Breviate of British Diplomatic Blue Books, 1919–1959*;[106] and Hilda Jones's *Catalogue of Parliamentary Papers*.[107] The House of Lords' papers take the same form as those of the Commons: procedural papers, the Journals, the Debates, House Papers, and Command Papers. Its Sessional Papers were bound and indexed in the nineteenth century as were those of the House of Commons, but fewer sets have been preserved. Each House sent documents to the other; thus a large number of Lords' papers are in the Commons' volumes with Commons' numbers. Since 1900, the Lords' Command Papers have been omitted from the Commons' volumes. Now the only duplication is in the case of reports of joint committees of both Houses. This reflects the decline not only in the quantity but also in the importance of the House of Lords' Papers. The Lords' indexes[108] provide a useful check with the Commons' indexes; no Lords' index has been published since 1920.

[103] Percy Ford and Grace Ford, *Select List of British Parliamentary Papers, 1900–1916: The Foundation of a Welfare State* (Oxford, B. Blackwell, 1957); *A Breviate of Parliamentary Papers, 1917–1939* (Oxford, Blackwell, 1951); *A Breviate of Parliamentary Papers, 1940–1954: War and Reconstruction* (Oxford, B. Blackwell, 1961).

[104] Margaret Isabella Adam, John Ewing, and James Munro (Edinburgh, Oliver and Boyd, 1913).

[105] Harold W. V. Temperley and Lillian M. Penson, *A Century of Diplomatic Blue Books, 1814–1914* (Cambridge, At the University Press, 1938).

[106] (Montreal, McGill University Press, 1963).

[107] Hilda Vernon Jones, *A Catalogue of Parliamentary Papers, 1801–1900, with a Few of Earlier Date* (London, P. S. King & Son, 1904).

[108] Great Britain, House of Lords, *General Index to Sessional Papers Printed by Order of the House of Lords or Presented by Special Command*, 3 vols. (London, G. E. Eyre and W. Spottiswoods, 1860–86). Vol. 1, 1801–59; vol. 2, 1859–70; vol. 3, 1871–85. From 1886 to 1920, annual indexes were published. Subsequently the only lists printed are unnumbered annual lists of titles.

The Foreign Office's *British and Foreign State Papers*[109] were formerly printed exclusively for the use of the British government and British diplomatic agents. They contain the major documents of the nineteenth and twentieth centuries which have been made public on political and commercial affairs and relations between nations. They include constitutions and organic laws of foreign countries as well as treaties. In 1922, with volume 116, *British and Foreign State Papers* absorbed *Hertslet's Commercial Treaties.* Each volume has a good index; the early volumes have country and subject indexes, and the later ones have added a chronological list of documents. There are four general indexes to the set.

The Foreign Office also publishes *Documents on British Foreign Policy, 1919–1939.*[110] E. L. Woodward and Rohan Butler, both historians, edited these volumes, which provide fuller coverage for the period than *Documents on International Affairs.* The first series begins in 1919 and covers events from the signing of the peace treaty ending World War I through the Hague Conferences in 1930. The second series begins in March, 1930, and ends on March 8, 1938, the day before the plebiscite was held in Austria. The third series covers the period from March 8, 1938, to September 3, 1939; it includes the documents necessary to study the origins of World War II.

The British have lists of diplomats, such as the *Colonial Office List;*[111] the *Diplomatic Service List,*[112] which succeeded the *For-*

[109] For full bibliographic information, see Chapter 10, note 63.

[110] Great Britain, 31 vols. (London, H. M. Stationery Office, 1946–). 1st series, 1919–29 (it actually covers 1919–February, 1922), 15 vols. (1949–67); 2d series, 1930–38, 9 vols. (1946–65); 3d series, March, 1938– September, 1939, 10 vols. (1949–61), vol. 10 is an index. Series 1A is to cover 1925 to 1959. It began publication with its first volume, *The Aftermath of Locarno, 1925–1926,* in 1966.

[111] 1862–1966 (London, H. M. Stationery Office, 1862–1966). The Colonial Office is now part of the Commonwealth Office, and the *Colonial Office List* has been combined with the *Commonwealth Relations Office Year Book* (1951–66) to form the *Commonwealth Office List,* 1967– . The *Colonial Office List* is divided into four parts: 1. the history, functions, and list of ministers, undersecretaries, and committees of the Colonial

eign Office List; and the *London Diplomatic List*,[113] which is an alphabetical list of representatives of foreign states and Commonwealth countries in London.

International

James Bennett Childs's *Government Document Bibliography*[114] lists the catalogs, indexes, and guides to the documents of the United States, the Confederate States, the states of the United States, foreign countries, and the League of Nations. The section on foreign countries is arranged alphabetically by the name of the country. Frequent brief annotations explain the scope and value of the particular title. For example, José Meyer's *Official Publications of European Governments* is described as a volume compiled on the basis of lists furnished by the various governments and the United States consular offices, including information from about thirty European governments.

Another bibliography is *A Study of Current Bibliographies of National Official Publications* put out by the International Committee for Social Sciences Documentation.[115] It lists national bib-

Office; 2. territories; 3. staff record of services; 4. Parliamentary and Non-Parliamentary Papers of colonial interest. There is a general index.

[112] (London, H. M. Stationery Office, 1966–). Annual. Succeeds the *Foreign Office List* (1806–1965) when the Foreign, Commonwealth, and Trade commissions merged on January 1, 1967, to form H. M. Diplomatic Service. The *Diplomatic Service List* has five parts: the home departments; British missions abroad; consular districts; chronological lists of secretaries of state, ministers of state, permanent undersecretaries, ambassadors, and high commissioners; and biographical notes and list of staff.

[113] (London: H. M. Stationery Office, 1964–). Annual.

[114] *Government Document Bibliography in the United States and Elsewhere*, 3d ed. (Washington, D.C., Government Printing Office, 1942, Paris, American Library in Paris, Reference Service on International Affairs, 1926). Partially reissued in revised printed form as *Official Publications of European Governments: An Outline Bibliography of Serials and Important Monographs, Including Diplomatic Documents, Issued by European Government Officers and Ministries* (Paris, 1929).

[115] *Étude des bibliographies courantes des publications officielles nationales: Guide sommaire et inventaire. A Study of Current Bibliographies of*

liographies, official journals, document bibliographies, and legislative publications of all independent states. The introductory matter is in French and English; the annotations, in French or English.

Winifred Gregory, the editor of the *Union List of Serials*, edited two other union lists that are still useful: *List of Serial Publications of Foreign Governments, 1815–1931*[116] and *International Congresses and Conferences, 1840–1937: A Union List of Their Publications Available in Libraries of the United States and Canada*.[117] The first title is a union list on the same general plan as the *Union List of Serials*, but it includes only government serials, that is, publications excluded from the *Union List of Serials*. *List of Serial Publications of Foreign Governments* lists the serial publications of foreign governments from the Congress of Vienna to the time of the rise of the dictators in the 1930's. Arranged alphabetically, with the exception of Russia which is listed separately at the end, it is subdivided by government departments and bureaus, with the indication of holdings of the various publications in some eighty-five American libraries.

In international relations there are two British and two American collections that are invaluable. The British series are *Survey of International Affairs* and *Documents on International Affairs*. *Survey of International Affairs*[118] is a prominent series of first-rate quality that reviews important international events throughout the world. Inaugurated by the Royal Institute of International Affairs about fifty years ago, this annual waits a few years before trying to

---

National Official Publications: Short Guide and Inventory, comp. by Jean Meyriat, UNESCO Bibliographical Handbook (Paris, UNESCO, 1958).

[116] Ed. for the American Council of Learned Societies, American Library Association, National Research Council (New York, H. W. Wilson Co., 1932).

[117] Edited under the auspices of the Bibliographical Society of America (New York, H. W. Wilson Co., 1938). Unfortunately, it excludes diplomatic congresses and conferences and those held under the League of Nations.

[118] 1920–23– (London, Oxford University Press, 1925–). Annual.

piece current history together. The different sections on the various areas of the world are written by experts. The volumes are well written, footnoted, and indexed.

Documents on International Affairs[119] is also prepared under the auspices of the Royal Institute of International Affairs to accompany and supplement the annual *Survey of International Affairs*. The editors for the *Survey* compiled the volume for 1960 and will compile the future volumes in succeeding years. The organization follows that of the *Survey*. The background for the documents, which include policy statements from the whole range of governments involved, can be found in the *Survey*.[120]

The American counterparts are *The United States in World Affairs* and *Documents on American Foreign Relations*. The Council on Foreign Relations publishes both of these annuals which, unlike the British, are up to date. The *United States in World Affairs*[121] is a concise review of world conditions as they relate to American foreign affairs. It includes a chronology of major events of the year. The text is documented with footnote references to standard available sources including its companion volume, *Documents on American Foreign Relations*.[122] This publication includes transcripts of the major treaties, agreements, diplomatic notes, policy statements, and public speeches bearing on foreign policy.

The *Foreign Affairs Bibliography: A Selected and Annotated List of Books on International Relations*[123] is an authoritative and selective bibliography of books and collections of documents in

[119] 1928– (London, Oxford University Press, 1929–). Annual.

[120] There is a consolidated index to both titles, the *Consolidated Index to the Survey of International Affairs, 1920–1938, and Documents on International Affairs, 1928–1938*, comp. by E. M. R. Ditmus (London, Oxford University Press, 1967).

[121] 1931– (New York, published for the Council on Foreign Relations by Harper & Brothers, 1932–). Annual.

[122] 1938/39– (New York, Council on Foreign Relations, 1939–).

[123] 4 vols. (New York, published for the Council on Foreign Relations by Harper & Brothers, 1933–55). Vol. 1, 1919–32; vol. 2, 1932–42; vol. 3, 1942–52; vol. 4, 1952–62 (New York, R. R. Bowker Co., 1964).

international relations. Based largely on the annotated notes appearing in the quarterly periodical *Foreign Affairs*, it tries to list the significant books, mostly in English and Western European languages. The entries are arranged under three major headings (general international relations; the world since 1914; and the world by regions) which are subdivided by subject and/or area. The bibliography covers history, politics, diplomacy, economics, international law, world organization, social problems, racial problems, and so on. There is an author index, which is currently continued in *Foreign Affairs*.

Index of Titles

282

General Index

Abbot Collection, the: 270
Abelard, Peter: 152
Abstracts: 57–58
Act Papers: 267–68; *see also* British government publications
Adams, James Truslow: 139–40
Africa: history, dictionaries, and encyclopedias, 81–84; biographical aids, 167
African Development Bank: 81
African Institute for Economic Development and Planning: 81
Almanacs: 86; newspaper, 87–88; British, 88–89; Canadian, 89; on Negroes, 89–90; on Congress, 90
Alonso, Benito Sanchez: 60
American Antiquarian Society: 22, 122
American Association for State and Local History: 109
American Council of Learned Societies: 156, 186
American Geographical Society: 130
American Historical Association: 32, 35, 104, 178, 182
American Library Association: 4, 31, 118
American Philosophical Society: 175
American Political Science Foundation: 168
American Revolution: 139–40
Ames, John G.: 237, 239–40, 255–56
Anderson, Frank M.: 176–77
Andrews, Charles McLean: 183
Archives: defined, 177; guides to, 178–83, 190–91; *see also* National Archives
Armstrong, Neil A.: 195
Armstrong, Robert D.: 183
Arnim, Max: 148
Asimov, Isaac: 88
Association of British Orientalists: 52

Association of Research Libraries: 124
Atlases: 129, 131; world geographical, 133–36; regional and topical, 136–39; historical, 139–41; on American history periods, 141–42; of world history, 142–43; for specialized periods in European history, 143–44; on world affairs, 144
Aufricht, Hans: 229
Australia: history encyclopedias, 85; biographical material on, 163–64
Austria: 149
Autobiographies: 150–51

Back, Harry: 66
Bainton, Roland H.: 59
Baker v. *Carr*: 214
Barnes, Thomas: 126
Barrau-Dihigo, Louis: 60
Bartlett, John: 195–96
Barzun, Jacques: 30
Bavarian Academy of Sciences, Historical Committee of: 165
Bayitch, Stojan A.: 50
Beaman, Middleton G.: 211–12
Beard, Charles A.: 95, 200
Beers, Henry Putney: 36
Bell and Howell Company: 118
Bemis, Samuel Flagg: 37, 183, 260–61
Beria, Lavrenti P.: 64
Berton, Peter: 56
Besterman, Theodore A.: 28–29
Bevans, Charles I.: 221
Bibliographies, geographical: 128–30
Bibliographies, government: 277–79
Bibliographies, history: 30–34, 146, 193; United States, 34–38; in special fields, 37–38, 47, 56–57; ancient, 38–39; medieval and Renaissance, 39–42; Great

297

For the Working Historian

THE RHETORIC OF HISTORY, by Savoie Lottinville. A critical examination of the structures and writing techniques essential to successful publication in the field of history. "Distilled wisdom regarding such things as foundations and concepts; opening scenes; heroes and villains; narrative drive, and the necessity of continuity and analysis. . . . In this work, as in his distinguished career, Lottinville has earned the thanks of every reader and every writer of history." — *San Francisco Chronicle.*

THE AMERICAN WEST: *New Perspectives, New Dimensions,* edited by Jerome O. Steffen. "This new book offers new vantage points from which to look at the people, culture and frontier history of the American West." — *Oklahoma Journal.* ". . . borders on the provocative as it explores new territory for the frontier historian, the Western environmentalist and behaviorist, and others in the field." — *Norman Transcript.*

HISTORICAL THOUGHT IN AMERICA: *Postwar Patterns,* by Timothy Paul Donovan. The "new" historians feel a strong sense of social responsibility demanding that they strive for greater objectivity than ever before, that they study past problems that bear most directly on our present dilemmas, and that they be willing to speculate on long-term changes in human society. "A provocative work that will help to create what Donovan calls 'the perfect historian.' . . . all historians should read it." — *History.* Also available in paperback.

UNIVERSITY OF OKLAHOMA PRESS

NORMAN